THE ELUSIVE REPUBLIC

The Elusive Republic

POLITICAL ECONOMY IN

JEFFERSONIAN AMERICA

BY DREW R. McCOY

PUBLISHED FOR THE

INSTITUTE OF EARLY AMERICAN HISTORY AND CULTURE

WILLIAMSBURG, VIRGINIA

BY THE UNIVERSITY OF NORTH CAROLINA PRESS

CHAPEL HILL

The Institute of Early American History and Culture
is sponsored jointly by the College of William and Mary in Virginia
and The Colonial Williamsburg Foundation.

© 1980 The University of North Carolina Press

Manufactured in the United States of America

Library of Congress Cataloging in Publication Data

McCoy, Drew R
The elusive Republic.

Includes index.
1. United States—Economic conditions—To 1865.
2. United States—Politics and government—1783–1809.
3. United States—Politics and government—1809–1817.
I. Institute of Early American History and Culture,
Williamsburg, Va. II. Title.
HC105.M235   320.9'73'046   79-20952
ISBN 0-8078-1416-4
ISBN 0-8078-4616-3 (pbk.: alk. paper)

The passage from *The Great Gatsby* quoted on page 3
is reprinted by permission of Charles Scribner's Sons.

04   03   02   7   6   5   4

FOR MY PARENTS

CONTENTS

ACKNOWLEDGMENTS

I am indebted to many people for assistance in the preparation of this book. Professor Merrill D. Peterson of the University of Virginia directed the dissertation upon which it is based, and I benefited from his expert guidance and judgment at all stages. W. W. Abbot and Robert Brugger also gave helpful readings of the dissertation during its preparation. Other friends and scholars, most notably Robert A. Emery and William G. Shade, assisted in the early stages of my work. Lance Banning, Gordon S. Wood, Joseph Ernst, and John Murrin offered additional commentary and encouragement along the way. I also owe a special debt to Professors Walter LaFeber and Michael Kammen of Cornell University, who first stimulated my interest in the subject a decade ago. Since that time they have continued to lend aid and encouragement to a former student.

I will always treasure my association with the Institute of Early American History and Culture in Williamsburg, Virginia, where I spent two years as a post-doctoral Fellow. Special thanks go to Thad W. Tate, Director of the Institute, and to Charles W. Royster, a former colleague who gave my manuscript a careful reading when it needed one most. The staff of the Institute has also applied its expert editorial skills to the final preparation of the work, and I would like to thank David Ammerman, Cynthia Carter, and Joy Dickinson Barnes for their kind and invaluable assistance in its completion.

Portions of this book have appeared in preliminary form in two articles in the *William and Mary Quarterly*: "Republicanism and American Foreign Policy: James Madison and the Political Economy of Commercial Discrimination, 1789 to 1794," 3d Ser., XXXI (1974), 633–646; and "Benjamin Franklin's Vision of a Republican Political Economy for America," 3d Ser., XXXV (1978), 605–628. I am grateful to the *Quarterly* for permission to incorporate material from these articles into the present work.

THE ELUSIVE REPUBLIC

*"He had come a long way
to this blue lawn, and his dream must have seemed
so close that he could hardly
fail to grasp it. He did not know that it was already behind him,
somewhere back in that vast obscurity
beyond the city, where the dark fields of the republic
rolled on under the night."*

F. Scott Fitzgerald,
The Great Gatsby

INTRODUCTION

Contemporary Americans all too often presume an unjustified familiarity with their Revolutionary forebears. It is easy to assume that our basic concerns were theirs, and especially that our understanding of the American Revolution and its legacy accurately reflects the meaning and significance they attached to it. While most of us recognize that our modern world of experience would be utterly foreign to the eighteenth-century mind, few acknowledge how frightening and even distasteful twentieth-century America might appear to the members of a Revolutionary generation that was steeped in the values and assumptions of a quite different age. It may be reassuring to think that modern America represents the fulfillment of the original spirit of the Revolution, but such a presumption is both dubious and dangerously misleading. If present-day Americans genuinely wish to come to grips with their Revolutionary heritage, they must begin with an understanding of how much has changed since the eighteenth century in the ways in which men think about society, economy, and government.

To men of the eighteenth century the creation of a republic entailed much more than simply replacing a king and hereditary privilege with an elective system of government. It was commonly assumed in Revolutionary America that a republican form of government was particularly precarious because it could succeed only in an extraordinary society of distinctively moral people. This prevalent belief in the fragility of republics generated among the Revolutionaries an intense concern with the fundamental character of their economy and society. After independence, when the thorny issues related to social and economic development became central to intellectual and political debate, Americans could agree almost without exception that the new nation should be republican, but within that broad and increasingly ambiguous consensus they differed sharply over a wide range of issues. And at stake, it always seemed to these republicans, was nothing less than their character as a people and hence the fate of the Revolutionary experiment itself.

The concept of "political economy" is not as widely used today as it was in the late eighteenth or early nineteenth centuries, and even then its meaning was not all that rigorous or precise. A Philadelphia merchant, Joshua Gilpin, noted in the early nineteenth century, for example, that although "the practice of political economy" was "coeval with the institution of society," the term itself "even yet has neither received so explicit a definition as it merits nor has it been reduced to the system of a general and acknowledged science." He went on to provide only a very broad definition of political economy as "the operation of government upon its domestic resources independent of its external or foreign administration." As Gilpin used the term, it was derived from the Aristotelian sense of "economics" as the art of managing a household; by direct analogy, the art of managing a state was referred to as "political economics."[2] Indeed, many eighteenth-century writers used political economy as Adam Smith did, to refer to "a branch of the science of a statesman or legislator" whose object was "to enrich both the people and the sovereign." In this sense of the term, "political economy" could refer specifically to the economic policy of a state.[3] But in an even broader, more general sense, the concept also signified the necessary existence of a close relationship between government, or the polity, and the social and economic order. Thus to the Revolutionaries in America, the notion of "political economy" reinforced the characteristically republican idea of a dynamic interdependence among polity, economy, and society.

Eighteenth-century thinkers also generally considered political economy under the broader rubric of moral philosophy. Before "economics" achieved the dubious status of pure science, it was not common practice to separate economics and ethics. The Revolutionaries lived during an age when a consideration of the normative dimension of economic life had not yet been sacrificed to the hubris of those who would claim to make economics into a "non-moral" science. The concept of "political economy," as distinct from "economics," is particularly symbolic of this eighteenth-century fusion of empirical science and ethical concerns.[4]

1. Joshua Gilpin, essay on political economy, Gilpin Papers, LXXV, Historical Society of Pennsylvania, Philadelphia.

2. See William Letwin, *The Origins of Scientific Economics: English Economic Thought, 1660–1776* (London, 1963), 233–234. See also Joseph Ernst, "Political Economy and Reality: Problems in the Interpretation of the American Revolution," *Canadian Review of American Studies*, VII (1976), 109–118, esp. 117 n. 1.

3. Adam Smith, *An Inquiry into the Nature and Causes of the Wealth of Nations*, ed. Edwin Cannan (New York, 1937 [orig. publ. London, 1776]), 397.

4. See Letwin, *Origins of Scientific Economics*; Glenn R. Morrow, *The Ethical and Economic Theories of Adam Smith: A Study in the Social Philosophy of the Eighteenth*

Above all, the Revolutionaries were acutely aware of the moral dimension of economic life, for they seemed obsessed with the idea that a republican polity required popular virtue for its stability and success. Simply stated, they assumed that a healthy republican government demanded an economic and social order that would encourage the shaping of a virtuous citizenry. In this sense, once the Revolutionaries succeeded in establishing independence from the British Empire, they had to do much more than merely define and put into practice the proper constitutional principles of republican government. They had to define, and then attempt to secure, a form of economy and society that would be capable of sustaining the virtuous character of a republican citizenry. They had to establish, in short, a republican system of political economy for America.

"In so complicated a science as political economy," Thomas Jefferson warned in 1816, "no one axiom can be laid down as wise and expedient for all times and circumstances, and for their contraries."[5] And indeed, most Americans of Jefferson's era were practical as well as flexible in their approach to the problems posed by economic and social development. No rigid principles or refined abstractions determined policies and programs, since even statesmen who were widely read in the "science" rarely considered themselves doctrinaire disciples of any formal school or system.[6] Jefferson's practicality in political economy, however, like that of his contemporaries, was contained in an intellectual universe of assumptions, values, and expectations that to a great extent defined the parameters and often the direction of his thinking. It was a distinctively eighteenth-century universe, a world of ideas with its own peculiar vocabulary, conceptual framework, and emotional context, irretrievably different from our modern world of political and economic assumptions. Perhaps the greatest contribution of recent studies of republican thought

---

Century (New York, 1923); and Norman S. Fiering, "President Samuel Johnson and the Circle of Knowledge," *William and Mary Quarterly*, 3d Ser., XXVIII (1971), 199–236, esp. 231–236.

5. Jefferson to Benjamin Austin, Jan. 9, 1816, Andrew A. Lipscomb and Albert Ellery Bergh, eds., *The Writings of Thomas Jefferson* (Washington, D.C., 1903–1904), XIV, 392.

6. See, for example, John Adams to Benjamin Rush, Dec. 22, 1806, Alexander Biddle, ed., *Old Family Letters* (Philadelphia, 1892), I, 120, with regard to Adams's complaint that he could find no one who pretended to understand the abstract system of "the French Œconomists," or physiocrats.

has been to remind twentieth-century Americans that they live in a profoundly different society and that great effort, imagination, and sensitivity are needed to comprehend the habits of thought and world view of their Revolutionary ancestors.[7]

Broadly defined, "republicanism" or "republican ideology" has come to refer to a peculiarly eighteenth-century political culture in which the idea of republican government was part of a much larger configuration of beliefs about human behavior and the social process. Profiting from the recent scholarship of Bernard Bailyn, Gordon Wood, and J.G.A. Pocock, among others, we can now speak of "republicanism" as a distinctive universe (or "paradigm") of thought and discourse that gave shape to contemporary perceptions of the American Revolution. The present study is designed to extend and deepen our understanding of "republicanism" by carrying it beyond the relatively narrow realm of political and constitutional thought that has dominated the attention of historians into the broader domain of political economy. In this regard, it will attempt to uncover, analyze, and give unity to a "lost" intellectual world of eighteenth-century political economy. In addition to placing the social and economic thought of articulate Americans in a meaningful ideological context, this study will analyze the impact of republican concerns on policymaking in post-Revolutionary America. Because a commitment to republican government demanded attention to the more general question of the structure and character of society, American statesmen were intensely concerned with the broader social and moral implications of the policies they pursued. In their quest to build a republican economy and society, therefore, they could perceive intimate connections between such seemingly remote and discrete matters as, for example, the need to open export markets for American produce and the need to sustain the virtuous character of a republican people.

There are many extremely useful studies of American economic and foreign policy for this entire period, but they almost uniformly wrench

---

7. For an excellent discussion of the growth of "republicanism" (or "republican ideology") as a concept in American historiography, see Robert E. Shalhope, "Toward a Republican Synthesis: The Emergence of an Understanding of Republicanism in American Historiography," *WMQ*, 3d Ser., XXIX (1972), 49–80. Our current understanding of American republicanism suffers from too narrow a focus on political and constitutional thought.

policies and programs out of their contemporary ideological context.[8] My purpose in much of what follows is to shed new light on certain often familiar subjects by viewing them from a different and hitherto neglected perspective. I do not claim, of course, that my approach to these matters is the only valid and illuminating one, and I would emphasize the selective character of the entire study. It is not intended to be a comprehensive consideration of American political economy, in any sense of that term, over a fifty-year period. My necessarily selective choice of topics for analysis has been guided in large part by a concern for thematic continuity and unity. Many studies dealing with political economy in this period, even the best ones, are diffuse and eclectic in their approach and thus fail to suggest any kind of convincing conceptual framework or overview. I hope to repair this deficiency without resorting to an overly narrow or confining focus. Above all, my selection of an organizing framework for the narrative that follows has been informed by my sense of eighteenth-century concerns and sensitivities. The first several chapters introduce the major themes of the study. These themes all focus, first, on the republican implications of contrasting visions of social development across space on the one hand, and through time on the other, and second, on the poignant struggle to adapt the traditional, classical republican impulse to modern commercial society. By the 1790s, at least two coherent "systems" of political economy can be identified in American thought and policy. The first five chapters of the present study are devoted to a discussion of matters bearing on the formation of these two systems, while the concluding five chapters are concerned with subsequent efforts to implement them under the Constitution.

My emphasis throughout this study will be on the ideological origins and the impact upon public policy of a Jeffersonian conception of republican political economy. By "Jeffersonian" I refer to a specific configuration of assumptions, fears, beliefs, and values that shaped a vision of expansion across space—the American continent—as a necessary alternative to the development through time that was generally thought

8. Two noteworthy exceptions are Edmund S. Morgan, "The Puritan Ethic and the American Revolution," *ibid.*, XXIV (1967), 3–43, and Roger H. Brown, *The Republic in Peril: 1812* (New York, 1964). Morgan has taken the first tentative step toward linking republicanism to economic thought and policy, while Brown's study suggests the utility of examining American foreign policy in the republican context.

to bring with it both political corruption and social decay. My analysis suggests that this Jeffersonian vision reflected the dominant ideological strain of republican political economy in Revolutionary and early national America. As a cast of mind, it will be explored in this study largely, but not exclusively, through a close consideration of such leading thinkers and policymakers as Benjamin Franklin, Thomas Jefferson, and especially James Madison. My approach will be to examine the outlook of these notably articulate men in the context both of the changing circumstances of early national America and of the broader range of contemporary eighteenth-century perception. Since the Jeffersonian vision grew out of an attempt to reconcile classical republicanism with more modern social realities and American conditions, it was not without its tensions, ambiguities, and even contradictions. It was never, in other words, a rigidly and unequivocally defined system of thought to which even Jefferson or Madison uniformly adhered. But it did represent a general vision of a republican America that motivated these two men in particular and also claimed the emotional allegiance of many Americans, particularly those who came to consider themselves Jeffersonian Republicans. For such republicans, the Jeffersonian vision embodied the broader meaning of the American Revolution in the realm of political economy.

Any analysis of specific policies and programs in political economy must be predicated on an understanding of how men in the eighteenth century conceived of the basic process of social and economic development and, consequently, of how this conceptualization related directly to the problem of creating and securing a republic in a new age of commercial complexity. Above all, American republicanism must be understood as an ideology in transition, for it reflected an attempt to cling to the traditional republican spirit of classical antiquity without disregarding the new imperatives of a more modern commercial society. Indeed, this republican ideology was often as remarkable for its complexity and ambiguity as it was for its compelling impact on the American mind. Whatever the partisan persuasion of most American statesmen, they generally thought in terms of constructing a national political economy that was compatible with a republican system of government. The crux of the matter, however, was to define republicanism in concrete and relevant terms, to determine the social and economic conditions necessary for its existence, and to identify the institutions and public policies that would best secure it. The period spanning the American Revolution and the War of 1812 was marked by an intense, and at times agonizing, effort to define the proper terms of a republican political economy. Most significantly, this search took place in an intellectual universe that, in its attempt to come to grips with a new world of economic experience, directed especially close attention to the progress, growth, and decay of societies.

Those who labour in the earth are the chosen people of God, if ever he had a chosen people, whose breasts he has made his peculiar deposit for substantial and genuine virtue. It is the focus in which he keeps alive that sacred fire, which otherwise might escape from the face of the earth. Corruption of morals in the mass of cultivators is a phaenomenon of which no age nor nation has furnished an example. It is the mark set on those, who not looking up to heaven, to their own soil and industry, as does the husbandman, for their subsistance, depend for it on the casualties and caprice of customers. Dependance begets subservience and venality, suffocates the germ of virtue, and prepares fit tools for the designs of ambition. This, the natural progress and consequence of the arts, has sometimes perhaps been retarded by accidental circumstances: but, generally speaking, the proportion which the aggregate of the other classes of citizens bears in any state to that of its husbandmen, is the proportion of its unsound to its healthy parts, and is a good-enough barometer whereby to measure its degree of corruption.

Thomas Jefferson, *Notes on the State of Virginia*

CHAPTER ONE

SOCIAL PROGRESS

AND DECAY IN

EIGHTEENTH-CENTURY

THOUGHT

Sometime during the summer or early fall of 1780, as the war for independence approached its most critical juncture and Americans faced an increasingly problematic future, the secretary of the French legation in Philadelphia, François Marbois, initiated a chain of events that would produce an intellectual and literary landmark of the Revolutionary age. As part of the French government's effort to secure useful information about its new and largely unknown ally, Marbois circulated a detailed questionnaire among influential members of the Continental Congress. When a copy of the questionnaire found its way to Thomas Jefferson, then the besieged governor of Virginia, he seized the opportunity to organize his wide-ranging reflections on the conditions and prospects of his native country. Many revisions and several years later, when the *Notes on the State of Virginia* publicly appeared, they included what was to become Jefferson's best-known commentary on political economy.[1] His celebration of "those who labour in the earth" as "the chosen people of God" has become a centerpiece of the republic's cultural heritage, a quintessential expression of its impassioned concern for the natural, earthbound virtue of a simple and uncorrupted people.

Jefferson's classic statement is so familiar that it might, at first glance, seem to require neither explanation nor analytical elaboration. But lurking beneath his deceptively simple paean to an agricultural way of life

1. Thomas Jefferson, *Notes on the State of Virginia*, ed. William Peden (Chapel Hill, N.C., 1955), 164–165.

was a more sophisticated perception of how societies normally changed through time as well as an acute understanding of the moral and political implications of a social process that he assumed was inevitable. His memorable observations on the comparative merits of agriculture and manufactures were directly informed by a characteristically eighteenth-century conception of social change.

Jefferson was responding in the *Notes* to Marbois's inquiry about the present state of commerce and manufactures in Virginia. Making a distinction customary of the times, Jefferson reported that the Revolution had encouraged the prolific production of very coarse clothing "within our families," but for the "finer" manufactures Virginians desired, he continued, they would undoubtedly continue to rely on importations from abroad. Recognizing that such a pattern would be considered unfortunate by "the political economists of Europe," who had established the principle "that every state should endeavour to manufacture for itself," Jefferson contended that it was instead a wise and necessary response to peculiar American conditions and to the lessons of history. In Europe, where the land was either fully cultivated or "locked up against the cultivator" by the bars of aristocratic tradition, manufacturing was "resorted to of necessity not of choice." New forms of employment had to be created, in other words, for those people who could not find occupations on the land. In America, by contrast, where "an immensity of land" courted the industry of even a rapidly expanding population, an alternative form of political economy that would not force men into manufacturing was both feasible and eminently desirable. Citing the "happiness and permanence of government" in a society of independent and virtuous husbandmen, Jefferson emphasized the moral and political advantages of America's social opportunity that far outweighed narrowly economic considerations. If his countrymen foolishly and prematurely embraced manufacturing, he predicted, a consequent and inevitable corruption of morals would necessarily endanger the fabric of republican government. Once large numbers of Americans abandoned secure employment on the land to labor in workshops, they would become dependent on "the casualties and caprice of customers" for their subsistence, and such dependence had historically bred a "subservience and venality" that suffocated "the germ of virtue" and prepared "fit tools for the designs of ambition." "It is the manners and spirit of a people which preserve a republic in vigour," Jefferson cautioned his readers, since "a degeneracy in these is a canker which soon eats to the heart of its laws and constitution."[2]

Jefferson's effusive optimism about his country's peculiar social potential could not obscure some nagging fears. He worried, on the one hand, that his contemporaries might blindly follow the maxims of European political economists, ignore his wisdom, and plunge into manufacturing. Education and a commitment to republican principles might defuse this particular danger, but a larger and less tractable problem loomed on the horizon. Jefferson recognized that the loathsome dependence, subservience, venality, and corruption that he so much dreaded—everything, in short, that he associated with European political economy—were in large part the unavoidable outgrowth of what he referred to as "the natural progress and consequence of the arts." He alluded here to a universal process that eighteenth-century social thinkers often described, a process whose repercussions might "sometimes perhaps" be "retarded by accidental circumstances," as Jefferson put it, but which inevitably had to be felt.[3] Like most enlightened thinkers of his age, Jefferson conceived of natural laws of social and cultural development that applied to America as much as to Europe. Vast resources of land might forestall the unfavorable consequences of this "natural progress" of the arts, but he never doubted that eventually America would be swept up in an inexorable logic of social change. Jefferson's plea in the *Notes on Virginia*, a plea that he would make throughout his public life, was that his countrymen not abuse or disregard the natural advantages that could postpone, but never prevent, a familiar and politically dangerous course of social development.

Jefferson's general conceptualization of the dynamics of social change was characteristic of post-Revolutionary Americans. Responding to a controversial piece of legislation in his state, George Mason, a fellow Virginian, had occasion in late 1786 to address several of these same issues in similar terms. In 1784 the general assembly had enacted a measure popularly known as the Port Bill, which attempted to limit the commonwealth's foreign trade to five coastal towns. Although the purpose of the act—the creation of a more centralized commercial system in the state that would release it from the pre-Revolutionary domination of

2. *Ibid.*
3. *Ibid.*, 165.

British merchants—was supported by an overwhelming majority of Virginians, many citizens, led by Mason, objected to this particular bill on both practical and ideological grounds. In the course of a lengthy memorial to the general assembly, Mason argued that Virginia was still at a relatively simple stage of social development and that legislative interference, promising to create large commercial cities, would only accelerate a dangerous process of social change. "If virtue is the vital principle of a republic, and it cannot long exist, without frugality, probity and strictness of morals," he queried, "will the manners of populous commercial cities be favorable to the principles of our free government? Or will not the vice, the depravity of morals, the luxury, venality, and corruption, which invariably prevail in great commercial cities, be utterly subversive of them?"[4] History, both ancient and more recent, supplied the unspoken but obvious answer.

Mason never doubted that the natural sequence of social development would culminate inevitably in the form of society he feared. He argued, rather, that Virginia not accelerate the process. There was no sense in incurring the many disadvantages of a more complex society before it was necessary. "Are not a people more miserable and contemptible in the last," he asked, "than in the early and middle stages of society? And is it not safer and wiser to leave things to the natural progress of time, than to hasten them, prematurely, by violence; and to bring on the community all the evils, before it is capable of receiving any of the advantages of populous countries?"[5]

Mason's battery of rhetorical queries suggests many of the tensions that troubled the eighteenth-century mind as it grappled with the wrenching repercussions of unsettling social and economic change. His admission that the advance of society to a more sophisticated form might have advantages is revealing, but he, along with most Americans of his age, seemed preoccupied with the deleterious consequences of this natural social development. Like Jefferson, Mason assumed the inevitability of a particular pattern of social growth, and they both perceived an intimate relationship between this pattern and the American experiment in republicanism. To understand fully the implications of their social analysis,

4. Robert A. Rutland, ed., *The Papers of George Mason, 1725–1792* (Chapel Hill, N.C., 1970), II, 862. For a further discussion of Mason's protest and for a history of the Port Bill, see Drew R. McCoy, "The Virginia Port Bill of 1784," *Virginia Magazine of History and Biography*, LXXXIII (1975), 288–303.

5. Rutland, ed., *Mason Papers*, II, 862–863.

and to appreciate the texture and resonance of American thinking in political economy in general, we must first turn to a consideration of the broader intellectual universe in which their perceptions were grounded.

[I]

The eighteenth century marked a watershed in the economic as well as the intellectual history of Western Europe, for the leading thinkers of that era had to assess the impact of a commercial revolution that had transformed nearly every aspect of European society since the fifteenth century. Today we tend to view this revolution as the preliminary stage of an even more fundamental "industrial revolution," but to men in the eighteenth century, who lacked our perspective, the commercialization of society in itself marked the birth of a distinctly modern order that represented a dramatic and dislocating break with the past. The rise of a flourishing international commerce, the development of more complicated national economies based on an advanced division of labor, and the revolution in public finance that brought with it funded public debts, large corporations, and the institutionalization of money markets were the major elements of this transformation in the economic life of Western Europe.[6] By stimulating curiosity about the historical development of societies, these changes encouraged attempts to explain how and why societies customarily changed through time and brought about efforts to evaluate the impact of these changes on the manners and morals of men. Appropriately, the eighteenth century witnessed vigorous debates on such matters as the civilizing versus the corrupting tendencies of commercial development, the definition and character of "luxury," and, above all, the question of whether some kind of fundamental decay was curiously inherent in social progress.

6. The literature on economic change in 18th-century Europe is voluminous. An excellent introduction to the situation in England, the focus of this great change, is T. S. Ashton, *An Economic History of England: The Eighteenth Century* (London and New York, 1955). See also Phyllis Deane, *The First Industrial Revolution* (Cambridge, 1965), and David S. Landes, *The Unbound Prometheus: Technological Change and Industrial Development in Western Europe from 1750 to the Present* (London, 1969), 1–123. A more specialized study of the financial revolution in England is P.G.M. Dickson, *The Financial Revolution in England: A Study in the Development of Public Credit, 1688–1756* (London, 1967). A brief descriptive account of the great social transformation in England in the 18th century

American thinkers were absorbed in these controversies by necessity as much as by choice. The colonists' sudden embrace of republicanism gave immediate and pressing relevance to the question of the relationship between economic change and public well-being. In this way the Revolution intensified an awareness of the broader cultural and moral implications of social change, an awareness that grew out of both recent colonial experience and the reflections of the historians, philosophers, and social commentators of the age. The convergence of experience and social theory in Revolutionary America was to produce a fervent aspiration to unprecedented success in harmonizing economic life, a wholesome society, and republican institutions. But behind the idealism, even utopianism, of the Revolutionary commitment lay an informed understanding of the imposing and perhaps insuperable problems in such a venture.

Eighteenth-century perceptions of social development were often shaped by a common conceptual approach. They were usually derived from ambitious attempts to apply scientific methods of inquiry to the study of man and society, an endeavor that produced a new historical sociology whose goal was the discovery of what was natural and normal in collective human development. This effort to create a "science of society" from a historical perspective owed much to the French philosopher Montesquieu and reached its fruition in the thought of his Scottish admirers, but it was inspired by a prevalent conviction of the age that social change could be understood in terms of a common process that eventually affected every society. It was generally believed that a comparative approach to history, based on the assumption of a universal human nature, might uncover predictable patterns of change that transcended accident or chance.[7]

As the men of the Enlightenment surveyed the terrain of their own relatively advanced society and speculated on its origins, they thought in terms of an evolutionary process that had discrete stages of development. All societies, they inferred from the evidence of history, normally pro-

---

can be found in M. Dorothy George, *England in Transition: Life and Work in the Eighteenth Century* (London, 1931).

7. See especially Gladys Bryson, *Man and Society: The Scottish Inquiry of the Eighteenth Century* (Princeton, N.J., 1945), chaps. 1 and 4; Peter Gay, *The Enlightenment: An Interpretation*, II, *The Science of Freedom* (New York, 1969), chap. 7; and Robert A. Nisbet, *Social Change and History: Aspects of the Western Theory of Development* (New York, 1969).

ceeded through several phases of organization from "rude" simplicity to "civilized" complexity. The number and specific characteristics of these stages varied somewhat from thinker to thinker, but the general pattern was consistent. By the second half of the century, especially among French and Scottish writers, the theory had taken firm shape and delineated four distinct and successive stages of social development, each based on a different mode of subsistence. This "four stages theory" was clearly reflected in the contemplations of a wide range of writers, from Helvétius, Turgot, and the physiocratic disciples of François Quesnay in France, to Adam Ferguson, Lord Kames, John Millar, and Adam Smith in Scotland. Their schematic understanding of socioeconomic development, which indirectly contributed to the rise of a new "classical" school of political economy, dominated sociological thought in the latter half of the eighteenth century.[8]

In simplest terms, the four stages were described as hunting, pasturage, agriculture, and commerce. In what Adam Smith referred to as the "lowest and rudest state of society"—a stage prior to any social organization of production—hunting, and to a lesser extent fishing, were the predominant modes of subsistence. A voluminous contemporary literature on the aboriginal inhabitants of America portrayed them as the perfect representatives of this universal first stage of social development. At the second stage, these primitive hunters were superseded by tribes of nomadic herdsmen or shepherds, such as those that had overrun and conquered the western provinces of the Roman Empire centuries earlier. The third, or agricultural stage, was peopled by more settled husbandmen who tilled the soil but who had, according to Smith, "little foreign commerce, and no other manufactures but those coarse and household ones which almost every private family prepares for its own use." As men advanced beyond this intermediate agricultural stage toward the highest, most complex levels of civilization, they eventually entered the fourth, or commercial stage. Represented by the most civilized areas of eighteenth-century Europe, where the development of commerce and the "finer" manufactures had progressed to a significant extent, this final form of social development was modern commercial society. It was characterized

8. For an exhaustive discussion of the "four stages" theory and its place in 18th-century social and economic thought, see Ronald L. Meek, *Social Science and the Ignoble Savage* (Cambridge, 1976).

by an advanced division of labor in the production process and the "polish" or "luxury" of a people of greatly refined manners and habits.[9]

As eighteenth-century analysts examined different societies of both the past and present, they discovered examples of each of the various stages, and they concluded that within any social system there was embedded a natural pattern of change that would normally manifest itself in time. According to most accounts, the basic stimulus to this change was population growth, which promoted a search first for supplementary sources of food and eventually for additional sources of employment that could support increased numbers of people.[10] Although the exact number of stages was often subject to individual interpretation, this general framework for describing the progress of societies provided the basis for virtually all discussions of social and economic development in the middle and late eighteenth century. During the American Revolution, for example, a writer in the *London Chronicle* offered the following typical assessment of the condition of the rebellious North American colonies:

There are five principal stages in the progress of mankind from the rudest state of barbarism to the highest state of politeness. Their first employment is hunting and fishing; their second pasturage, their third agriculture, their fourth manufactures, and their fifth trade and commerce. The Americans, at least the greatest part of them, are in the third of these stages; and beyond it they are not likely to advance for a considerable time, for this very obvious reason, that being possessed of an immense tract of country, and that, too, fertile in the highest degree, they will naturally employ themselves in cultivating the soil, before they begin to think of manufacturing its produce.[11]

In addition to shaping European assessments of the American condition, this conceptual framework became central to the way in which Americans themselves understood their society and its probable future.

Of tremendous significance in this formulation was the idea that each

9. Adam Smith, *An Inquiry into the Nature and Causes of the Wealth of Nations*, ed. Edwin Cannan (New York, 1937 [orig. publ. London, 1776]), 653, 655. In addition to Meek, *Social Science and the Ignoble Savage*, see Joseph Cropsey, *Polity and Economy: An Interpretation of the Principles of Adam Smith* (The Hague, 1957), 56–58, and Andrew S. Skinner, "Adam Smith: An Economic Interpretation of History," in Andrew S. Skinner and Thomas Watson, eds., *Essays on Adam Smith* (London, 1975), 154–178.

10. Roy Pascal, "Property and Society: The Scottish Historical School of the Eighteenth Century," *Modern Quarterly*, I (1938), 167–179.

11. *London Chronicle*, Jan. 24, 1778, printed in *Pennsylvania Magazine of History and*

stage of development was characterized not only by a particular form of social and economic organization, but also by appropriate and well-defined patterns of human behavior. Men's manners, habits, customs, and morals changed, in other words, as society advanced. Assessing the cultural consequences of social development thus proved to be an important but complex matter. Modern commercial society was very different in its economic organization from earlier, ruder societies. "In every improved society," Smith observed, the farmer was "generally nothing but a farmer" and "the manufacturer, nothing but a manufacturer," and he also noted that the labor "necessary to produce any one complete manufacture" was "almost always divided among a great number of hands." What had been "the work of one man in a rude state of society," in short, was "generally that of several in an improved one."[12] The establishment of this thorough division of labor created an intricate network of exchanges among men that destroyed the crude self-sufficiency characteristic of less civilized societies, where "every man endeavours to supply by his own industry his own occasional wants as they occur." In a commercial society, where "every man . . . lives by exchanging, or becomes in some measure a merchant," productivity was both increased and diversified. Men were no longer satisfied with the bare "necessaries" they could produce within their own households, but desired instead to produce and consume the more refined "conveniencies" and "luxuries" that an advanced division of labor made possible.[13] As men's tastes and patterns of consumption changed, so too did their habits, manners, and morals. Modern commercial society was creating new men as well as new economic institutions. Eighteenth-century thinkers could usually agree that the commercialization of society had serious consequences; their problem was to determine if those consequences were predominantly favorable, unfavorable, or some strange combination of both.

The troublesome term "luxury" was usually the focus of any consideration of the moral qualities of modern commercial society. Luxury had been present as a concept in Western culture as far back as classical antiquity, when Plato had established both general standards for defining it and a remarkably residual hostility toward it. In broadest terms,

---

Biography, VII (1883), 195–196. Meek, *Social Science and the Ignoble Savage*, has the most thorough discussion of the prevalence of this general conceptualization.

12. Smith, *Wealth of Nations*, ed. Cannan, 5.

13. *Ibid.*, 259, 22.

luxury traditionally referred to the dangerous forms of sensual excess that accompanied men's indulgence in artificial and superfluous pleasure. During the Middle Ages, when luxury had been considered one of the seven deadly sins, it had been associated with debilitating and anti-social behavior that clogged the individual mind, corrupted society, and endangered the public welfare. The eighteenth century, however, marked a transitional period in the Western understanding of luxury. As men were compelled to respond to the materialistic impulses of the rich new world around them, their confrontation of luxury became an increasingly ticklish and demanding matter. Traditional moral standards were called into question, and there was much disagreement about the precise meaning of the term and its proper application. As society advanced through the stages of development, what had formerly been considered "luxury" was now viewed by many observers as mere "convenience" or rational improvement.[14] Thus the English bishop William Warburton characteristically referred to luxury as "this ambiguous term," asserting that there was "no word more inconstantly used and capriciously applied to particular actions."[15]

In his *Essay on the History of Civil Society*, first published in 1767, Adam Ferguson struggled to offer an objective definition of the term. Men might agree that luxury signified the "complicated apparatus which mankind devise for the ease and convenience of life," including "their buildings, furniture, equipage, cloathing, train of domestics, refinement of the table, and, in general, all that assemblage which is rather intended to please the fancy, than to obviate real wants, and which is rather ornamental than useful." The problem, however, was that men were now "far from being agreed on the application of the term *luxury*, or on that degree of its meaning which is consistent with national prosperity, or with the moral rectitude of our nature."

14. The secondary literature on the notion of "luxury" in 18th-century thought is scattered. The best single study is Simeon M. Wade, Jr., "The Idea of Luxury in Eighteenth-Century England" (Ph.D. diss., Harvard University, 1968). See also John Sekora, *Luxury: The Concept in Western Thought, Eden to Smollett* (Baltimore, 1977), esp. chaps. 1–3. A brief but useful discussion of French thought on luxury can be found in Ellen Ross, "Mandeville, Melon, and Voltaire: The Origins of the Luxury Controversy in France," in Theodore Besterman, ed., *Studies on Voltaire and the Eighteenth Century*, CLV (Oxford, 1976), 1897–1912.

15. Quoted in Susie I. Tucker, *Protean Shape: A Study in Eighteenth-Century Vocabulary and Usage* (London, 1967), 146.

It is sometimes employed to signify a manner of life which we think necessary to civilization, and even to happiness. It is, in our panegyric of polished ages, the parent of arts, the support of commerce, and the minister of national greatness, and of opulence. It is, in our censure of degenerate manners, the source of corruption, and the presage of national declension and ruin. It is admired, and it is blamed; it is treated as ornamental and useful; and it is proscribed as a vice.[16]

As Ferguson here suggested, an eighteenth-century thinker's concept of luxury generally mirrored his attitude toward the contemporary commercial revolution. While some observers voiced only fear and were unequivocal in their condemnation of the commercialization of life, there were new optimists who, for the first time in Western thought, attempted an unqualified defense of commerce and the luxury it brought with it. These two extreme positions defined the spectrum of debate, with most thinkers exploring some intermediate, more balanced perspective that often led to a guarded ambivalence.[17]

At one end of the spectrum, traditional moralists continued to denounce luxury and modern commercial society in familiar terms. They asserted that luxury reflected as well as encouraged an unprincipled pursuit of private gain and an enervating indulgence of sordid and debauching human appetites. As society became commercialized, it was charged, men became increasingly selfish, greedy, and hedonistic, concerned more with their own personal wealth and comfort than with the welfare of society as a whole. It was common, in this regard, for eighteenth-century critics of luxury to compare contemporary society unfavorably to the ancient republic of Sparta, where commerce and the accumulation of private wealth had been banished in the interest of austerity and a virtuous, self-denying attention to the public good. According to these admirers of Sparta, commerce inevitably unleashed human avarice, and such a removal of necessary restraints promoted a devastating inequality among men that made a just social order impossible. As Jean Jacques

16. Adam Ferguson, *An Essay on the History of Civil Society* (Edinburgh, 1767), 375.

17. Relevant secondary material includes: E.A.J. Johnson, *Predecessors of Adam Smith: The Growth of British Economic Thought* (New York, 1937), esp. 281–300; W. L. Taylor, *Francis Hutcheson and David Hume as Predecessors of Adam Smith* (Durham, N.C., 1965), esp. 55–62, 103–117; Joseph J. Spengler, *French Predecessors of Malthus: A Study in Eighteenth-Century Wage and Population Theory* (Durham, N.C., 1942); and J.G.A. Pocock, "Civic Humanism and Its Role in Anglo-American Thought," in *Politics, Language, and Time: Essays in Political Thought and History* (New York, 1971), 80–103.

Rousseau and traditional moralists of his ilk warned, modern man's infatuation with commerce and the pursuit of riches only led to social chaos, empty individualism and privatism, and the disintegration of any meaningful form of human community.[18]

Rousseau was undoubtedly the most sensitive, perceptive, and challenging eighteenth-century critic of luxury and the new social order, for he delved deepest into what he understood to be the emotional and psychological malaise of contemporary civilization. His *Discours sur les sciences et les arts* (1749–1750), soon followed by his *Discours sur les fondémens de l'inégalité parmi les hommes* (1753–1754), provided a vigorous and categorical dissent against the new idea that the commercialization of human life was both natural and fundamentally salutary. Social development and the concomitant progress of the arts and sciences, as it was celebrated by Voltaire and other enlightened optimists throughout Europe, appeared instead to Rousseau as a degenerative process that divorced the human soul from its natural qualities of simplicity, goodness, and compassion. From his perspective, modern society created a multitude of artificial needs and desires in men to which they became enslaved. He pointed especially to the anxious, even frenetic, drive to achieve wealth and status that could never fully satisfy an illusory craving for social distinction. Harshness, competitiveness, jealousy, treachery, and hypocrisy came to characterize men's lives as they retreated ever further from the true inner springs of human action that were revealed in Rousseau's purely hypothetical state of nature, where primitive, pre-social men did not add unnecessary layers of greed and deception to their autonomous and spontaneously compassionate souls. For Rousseau, the "politeness" and urbanity of eighteenth-century Europe were only a misleading and superficial gloss on the profound unhappiness and alienation that lay beneath. Trapped in a new world of acquisitiveness and vanity, men had lost contact with their true selves and were now obsessed with luxury in a way that brought to a head the sickness of a materialistic civilization.[19]

18. See also R. H. Tawney, *Religion and the Rise of Capitalism: A Historical Study* (New York, 1926), esp. chap. 3.

19. See Judith N. Shklar, *Men and Citizens: A Study of Rousseau's Social Theory* (London, 1969); Ramon M. Lemos, *Rousseau's Political Philosophy: An Exposition and Interpretation* (Athens, Ga., 1977); and, above all, Mario Einaudi, *The Early Rousseau* (Ithaca,

By demanding unequivocally that his contemporaries confront the monstrous inequality, personal alienation, and loss of natural virtue that he associated with modern progress, Rousseau was often mistakenly viewed as a naive reactionary—a primitivist who foolishly wished to undo the civilization process and return society to a state of barbarous simplicity. Although Rousseau's analysis of the ills of modern commercial society drew on a traditional, and perhaps anachronistic, moral animus against luxury that had its roots in ancient philosophy and Christian theology, he clearly understood the futility of idle primitivist fantasies, and his outlook was far more sophisticated and psychologically acute than his critics were prone to admit. The adamant stridency of Rousseau's protest attests, above all, to the powerful appeal of the alternative persuasion he attacked. In one sense, he was launching a frontal assault on a purportedly enlightened view of the world that, in his eyes, represented a total reversal of Western thought.[20]

The new vision of man and society to which Rousseau objected so vehemently found vigorous expression in the pro-luxury writings of, among others, Voltaire, Jean-François Mélon, and the infamous Bernard Mandeville. If Rousseau's early tracts represent one end of the spectrum in the luxury controversy, the other extreme found its clearest voice in Mandeville's controversial *The Fable of the Bees* (1714). More than any other single figure, Mandeville set the tone for the eighteenth-century debate on luxury. In a ponderous social allegory that was judged by most of his contemporaries to be perversely cynical, this Anglo-Dutch physician and satirist appeared to defend as natural, necessary, and socially beneficial the commerce, luxury, and unfettered pursuit of individual gain that were part of the new economic order. Since men inevitably and quite naturally pursued their private pleasure, Mandeville suggested, it was foolish to expect them to behave "virtuously" in the traditional sense of that term. Moreover, in addition to flying in the face of normal human tendencies, classical austerity and self-denial were incompatible with social greatness, for only a desire to enjoy the pleasures of wealth and refinement could elicit the human exertion that raised society above the

---

N.Y., 1967). Einaudi's provocative study has tremendously influenced my brief discussion of Rousseau.

20. Einaudi, *Early Rousseau*, 56–60. See also Bertrand de Jouvenel, "Jean-Jacques Rousseau," *Encounter*, XIX (December 1962), 35–42.

level of brutal savagery. In its simplest terms, Mandeville's message in the *Fable* was that every powerful and prosperous modern society was, by necessity, built squarely upon the worldly foundations of "corruption"; namely, materialism, money grubbing, and pleasure seeking. He thus advanced the revolutionary idea that the private pursuit of sensual gratification, far from being reprehensibly enervating and selfish, was instead a positive force that unleashed the latent productive power of society.[21]

Since no state could be opulent and traditionally virtuous at the same time, it followed from Mandeville's logic that attempts by modern men to practice the classical or Christian virtues were misguided and would only bring society crashing down in ruins.[22] According to him, the consumption of even the most frivolous luxuries by the rich and powerful members of society should be welcomed rather than condemned. If nothing else, their propensity for extravagant consumption inadvertently created new forms of employment for the poverty-stricken masses of men who might otherwise be idle and starve. Although Mandeville's vision of progress through luxury excluded these members of a permanent lower class from participation in the new feast of consumption, he nevertheless stressed that the ostensibly decadent desire of the opulent classes to reap the pleasurable rewards of a materialistic age was actually a boon to the drudges of society. By generating employment that might at least support these "labouring poor" at a bare subsistence level, an economy built on the pursuit of luxury benefited all elements of a rigidly stratified society by detonating its explosive productive potential.[23]

Mandeville was groping in the *Fable* toward a new, utilitarian concept of virtue, by which any action that contributed to the welfare of society in the long run, even if it were the immediate consequence of traditional vices like greed, ambition, or avarice, could be considered virtuous in a more modern, realistic sense. The subtitle of his notorious allegory— "private vices, publick benefits"—captured the essence of this argument, which suggested that avaricious, self-aggrandizing behavior paradoxi-

---

21. Bernard Mandeville, *The Fable of the Bees: or, Private Vices, Publick Benefits*, ed. F. B. Kaye (Oxford, 1924 [orig. publ. London, 1714]). For a useful discussion of Mandeville's philosophy, see Hector Monro, *The Ambivalence of Bernard Mandeville* (Oxford, 1975).

22. Monro, *Ambivalence of Mandeville*, 4.

23. Wade, "Idea of Luxury," chap. 2; Sir Leslie Stephen, *History of English Thought in the Eighteenth Century* (New York, 1876), II, chap. 9; and Joyce Appleby, "Ideology and Theory: The Tension between Political and Economic Liberalism in Seventeenth-Century England," *American Historical Review*, LXXXI (1976), 499–515.

cally but inevitably furthered the public welfare or common good by contributing to the construction of a prosperous, thriving, and powerful commercial society.[24]

On the Continent, Mandeville's sentiments were most clearly corroborated in Mélon's *Essai politique sur le commerce* (1734). Mélon emphatically agreed that luxury was an inextricable part of modern society that, were it banished in order to restore primitive virtue, would only reduce civilized men to the wild lives, fierce manners, and barbarous isolation of the Hurons or the Iroquois of North America. Another French philosopher who admired both Mandeville and Mélon (and despised Rousseau) was the famed Voltaire, whose *Defence du Mondain* (1737) and other polemical tracts ridiculed reactionary moralists for blindly celebrating the rusticity and poverty of ancient republics. In his didactic pro-luxury poems, Voltaire presented a sparkling vision of a bright new world of sensual experience, where civilized men of polished manners were free to enjoy the refined pleasures that came with social progress.[25]

Although few of Mandeville's contemporaries were prepared to embrace his ideas, at least not in the extreme and shocking terms suggested in *The Fable of the Bees*, many of them agreed with Mélon and Voltaire that some accommodation with the new order was necessary. Probably the most influential defender of "polished ages" in the eighteenth century was the Scottish philosopher and historian David Hume, who persuasively explored the limitations of the traditional condemnation of commerce and luxury that remained very much alive. Hume's defense of commercial society was spirited and unequivocal, but it was also an attempt to mediate the claims of the two extreme and, from his point of view, absurd perspectives of his age, that of the Mandevillian "libertines" who praised even vicious luxury, and that of the naive moralists who, like Rousseau, found in even the most innocent luxury a devastating source of corruption.[26]

24. Monro, *Ambivalence of Mandeville*, esp. chaps. 1, 4, 7, and 8.

25. Ross, "Mandeville, Melon, and Voltaire," in Besterman, ed., *Studies on Voltaire*, CLV, 1905–1912; Einaudi, *Early Rousseau*, chap. 2.

26. Hume developed the brunt of his argument in two essays, "Of Commerce" and "Of Refinement in the Arts," first published in *Political Discourses* (Edinburgh, 1752). These and other relevant essays are conveniently reprinted in Eugene Rotwein, ed., *David Hume: Writings on Economics* (Madison, Wis., 1970 [orig. publ. 1955]). For secondary material on Hume's political economy, see, in addition to Rotwein's introduction to the above, the following: Johnson, *Predecessors of Adam Smith*, 281–300; Taylor, *Hutcheson and Hume*,

In making his case for the civilizing influence of commerce, Hume emphasized that the advance of commerce and the mechanical arts, on the one hand, and of the liberal and fine arts, on the other, were dynamically interdependent. "The same age, which produces great philosophers and politicians, renowned generals and poets," he wrote, "usually abounds with skillful weavers, and ship-carpenters." His point was straightforward: the spirit of an age affected "all the arts," and thus "the minds of men, being once roused from their lethargy, and put into a fermentation, turn themselves on all sides, and carry improvements into every art and science." As society became commercialized, the social as well as economic ties between men promoted all kinds of beneficial intercourse, resulting in a more civilized, refined, and learned culture. "Thus *industry, knowledge,* and *humanity,*" Hume summarized, "are linked together by an indissoluble chain, and are found, from experience as well as reason, to be peculiar to the more polished, and, what are commonly denominated, the more luxurious ages."[27]

Hume understood that this logic would fall on deaf ears among those of his readers who were conditioned to believe that any "refinement on the pleasures and conveniences of life" had a natural tendency "to beget venality and corruption." Acknowledging the prevalent temptation of his age "to declaim against present times, and magnify the virtue of remote ancestors," he opened fire on the crude fallacies in this traditional mode of thought. Was it really necessary to remind his contemporaries that "treachery and cruelty, the most pernicious and most odious of all vices," were far more common to rude, unpolished societies than to the allegedly corrupt nations of modern Europe? Philosophers could extol the virtues of primitive, pre-commercial societies as long as they had naive listeners to indulge; but every sane man, upon reflection, undoubtedly "would think his life or fortune much less secure in the hands of a MOOR or TARTER, than in those of a FRENCH or ENGLISH gentleman, the rank of men the most civilized in the most civilized nations."[28] For Hume, it was absurd to confuse the brutal savagery of primitive hunters and warriors with virtue. Men became truly virtuous when they exercised their natural

---

esp. 106–117; Gay, *Enlightenment,* II, 344–368; John B. Stewart, *The Moral and Political Philosophy of David Hume* (New York, 1963), esp. 172–195; and Wade, "Idea of Luxury," esp. chaps. 1 and 4.

27. "Of Refinement in the Arts," Rotwein, ed., *David Hume,* 22–23.

28. *Ibid.,* 27, 29.

powers of mind and body—their art and industry—to civilized ends. "Acknowledge, therefore, O man," he advised, "the beneficence of nature; for she has given thee that intelligence which supplies all thy necessities. But let not indolence, under the false appearance of gratitude," he added, "persuade thee to rest contented with her presents. Wouldest thou return to the raw herbiage for thy food, to the open sky for thy covering, and to stones and clubs for thy defence against the ravenous animals of the desert? Then return also to thy savage manners, to thy timorous superstition, to thy brutal ignorance; and sink thyself below those animals, whose condition thou admirest, and wouldest so fondly imitate."[29]

Just as the ancient republic of Sparta was a positive symbol of disinterested virtue to anti-commercial moralists of the eighteenth century, to Hume and to many of his sympathizers it was a negative symbol of barbaric and uncivilized ferocity—a society whose exclusion of commerce and luxury had been violent, unnatural, and stultifying.[30] According to Hume, Sparta stood as a warning to modern societies, not as a model, for it demonstrated that men could not be governed by a disinterested passion for the public good without an unacceptably tyrannical enforcement of perfect equality and austerity. It was far more natural, realistic, and just, he asserted, "to govern men by other passions, and animate them with a spirit of avarice and industry, art and luxury."[31] Since men would ordinarily lapse into an indolent and savage dissipation in the absence of the incentives to industry and exertion that luxury offered, they had to be indulged, and even encouraged, in their proclivity for luxury. By putting a premium on the stimulation of constructive human endeavor, Hume succeeded in couching an essentially Mandevillian argument in more palatable terms. Unlike Mandeville, he conceded the dangers of what he termed vicious or excessive luxury; but who could doubt, Hume asked, that commerce and luxury were the necessary catalysts in the shaping of any meaningful form of human civilization? "When excessive," luxury was "the source of many ills." Nevertheless, it was "in general preferable to sloth and idleness, which would commonly

---

29. "The Stoic," reprinted in T. H. Green and T. H. Grose, eds., *Essays: Moral, Political, and Literary, by David Hume* (London, 1882), I, 204. See also E. J. Hundert, "The Achievement Motive in Hume's Political Economy," *Journal of the History of Ideas*, XXXV (1974), 139–143.

30. Elizabeth Rawson, *The Spartan Tradition in European Thought* (London, 1969), 344–367.

31. "Of Commerce," Rotwein, ed., *David Hume*, 13.

succeed in its place, and are more hurtful both to private persons and to the public. When sloth reigns, a mean uncultivated way of life prevails amongst individuals, without society, without enjoyment."[32]

Hume's assault on the anti-luxury tradition was echoed in the writings of many other philosophers and polemicists who were just as anxious to contend that commerce was not inseparably tied to dissipation. "The refinements, elegancies and ornaments of civil life," William Temple concurred, "do not make intemperance and debauchery necessary; neither will the exclusion of them make a people abstemious, chaste, virtuous, and sober." A people could indeed "be all that is bad without commerce and the refinements of civil life, and all that is good with them," since "a simple life" certainly did not "extinguish the force of the selfish and cruel passions." On the contrary, these destructive passions appeared "in more horrible shapes" among the primitive North American natives than among the nations that practiced "refined luxury" and cultivated those "arts and ornaments of civil life" that restrained "in a great measure their ferocity."[33] Rousseau may have been impressed by the virtues of the "noble savage," but defenders of a new commercial age like Hume and Temple were appalled by the bestiality of the "ignoble savage" who roamed the forests of North America.

Hume's relatively moderate defense of luxury expressed a point of view that would attract considerable support in America as well as in Europe. Virtually all eighteenth-century thinkers agreed on one point: once men moved beyond the most primitive stage of social development represented by the natives of the New World, they came under the influence of "artificial needs" quite different from the simple subsistence needs that men shared with other forms of animal life. As self-conscious members of civil society, men inevitably compared their situation with that of their fellows in a process that generated a wide range of imaginary needs that became just as urgent as the more fundamental drive for subsistence. "Food and clothing constitute our only real needs," explained the French writer François Véron de Forbonnais, who characteristically distinguished between "les besoins réel" that men experienced

---

32. "Of Refinement in the Arts," *ibid.*, 32.

33. [William Temple], "A Vindication of Commerce and the Arts . . ." (London, 1758), reprinted in John R. McCulloch, ed., *A Select Collection of Scarce and Valuable Tracts on Commerce . . .* (London, 1859), 531. Temple was attempting to refute the traditional condemnation of luxury included in William Bell's prizewinning essay, *A Dissertation on the*

in a state of nature and "les besoins d'opinion" that arose in civil society. Just as "the idea of comfort comes to men only as a consequence of this first urge," luxury was "in its turn a consequence of comparing our condition with the superfluous comforts enjoyed by other individuals."[34] The controversial issue was whether these emulative urges stimulated progress or degeneration. "Men in society continually compare themselves to one another," Charles-François de Saint-Lambert noted in his article on luxury in the *Encyclopedia*, as they endeavor "unceasingly to establish the idea of their superiority, first in their own minds, then in the minds of others."[35] To Rousseau and other traditionalists, this compulsive desire for distinction imposed an impossible psychological burden on the individual that could end only in frustration, unhappiness, and alienation. To Saint-Lambert, however, as to Hume, it indirectly encouraged the industrious production of useful wealth that fostered a richer, more refined civilization. As long as men's selfish appetites did not run completely amok, their desire for wealth and distinction "supports, enriches, and gives life to every important society."[36]

Similarly, Josiah Tucker, the English clergyman and social commentator, admitted that the passion of self-love could be overindulged to the point of abuse, but he was more concerned with the consequences of the lethargy and apathy that would exist in its absence. Despite undeniable dangers, the restless appetites that arose from self-love should not be discouraged, because were they "once restrained, or greatly weakened, human Nature would make but feeble Efforts towards any thing great or good."[37] As the Scottish political economist Sir James Steuart aptly noted, these appetites offered the modern alternative to the enforced slave labor of earlier times, for men were now incited to labor not *"because they were slaves to others"* but because they were *"slaves to*

Following Subject: *What Causes Principally Contribute to Render a Nation Populous? And What Effect has the Populousness of a Nation on its Trade?* (Cambridge, 1756).

34. "Commerce," translated and reprinted in Nelly S. Hoyt and Thomas Cassirer, eds., *Encyclopedia: Selections* (Indianapolis, Ind., 1965), 49–50.

35. *Ibid.*, 217, 203–234.

36. *Ibid.*, 230.

37. *The Elements of Commerce and Theory of Taxes* (privately printed, 1755), published in Robert Livingston Schuyler, ed., *Josiah Tucker: A Selection from His Economic and Political Writings* (New York, 1931), 59. See also Walter Ernest Clark, *Josiah Tucker, Economist: A Study in the History of Economics* (New York, 1903).

their own wants."[38] Adapting the arguments of both Mandeville and Hume, Tucker appropriately observed that "every Man should be allowed, and even encouraged to be industrious in all such Ways as will serve himself and the Public together," because this unleashing of human energy was "the Foundation both of private Industry, and of national Prosperity and universal Plenty."[39]

[I I]

Although a wide variety of writers followed Hume in escaping the rigid confines of a traditional denunciation of sensuality, it is revealing that most of them conceded the potential dangers of luxury. Even those observers who celebrated the benefits of commerce often continued to worry about its concomitant capacity to have a deleterious influence on the strength and character of a society. More often than not, ambivalence characterized the writings of defenders of commerce who rejected Rousseau's extreme position but were not entirely comfortable in doing so. Among mid-eighteenth-century Englishmen who saw their country as an alarming replica of degenerate and declining Rome, John Brown, a belletrist and preacher, characteristically bemoaned the "vain, luxurious, and selfish EFFEMINACY" that had overtaken England's commercialized society. In a controversial tract that provoked a raging debate among his countrymen (and was also to become part of John Witherspoon's course in moral philosophy at Princeton and widely read throughout America), Brown examined a paradox central to the writings of the illustrious Montesquieu; to wit, that commerce always had the power to corrupt, as well as to polish manners and morals.[40]

38. Sir James Steuart, *An Inquiry into the Principles of Political Oeconomy*, ed. Andrew S. Skinner (Chicago, 1966 [orig. publ. London, 1767]), I, 51. For a broader discussion of Steuart's approach to political economy, see S. R. Sen, *The Economics of Sir James Steuart* (Cambridge, Mass., 1957).

39. Josiah Tucker, *Four Tracts, Together with Two Sermons, on Political and Commercial Subjects* (Gloucester, 1774), 14.

40. John Brown, *An Estimate of the Manners and Principles of the Times*, 2d ed. (London, 1757), 29. See also Book XX of Montesquieu's *De l'Esprit des lois* (Paris, 1748). For the reference to Brown's influence in America, see Douglass G. Adair, "The Intellectual Origins of Jeffersonian Democracy: Republicanism, the Class Struggle, and the Virtuous Farmer" (Ph.D. diss., Yale University, 1943), 53, and Bernard Bailyn, *The Ideological Origins of the American Revolution* (Cambridge, Mass., 1967), 87. An excellent discussion

In typical eighteenth-century fashion, Brown noted that the impact of commerce on human society proceeded through several successive stages. In the first, commerce supplied mutual necessities, prevented mutual wants, extended mutual knowledge, eradicated mutual prejudice, and spread mutual humanity. In its middle and more advanced stage, it provided conveniences, increased population, coined money, gave birth to the arts and sciences, created equal laws, and diffused general plenty and happiness. But in its third and highest stage, Brown warned, commerce seemed to change its nature and effects; it brought in superfluity and vast wealth, promoting avarice, gross luxury, and effeminacy among the higher ranks of men. "In its first and middle stages," he observed, commerce "is beneficent; in its last, dangerous and fatal." It first polished and strengthened societies, but then corrupted, weakened, and destroyed them.[41] Brown was saved from a fatalistic despair about England's future only by the cautious hope that the social cycle he described might not be inevitable. Perhaps it was possible, in other words, to retain the necessary benefits of commerce while preventing or staving off its harmful and destructive tendencies. Thus he proposed that "Commerce and Wealth be not discouraged in their Growth; but checked and controuled in their Effects." Brown appeared to recognize, however, that this deceptively simple formula raised as many problems as it solved.[42]

Despite his gloomy evaluation of England's present condition, Brown was pointedly disputing a common tendency among eighteenth-century thinkers to employ a traditional biological analogy. Dating back to the ancient Greeks, that analogy likened political societies to organisms that were born, matured, decayed, and died. According to this view, societies, like men, always had an age, and they naturally proceeded from "youth" through "manhood" to maturity and "old age." This metaphor suggested a cyclical view of historical development in which change, or the process of time, was eventually and inevitably associated with decay. Social maturity had definite advantages over youth, but it also presaged the inevitable onset of corruption and dissolution.

of Brown's *Estimate* and the furor it provoked can be found in Wade, "Idea of Luxury," chaps. 5–9.

41. Brown, *Estimate of Manners and Principles*, 151, 151–153.

42. *Ibid.*, 217. For an earlier and parallel statement of Brown's view of the stages of commerce, see Richard Jackson to Benjamin Franklin, June 17, 1755, in Leonard W. Labaree *et al.*, eds., *The Papers of Benjamin Franklin* (New Haven, Conn., 1959–), VI, 81–82.

Brown was not alone in attempting to discourage the facile application of this traditional analogy, but the metaphor of a cyclical social process, with all of its pessimistic implications, retained a significant, if not dominant, place in the eighteenth-century mind.[43] Many observers feared, indeed, that progress, development, and decay might take place simultaneously; even a fulsome pride in man's material and technological achievements did not preclude expressions of historical pessimism that emphasized cultural decadence or moral and spiritual decay. As Saint Augustine had suggested centuries earlier, man's possession of faculties crucial to his material and intellectual progress on earth (his covetousness of gain and his lust for knowledge, for example) could also contribute to a parallel decay of the spirit and soul.[44] It is not surprising, therefore, that as men in the eighteenth century viewed the progress of societies through the stages of development, from rudeness to civilization and from youth to maturity, they very often had a mixed or ambivalent judgment of the process.

Although the Enlightenment has customarily been linked to the rise of confidence in the potential for human progress, such an unqualified association can be seriously misleading. There can be no doubt that the age of the Enlightenment eventually saw the birth of a new metaphor of growth, of a vision of unending social progress without decline or decay that culminated in the effusive optimism of William Godwin and the marquis de Condorcet at the end of the century. Nevertheless, many of the most enlightened perceptions of social growth in the eighteenth century were permeated with a nagging skepticism. As Peter Gay has reminded us, the philosophes usually saw progress as circumscribed and impermanent, always bringing with it evils as well as blessings, and this apparent "law of compensation" applied especially to their understand-

43. Brown, *Estimate of Manners and Principles*, 213–214. For an extended and detailed analysis of this pattern of thought from classical antiquity to the present, see Nisbet, *Social Change and History*, esp. chap. 3. See also Henry Vyverberg, *Historical Pessimism in the French Enlightenment* (Cambridge, Mass., 1958); Lois Whitney, *Primitivism and the Idea of Progress in English Popular Literature of the Eighteenth Century* (Baltimore, 1934); Gay, *Enlightenment*, II, esp. 100–107; and Stow Persons, "The Cyclical Theory of History in Eighteenth Century America," *American Quarterly*, VI (1954), 147–163. For examples of the application of the analogy by American writers, see Oliver Noble, *Some Strictures upon . . . the Book of Esther* (Newburyport, Mass., 1775), 7, and William Henry Drayton, *A Charge, on the Rise of the American Empire . . .* (Charleston, S.C., 1776), 2–3.

44. Nisbet, *Social Change and History*, 90–97.

ing of the movement of society through its customary stages of development.[45] Perhaps the most systematic, perceptive analysis of social progress in the mid-eighteenth century came in the writings of the Scottish school of "sociological historians," whose perspective much influenced American thinkers. The rudimentary social science of Adam Ferguson, Lord Kames, John Millar, and, most notably, Adam Smith—which arose in the context of the commercialization of Scottish society itself—reveals quite well how an attention to this law of compensation prevented an unqualified optimism about the reality and potential of human progress.[46]

On the whole it can be said that the Scots had a positive view of social development and welcomed it. Adam Smith approved of the structural consequences of the commercialization of society, for he saw economic change as a peaceful way of bringing about a desirable social transformation. In his scheme of "philosophical history," the advance of Western Europe to the fourth, or commercial, stage of development had marked the decline of the rigidly hierarchical feudal order of the last phase of the third, or agricultural, stage, where great proprietors had maintained large numbers of tenants and retainers in abject dependence. The transition to a modern market economy had been initiated, as Smith described it, by accident, when feudal barons, rather than continuing to use their agricultural surplus exclusively for the support of their retainers, had indulged their vanity by bartering it for the new luxuries offered by merchants and manufacturers. The long-term consequences of this unthinking decision were momentous. Former retainers eventually gained a new measure of comparative independence and greater personal liberty; the great proprietors gradually lost their absolute judicial and military power, resulting in regular and orderly government in the countryside; and the social foundations were laid for greater productivity and sus-

45. Gay, *Enlightenment*, II, 101–107, 362–368. See also Vyverberg, *Historical Pessimism*, esp. 1–6, 229–231.

46. In addition to Bryson, *Man and Society*, and Cropsey, *Polity and Economy*, see David Kettler, *The Social and Political Thought of Adam Ferguson* (Columbus, Ohio, 1965), and the several studies by William C. Lehmann: *Adam Ferguson and the Beginnings of Modern Sociology: An Analysis of the Sociological Elements in His Writings with Some Suggestions as to His Place in the History of Social Theory* (New York, 1930); *John Millar of Glasgow, 1735–1801: His Life and Thought and His Contributions to Sociological Analysis* (Cambridge, 1960); and *Henry Home, Lord Kames, and the Scottish Enlightenment: A Study in National Character and in the History of Ideas* (The Hague, 1971).

tained economic growth. To this extent, Smith and his fellow Scots applauded the broader, sociological consequences of the rise of modern commercial society.[47]

They also tended to agree with their countryman Hume that the commercialization of society had a predominantly salutary effect on men's habits and manners—at least initially. "Whenever commerce is introduced into any country," Smith observed in his *Lectures*, "probity and punctuality always accompany it." Men became industrious, sober, disciplined, frugal, honest, and imbued with a contractual understanding of justice; these were major virtues that were unknown in rude or barbarous countries.[48] By arousing men from their customary lethargy, commerce served society well, for commercial men who regularly exercised their art and industry created, in addition to new wealth, a civilized culture of softened, more humane manners and morals. Thus to the extent that commerce encouraged cultural progress by replacing the inhumanity of the savage and the unproductive indolence of the feudal landowner with moderation, sincerity, and industry, Smith welcomed the advance of society toward the higher stages of development.[49]

But there were also many doubts and misgivings among the Scots. Without exception, their analysis of the commercialization process was clouded by ambivalence. Henry Home, Lord Kames, echoed the sentiments of John Brown, for instance, when he admitted that all too often commerce and luxury proceeded beyond the ameliorative stage and began to have a corrupting influence on social character. "Nations originally are poor and virtuous," Kames noted in his *Sketches of the History of Man*, published in 1774. "They advance to industry, commerce, and perhaps to conquest and empire," he continued, undoubtedly thinking of the Roman example that so preoccupied the eighteenth-century mind. "But this state is never permanent: great opulence opens a wide door to

47. Smith, *Wealth of Nations*, ed. Cannan, Book III, chaps. 2–4, 361–396. See also Skinner, "Adam Smith," in Skinner and Watson, eds., *Essays on Adam Smith*, and D. A. Reisman, *Adam Smith's Sociological Economics* (London, 1976), esp. chaps. 3 and 5.

48. Adam Smith, *Lectures on Justice, Police, Revenue, and Arms*, ed. Edwin Cannan (Oxford, 1896), 253.

49. *Ibid.*, 253–259; Reisman, *Smith's Sociological Economics*, chap. 3; Kettler, *Social and Political Thought of Ferguson*, chaps. 6–7. For a broader discussion of this defense of commercial men, see Ralph Lerner, "Commerce and Character: The Anglo-American as New-Model Man," *William and Mary Quarterly*, 3d Ser., XXXVI (1979), 3–26.

indolence, sensuality, corruption, prostitution, perdition."[50] As luxury surpassed a healthy degree, men's social affections waned, rendering them as inactive and selfish as brute savages. As the polish of a culture corroded into corruption, there was, as Adam Ferguson put it, suggesting the cyclical pattern, "a kind of spontaneous return to obscurity and weakness."[51]

The pitfalls of the degenerative process that Kames and Ferguson described extended beyond the decay of men's manners and morals; it also created grave structural problems in the organization of society. The progress of the division of labor, with its specialization and increased productivity, was the earmark of modern commercial society, but this progress invariably had disturbing consequences as well. As Rousseau had suggested, it tended to produce glaring inequalities of wealth, status, and power, whereby a mass of poverty-stricken laborers became danger-ously dependent on a privileged class of property-owning employers.[52] Although modern commercial society may have initially marked an im-provement over the stark inequality and dependency of feudal society, the Scots agreed that the modern social form eventually produced its own system of inegalitarian subjection. "In every commercial state, notwith-standing any pretension to equal rights," Ferguson conceded, "the ex-altation of a few must depress the many."[53] This concern among the Scots with a modern form of inequality was often directed at the hordes of so-called "labouring poor," whose depressed condition so bedeviled eighteenth-century reformers, including Adam Smith.

Although Smith emphatically approved of an advanced division of labor as the basis of continuing economic growth and social progress, he was also concerned with its concomitant tendency to relegate the labor-ing classes to a brutish existence that crippled their minds and bodies. Smith believed that a man's character was formed to an overwhelming

50. Henry Home, Lord Kames, *Sketches of the History of Man* (Edinburgh, 1813 [orig. publ. 1774]), I, 525.

51. Ferguson, *Essay on History of Civil Society*, 318.

52. Einaudi, *Early Rousseau*, chaps. 6 and 9. In addition to the writings of Rousseau cited earlier, see his *Discours sur l'Economie politique* (1754–1755), conveniently reprinted in Jean Jacques Rousseau, *The Social Contract, and Discourses*, trans. G.D.H. Cole (New York, 1950), 285–330.

53. Ferguson, *Essay on History of Civil Society*, 285, cited in Gay, *Enlightenment*, II, 342.

extent by his profession or his function in the production process. As the division of labor became more specialized in modern commercial society, so too did the activities of individual working men, and the result, Smith argued, was a frightening dehumanization of the laboring classes.[54] In the *Wealth of Nations*, he offered a vivid description of the enfeebled, even mutilated, minds of workers who were engaged in advanced forms of manufacturing—such as those who spent their lives putting the heads on pins:

In the progress of the division of labour, the employment of the far greater part of those who live by labour, that is, of the great body of the people, comes to be confined to a few very simple operations, frequently to one or two. But the understandings of the greater part of men are necessarily formed by their ordinary employments. The man whose whole life is spent in performing a few simple operations, of which the effects too are, perhaps, always the same, or very nearly the same, has no occasion to exert his understanding, or to exercise his invention in finding out expedients for removing difficulties which never occur. He naturally loses, therefore, the habit of such exertion, and generally becomes as stupid and ignorant as it is possible for a human creature to become.[55]

Because of their debased condition, these new "savages" were poor candidates for good citizens and soldiers; hence their deplorable situation had far-reaching consequences for society as a whole. "Of the great and extensive interests of his country," Smith wrote of the worker,

he is altogether incapable of judging; and unless very particular pains have been taken to render him otherwise, he is equally incapable of defending his country in war. His dexterity at his own particular trade seems, in this manner, to be acquired at the expence of his intellectual, social, and martial virtues. But in every improved and civilized society this is the state into which the labouring poor, that is, the great body of the people, must necessarily fall, unless government takes some pains to prevent it.[56]

54. For excellent discussions of this matter, see Reisman, *Smith's Sociological Economics*, chaps. 3 and 6; Robert L. Heilbroner, "The Paradox of Progress: Decline and Decay in *The Wealth of Nations*," in Skinner and Watson, eds., *Essays on Adam Smith*, 524–539; and E. G. West, "Adam Smith and Alienation: Wealth Increases, Men Decay?" *ibid.*, 540–552.
55. Smith, *Wealth of Nations*, ed. Cannan, 734.
56. *Ibid.*, 735.

"To remedy these defects," Smith grimly concluded, "would be an object worthy of serious attention."[57] He could never conceive of entrusting this "great body of the people" with political power, since he feared that their condition would permit them to be nothing other than the tools of their employers. Unable to participate responsibly in the political process, the laboring poor in modern commercial society had been rendered unfit for any form of democracy by the impact of an advanced division of labor.[58]

Ferguson, Kames, and Millar seemed just as troubled as Smith by this phenomenon. An excessive division of labor that led to monotonous work habits, wrote Kames, "confines the mind to a single object and excludes all thought and invention: in such a train of life the operator becomes dull and stupid like a beast of burden." "Men by inaction," he lamented, "degenerate into oysters."[59] By contrast, ironically, the mass of the people in ruder, less civilized societies seemed to have a much more elevated character. In the so-called "barbarous societies" of hunters, shepherds, "and even of husbandmen in that rude state of husbandry which precedes the improvement of manufactures, and the extension of foreign commerce," Smith wrote, the varied occupations of every man obliged him "to exert his capacity, and to invent expedients for removing difficulties which are continually occuring." In this way invention was "kept alive," and the minds of men were not "suffered to fall into that drowsy stupidity, which, in a civilized society, seems to benumb the understanding of almost all the inferior ranks of people."[60] Because of Smith's perception of this dramatic contrast, he was even prone on occasion to wax eloquent about the superiority of the traditional agricultural way of life in contemporary Europe to the more modern life-style of urban skilled laborers. He greatly resented the increasingly popular habit of denigrating the simple farmer, whose versatile skills and nimble mind actually gave him a character "much superior" to that of the manufacturer. "How much the lower ranks of people in the country are really superior to those of the town," Smith sniffed, "is well known to every

57. Smith, *Lectures*, ed. Cannan, 259.

58. Reisman, *Smith's Sociological Economics*, 205–207.

59. Kames, *Sketches of History of Man*, I, 152–153. For comparable statements from Ferguson and Millar, see the discussion in Reisman, *Smith's Sociological Economics*, 153–154.

60. Smith, *Wealth of Nations*, ed. Cannan, 735. See also Heilbroner, "Paradox of Progress," in Skinner and Watson, eds., *Essays on Adam Smith*, 530–532.

man whom either business or curiosity has led to converse much with both."[61]

To the Scots, in short, the advance of society was never the unmixed blessing that Mandeville had celebrated. They never doubted that social and economic development had serious, apparently unavoidable pitfalls. They were willing to pay this price for progress, but they could also never bury completely their uneasy misgivings. As society advanced naturally toward the higher stages of development, the civilizing effects of commerce were ironically threatened by a fundamental deterioration of the human condition best exemplified in the degradation of a new class of modern savages. Beyond a certain point, the civilizing process seemed to turn to one of corruption; the commercialization of society promised to humanize men but, as the law of compensation took its toll, also to debase them. The gloomier side of the Scots' assessment of social progress was to become particularly relevant to the fears and concerns of American republicans, because the brutish creatures Smith described, the so-called "labouring poor," were incompatible with the dramatically new form of government and society that the Revolutionaries aspired to build.

[III]

Even a cursory examination of the eighteenth-century confrontation with economic growth would be incomplete without some discussion of the role of government, a matter that, as George Mason's later concern with the Port Bill suggests, was also to be of central importance to American republicans. It is worth emphasizing that when Adam Smith discussed the devastating repercussions of an advanced division of labor, he pinned no specific blame on the political system. He was concerned here with the ramifications of a natural process that was theoretically unrelated to government action. In fact, rather than attribute this particular problem to political machinations that interfered with a beneficent natural order, he suggested that compensatory governmental measures were necessary to ameliorate the unfavorable conditions brought about by this brand of natural progress.[62]

61. Smith, *Wealth of Nations*, ed. Cannan, 127. See also Heilbroner, "Paradox of Progress," in Skinner and Watson, eds., *Essays on Adam Smith*, 358.

62. Smith, *Wealth of Nations*, ed. Cannan, 736–738; Reisman, *Smith's Sociological Economics*, chap. 7.

Nevertheless, the thrust of Smith's teaching in political economy, as anyone who has ever heard of the "invisible hand" would readily insist, was that meddlesome government was the primary culprit in Europe's social and economic difficulties. This dimension of Smith's approach can easily be overemphasized, for he objected more to specific kinds of governmental interference, which he lumped under the rubric of "the mercantile system" or "the policy of Europe," than to the general presence of government in the social and economic process. The eighteenth century was still an age of *political* economy, and Smith, as part of his age, assumed that government was to a great extent inextricably tied to the operation of a country's society and economy.[63] Even the French physiocrats, who were apostles of the "rule of nature" in economic life, assumed that a powerful government was necessary to implement and enforce economic natural law. They did not question monarchy, absolutism, or the interventionist state; they merely wanted government to behave differently.[64] Both Smith and the physiocrats objected to specific abuses of this necessary role of government, systematic abuses that compounded the problems experienced by the nations of modern Europe as they underwent the process of commercialization. In its simplest terms, Smith's momentous indictment of what has come to be known as "mercantilism" can be viewed as part of a broader eighteenth-century controversy over the relationship between government and social change—a controversy that was closely tied to the contemporaneous problem of determining whether certain patterns of change were properly understood as progress, decay, or some strange amalgam of both.

Much of this debate in political economy took the form of reactions to the new activities and functions of government in the eighteenth century.

63. See especially, Jacob Viner, "Adam Smith and Laissez Faire," in John Maurice Clark *et al.*, *Adam Smith, 1776–1926: Lectures to Commemorate the Sesquicentennial of the Publication of "The Wealth of Nations"* (Chicago, 1928), 116–155; Glenn R. Morrow, *The Ethical and Economic Theories of Adam Smith: A Study in the Social Philosophy of the Eighteenth Century* (New York, 1923); Élie Halévy, *The Growth of Philosophic Radicalism*, trans. Mary Morris (London, 1928), chap. 3; and William Letwin, *The Origins of Scientific Economics: English Economic Thought, 1660–1776* (London, 1963), chap. 8. Also useful for its general discussion of the political dimension of 18th-century economic thought is Walton H. Hamilton and Douglass Adair, *The Power to Govern: The Constitution—Then and Now* (New York, 1937), esp. chap. 4.

64. Elizabeth Fox-Genovese, *The Origins of Physiocracy: Economic Revolution and Social Order in Eighteenth-Century France* (Ithaca, N.Y., 1976); Mario Einaudi, *The Physiocratic Doctrine of Judicial Control* (Cambridge, Mass., 1938).

In England, the growth of a modern fiscal system in the wake of the Glorious Revolution and the ensuing decades of war drew fire from a vocal opposition that viewed this financial revolution as a dangerous innovation. The funding of the national debt, the creation of the Bank of England and other large moneyed companies, and the establishment of a permanent stock and money market were an integral part of England's "revolution settlement." The boom in speculation and the rise of a new class of "moneyed men" that accompanied the system and culminated in the infamous South Sea Bubble of 1720 became the focus of a prolonged and heated controversy whose influence on the development of American republican thought has been clearly established. The "country" opposition to an allegedly corrupting connection between the English government and the new economic order—corruption manifested in ministerial influence in Parliament, the public support of "stockjobbers" and other dependents, and the like—percolated quickly to America where, in the end, it shaped both the ideology of the Revolution and the Jeffersonian opposition to the Federalists in the 1790s.[65] The recent historiographical emphasis on the financial revolution and the "country" reaction it provoked has tended to obscure, however, other dimensions of eighteenth-century political economy that can be useful in furthering our understanding of American republican perspectives.

Both in England and on the Continent men vigorously debated the proper role of government in promoting different kinds of economic activity. Smith and the physiocrats were in the vanguard of a movement to combat the common belief that foreign commerce and manufactures were the crucial sectors of any national economy and, as such, that they were deserving of special political attention and support. To Smith, the "mercantile system" or "policy of Europe" involved an elaborate system of privileges extended to merchants and manufacturers in order to promote their private interests, which according to faulty mercantilist logic coincided with the national interest. In France, the physiocrats were part

65. Dickson, *Financial Revolution in England*; Isaac Kramnick, *Bolingbroke and His Circle: The Politics of Nostalgia in the Age of Walpole* (Cambridge, Mass., 1968); J.G.A. Pocock, *The Machiavellian Moment: Florentine Political Thought and the Atlantic Republican Tradition* (Princeton, N.J., 1975), chaps. 13–15; Lance Banning, *The Jeffersonian Persuasion: Evolution of a Party Ideology* (Ithaca, N.Y., 1978); Rodger D. Parker, "The Gospel of Opposition: A Study in Eighteenth-Century Anglo-American Ideology" (Ph.D. diss., Wayne State University, 1975).

of a general revolt against the legacy of the seventeenth-century regime of Louis XIV and his chief minister, Jean Baptiste Colbert. Beginning in the early eighteenth century and reaching a peak in the late 1740s and early 1750s, French commentators attacked Colbert's notorious system of state subsidization of manufacturing establishments, particularly in the luxury industries.[66] The general complaint in both countries was that these political preferences operated to the disadvantage of agriculture, in the process stifling productivity, encouraging rural depopulation, and promoting unnecessary social misery.

According to Smith, the mercantile system of political economy—whose goal, as he described it, was "to enrich a great nation rather by trade and manufactures than by the improvement and cultivation of land, rather by the industry of the towns than by that of the country"—ultimately rested on deception.[67] The inhabitants of the towns, the merchants and manufacturers, had duped both government officials and the inhabitants of the countryside into believing that "the private interest of a part, and of a subordinate part of the society" was identical to "the general interest of the whole."[68] Writing a year prior to the publication of the *Wealth of Nations*, the English polemicist George Whatley pithily expressed Smith's point of view when he suggested that most of the statutes, acts, edicts, and arrets that clogged the administrations of Europe were "either political Blunders, or Jobbs obtain'd by artful Men, for private Advantage, under Pretence of public Good."[69] Smith contended that a "profusion of government" had retarded the natural growth of England's economy by diverting capital away from agriculture, always the most productive form of investment, into less productive channels. The new and overgrown government bureaucracy was itself a devastating drain on resources, but Smith's concern extended beyond this specific problem.[70] He believed that equal amounts of capital in-

---

66. A. W. Coats, "Adam Smith and the Mercantile System," in Skinner and Watson, eds., *Essays on Adam Smith*, 218–236; Spengler, *French Predecessors of Malthus*, esp. chaps. 2 and 5.

67. Smith, *Wealth of Nations*, ed. Cannan, 591.

68. *Ibid.*, 128.

69. [George Whatley], *Principles of Trade . . .* , 2d ed. (London, 1774), 33.

70. Smith, *Wealth of Nations*, ed. Cannan, 328, 325–329. Smith deplored the waste of public revenue "in maintaining unproductive hands," such as those "who compose a numerous and splendid court, a great ecclesiastical establishment, great fleets and armies, who

vested in different ways produced varying quantities of productive labor and useful wealth, and he established a hierarchy, a natural progression of decreasing utility, in which investment in agriculture ranked as most productive, manufacturing second, and the various forms of domestic and foreign commerce last. In the absence of interference from government, he argued, capital naturally flowed into these channels in the most beneficial sequence. Under such conditions, it could be expected that a nation would not develop extensive manufactures or a prolific carrying trade until the more productive agricultural sector of the economy had been fully developed. The disastrous effect of the mercantile system in Europe, however, was precisely to upset and even invert this natural order.[71] Smith ultimately pointed to England's North American colonies to illustrate the advantages of a contrasting system of "natural liberty," where the unimpeded investment of virtually all capital in agriculture, he contended, was "the principal cause" of the colonies' "rapid progress" toward "wealth and greatness."[72]

Writers throughout Europe shared Smith's general concern with the languishing state of agriculture under a mercantile system such as England's. In France, the physiocrats were alarmed by the disastrous consequences of a political system that put a premium on the production of manufactures, especially luxury manufactures, at the expense of the cultivation of the countryside.[73] Quesnay and his disciples were obsessed with improving the underdeveloped state of French agriculture, which they traced to a burdensome system of taxation and a battery of mercantilist privileges that had upset the natural order of economic life. The force of this misguided political system, they charged, drew human energy away from the production of useful "necessaries" that supported

in time of peace produce nothing, and in time of war acquire nothing which can compensate the expence of maintaining them, even while the war lasts." These sycophants produced nothing themselves and were maintained "by the produce of other men's labour." *Ibid.*, 325.

71. *Ibid.*, Book II, chap. 5, and Book IV. See especially C. R. Fay, "Adam Smith, America, and the Doctrinal Defeat of the Mercantile System," *Quarterly Journal of Economics*, XLVIII (1933–1934), 304–316; R. Koebner, "Adam Smith and the Industrial Revolution," *Economic History Review*, 2d Ser., XI (1958–1959), 381–391.

72. Smith, *Wealth of Nations*, ed. Cannan, 347.

73. In addition to the studies by Spengler and Fox-Genovese cited above, useful secondary works include: Ronald L. Meek, *The Economics of Physiocracy: Essays and Transla-*

the mass of the people to the fabrication of frivolous "superfluities" that were consumed only by a wealthy elite. Such an artificial diversion of capital from agriculture to manufactures, Quesnay wrote, had become the lamentable rule in "poor kingdoms where the greater part of the overabundant luxury manufactures are kept going by means of exclusive privileges."[74] A system of fashion and luxury, enforced by political means, thus took precedence over more fundamental subsistence needs, and the human costs were staggering. Large numbers of people were steadily drawn away from the countryside, off the land, into less productive occupations in crowded urban areas. The ultimate result of this rural depopulation was the widespread poverty, moral decadence, and shameful squandering of resources—both natural and human—that characterized a stagnant socioeconomic order where depressed laboring classes were systematically manipulated to support the extravagantly corrupt life-style of a politically privileged minority.[75]

[IV]

Neither Adam Smith nor most of the French commentators who shared his concerns ever embraced in its totality the formal physiocratic system of political economy, which had a rigorous technical and philosophical basis. And although the writings of the physiocrats were far from un-

---

tions (Cambridge, Mass., 1963); Werner Sombart, *Luxury and Capitalism*, trans. W. R. Dittmar (New York, 1938 [orig. publ. Munich and Leipzig, 1913]); Martin Albaum, "The Moral Defenses of the Physiocrats' Laissez-Faire," *Jour. Hist. Ideas*, XVI (1955), 179–197.

74. The quote is from "General Maxims for the Economic Government of an Agricultural Kingdom," translated by Ronald L. Meek and printed in Meek, *Economics of Physiocracy*, 245. Meek's volume, which includes translations of the physiocrats' writings and several of his own interpretive essays, is an indispensable introduction to the physiocrats.

75. Many non-physiocrats shared these general concerns, most notably Rousseau. Joseph Spengler's *French Predecessors of Malthus* is the best general account of the broader context of the public discussion of which the physiocrats were a crucial part. Also useful are Kingsley Martin, *The Rise of French Liberal Thought: A Study of Political Ideas from Bayle to Condorcet*, ed. J. P. Mayer, 2d ed. rev. (New York, 1954 [orig. publ. 1929]), chap. 9; William H. Wickwar, "Helvétius and Holbach," in F.J.C. Hearnshaw, ed., *The Social and Political Ideas of Some Great French Thinkers of the Age of Reason* (New York, 1930), 195–216; and Everett C. Ladd, Jr., "Helvétius and d'Holbach: 'La moralisation de la politique,'" *Jour. Hist. Ideas*, XXIII (1962), 221–238.

known across the Atlantic, there were few dedicated disciples in America either.[76] Nevertheless, the physiocrats articulated most clearly a resonant cluster of fears and concerns that were to find extensive expression among republican thinkers in America. Americans understood how a society could grow old naturally as it proceeded through the customary stages of social organization, and they were very much concerned, as Jefferson revealed in his commentary in the *Notes on Virginia*, with the potentially corrupting effects of this unavoidable development through time. But they also recognized that a society could be prematurely pushed into decay, and its predicament unnecessarily aggravated, by the insidious operations of a mercantilist government that embraced faulty economic principles and catered to the demands of privileged groups and special interests. As many of the anti-mercantilist writers in France noted, the real tragedy of their country's situation was that it was unnecessarily premature. After all, the introduction of extensive luxury manufacturing need normally occur only after a country's agricultural potential had been fully realized. Applied to America, with its vast resources of uncultivated land, this cast of mind would identify the specter of political corruption, especially in the form of a government dedicated to the kinds of economic practices that Smith and the physiocrats condemned, as a more immediate threat to social well-being than the inevitable ravages of time.

When the Revolutionaries in America forged a commitment to republicanism, in sum, they were confronted almost immediately with several fundamental and interrelated questions, all of which were rooted in this broader universe of eighteenth-century perceptions and concerns. At which stage or stages of social development was republicanism viable? Did American society correspond to such a stage? If so, for how long could the country remain at a republican stage of social development? And finally, what was the proper role of government in consolidating a republican order in America? Together, these questions established a basic context for public debate in political economy that would prevail during the half century from the Revolution to the War of 1812. This context first began to take form in the 1760s and 1770s with the burgeoning revolt against English "corruption." From one perspective,

76. Two noteworthy exceptions were Benjamin Franklin, who directly absorbed physiocratic doctrine into his thinking, and George Logan, a friend of Franklin's and a prominent Jeffersonian after 1790. Both will receive attention in the chapters below.

the mother country represented to the Revolutionaries the perfect example of an old, highly developed society that demonstrated all too well the insidious tendencies of the Scots' "law of compensation." For as Adam Smith observed, and as most Americans came to agree, it was cruelly ironic that in England, the most civilized country of all, "the people who cloathe the whole world are in rags themselves."[77]

77. Smith, *Lectures*, ed. Cannan, 257.

CHAPTER TWO

THE REPUBLICAN REVOLUTION

In the eyes of the American Revolutionaries, England had degenerated by the 1770s into a state of irredeemable corruption. When the British radical Richard Price described his own country in 1776 as "enervated by luxury; encumbered with debts; and hanging by a thread," he voiced the consensus of the insurgents across the Atlantic.[1] The Revolutionaries had little doubt, moreover, that England's contagion would engulf the colonies if the imperial connection was not severed. On this level, the Revolution became a struggle to establish a society that would escape the decay and corruption that had overtaken so much of the Old World. The task of securing such a republic in late eighteenth-century America posed a formidable challenge, however, in no small part because the ideology of "republicanism" that guided the Revolution was so fragile, torn by serious tensions and ambiguities. In one very fundamental sense, it was an ideology in flux, caught precariously between traditional concerns anchored in classical antiquity and the new and unstable conditions of an expansive commercial society.

The Revolutionaries shouldered a burden that was common to the intellectual life of their age—the burden of bridging the widening gap between traditional and modern ways of thought in the context of extensive, often unsettling, social and economic change. They enthusiastically embraced the republican spirit of classical antiquity that expressed "virtue" in terms of a primitive economy, but they also seemed to realize that this spirit had to be accommodated to their own dynamic world of commercial complexity. They vigorously denied that classical ideals should be surrendered completely to the demands of this new world, as Bernard Mandeville and his sympathizers suggested, but they

---

1. Richard Price, *Observations on the Nature of Civil Liberty* . . . (London, 1776), 98. See also Bernard Bailyn, *The Ideological Origins of the American Revolution* (Cambridge, Mass., 1967), chap. 4, and Gordon S. Wood, *The Creation of the American Republic, 1776–1787* (Chapel Hill, N.C., 1969), chaps. 1 and 3.

also understood that these ideals could not always be implemented or even interpreted literally. Although Americans might be committed in spirit to the simple values of a pre-commercial "Christian Sparta," their economy and society bore little resemblance to that ancient model. Because the Revolutionaries ultimately wished to be a more productive, civilized people than the primitive Spartans whose virtues they so much admired, a republican political economy in America would somehow have to straddle antiquity and modernity.[2]

The revolt against England went far beyond a repudiation of monarchical government; it entailed a passionate rejection of the British form of political economy. Historians of American "republicanism" have paid too little attention to the Revolutionaries' perception of British mercantilism as an economic system that reflected the tragedies of national corruption and "old age." Similarly, insufficient attention has been directed to the forging of an alternative conception of republican political economy. Perhaps more than any other colonial American, Benjamin Franklin thoughtfully analyzed and articulated this dimension of the Revolution. He developed his view of mercantilist England within a familiar eighteenth-century framework of assumptions about social development, and his contrasting vision of an independent, republican America deserves careful scrutiny. It was a broad vision that would have a great and lasting appeal for his countrymen and a significant influence on American public policy for decades to come.[3]

[I]

As a political economist, Franklin is probably best remembered for his analysis of population growth in North America. His famous formula of a doubling of the colonial population approximately every twenty years was first propounded in an essay of 1751, "Observations Concerning the

2. The best discussion of the social dimension of American "republicanism" is in Wood, *Creation of the American Republic*, esp. chaps. 2, 3, and 10. The reference to a "Christian Sparta" is from Samuel Adams, *ibid.*, 114–118.

3. The secondary literature pertaining to Franklin's political economy is voluminous, but there is neither a satisfactory synthesis nor any attempt to place him in a republican context. Particularly useful for understanding Franklin are Gerald Stourzh, *Benjamin Franklin and American Foreign Policy*, 2d ed. (Chicago, 1969), esp. 54–65, 75–82, 104–114, and 241–259, and Paul W. Conner, *Poor Richard's Politicks: Benjamin Franklin and*

Increase of Mankind." This essay contained a general theoretical consideration of the conditions that promoted or retarded the increase of population, as well as a vivid comparison of the demographic situations of Europe and North America.[4] Franklin argued that population increased in proportion to the number of marriages, which in turn depended on the ease and convenience of supporting a family. Crucial factors in this regard were the available supply of land and the density of population. In the "full settled" countries of Europe, marriages were discouraged by the difficulty of earning a comfortable living. Those who could not get land, Franklin explained, "must Labour for others who have it; when Labourers are plenty, their Wages will be low; by low Wages a Family is supported with Difficulty; this Difficulty deters many from Marriage, who therefore long continue Servants and single." By contrast, in America, where land was still plentiful and cheap, a young laboring man could look forward to owning a successful farm, and he would therefore marry early in life and become capable of supporting a large family. From this condition arose the dramatic difference in the rates of population growth between densely populated Europe and sparsely populated North America.[5]

Franklin's demographic analysis built on several ideas common to eighteenth-century political economy. His focal concern with population density reflected the prevalent belief that an increase in the number of inhabitants propelled a society through its customary stages of develop-

---

His New American Order (New York, 1965), esp. chap. 3. See also: W. A. Wetzel, *Benjamin Franklin as an Economist* (Baltimore, 1895); Lewis J. Carey, *Franklin's Economic Views* (New York, 1928); Earle D. Ross, "Benjamin Franklin as an Eighteenth-Century Agricultural Leader," *Journal of Political Economy*, XXXVII (1929), 52–72; A. Whitney Griswold, "Three Puritans on Prosperity," *New England Quarterly*, VII (1934), 475–493; Alfred Owen Aldridge, "Franklin as Demographer," *Journal of Economic History*, IX (1949), 25–44; Charles L. Sanford, "An American *Pilgrim's Progress*," *American Quarterly*, VI (1954), 297–310; and Walter LaFeber, "Foreign Policies of a New Nation: Franklin, Madison, and 'The Dream of a New Land to Fulfill with People in Self-Control,' 1750–1804," in William Appleman Williams, ed., *From Colony to Empire: Essays in the History of American Foreign Relations* (New York, 1972), 10–37. My own brief examination of Franklin's political economy, which parallels much of the discussion in this chapter, can be found in "Benjamin Franklin's Vision of a Republican Political Economy for America," *William and Mary Quarterly*, 3d Ser., XXXV (1978), 605–628.

4. The essay can be found in Leonard W. Labaree *et al.*, eds., *The Papers of Benjamin Franklin* (New Haven, Conn., 1959–), IV, 225–234.

5. *Ibid.*, 227, 228.

ment, and he went on to explore the corollary that a people's employments depended upon a country's population density. As long as land was abundant and available for settlement, a society would not advance beyond the relatively youthful stage of agriculture, when the overwhelming majority of men were independent and comfortable farmers. As a society aged, however, and population began to press on the supply of land, many individuals were forced to seek other modes of subsistence, usually in manufacturing. Generally, these men were not independent or self-employed; they were dependent wage-laborers who worked for "a master." As Franklin wrote in 1760, "Manufactures are founded in poverty," for "it is the multitude of poor without land in a country, and who must work for others at low wages or starve, that enables undertakers to carry on a manufacture." He added that "no man who can have a piece of land of his own, sufficient by his labour to subsist his family in plenty, is poor enough to be a manufacturer and work for a master." Franklin thus expressed the common eighteenth-century notion that progress, or the advance of society to more complex stages of development through population growth, entailed an alarming increase in poverty, inequality, dependence, and misery. "It is a striking observation of a very *able pen*," he noted, perhaps referring to his own essay on population, "that the natural livelihood of the thin inhabitants of a forest country, is hunting; that of a greater number, pasturage; that of a middling population, agriculture; and that of the greatest, manufactures; which last must subsist the bulk of the people in a full country, or they must be subsisted by charity, or perish."[6]

Before the Revolution, the demographic roots of Franklin's political economy helped form his image of England as an aged, overpopulated, and starkly inegalitarian society. Unlike her colonies in North America, England had no immediate recourse to virgin land, and the English situation was in large part the classic case of a fully peopled country in which, as Thomas Jefferson would explain in the *Notes on Virginia*, extensive manufacturing had necessarily developed to support a redundant population.[7] In this respect, England's system of manufacturing was the unavoidable means of rescuing large numbers of its people from

6. Franklin, "The Interest of Great Britain Considered," *ibid.*, IX, 73–74. For a similar explanation of this progression, see also "The North American, No. II," *Boston-Gazette and Country Journal*, Jan. 9, 1769.

7. See the discussion in chap. 1 above, pp. 13–15. For an English writer's explanation of his country's situation, see Arthur Young, *Political Arithmetic . . .* (London, 1774), 80–84.

idleness and starvation, since it offered employment for those who could no longer work on the land. But such a system usually provided little more than employment at a bare subsistence level. In Franklin's eyes, Britain thus qualified as an old, "full settled," highly stratified country, suffering from the serious inequalities and dependencies of an advanced stage of social development.

During the turbulent years of the Anglo-American crisis, Franklin came to hold a bitterly negative view of English society. His bitterness arose from a growing recognition that more was involved in the British dilemma than the natural consequences of population pressure on the supply of land, for he saw England's social pathology to be exacerbated by the operation of its government. The country was the victim of more than natural and ineluctable forces; its predicament was aggravated by a misguided political system. During his tenure as a colonial agent in England during the 1760s, Franklin came under the direct influence of the French "economistes" or physiocrats.[8] His encounter with them, both personally and with their writings, sharpened many of his economic beliefs and confirmed a basically anti-mercantilist outlook that informed his perception of British colonial policy as well as his broader understanding of England's political economy. He did not need the physiocrats to convert him to a preference for agriculture, but their carefully reasoned, "scientific" indictment of the mercantilist penchant for subsidizing foreign commerce and manufactures prompted him to cast his beliefs into more systematic form. The central physiocratic axioms—that agriculture was the only true source of wealth and that political interference with this natural order of economic life was pernicious—Franklin adopted almost without reservation.

As he read the physiocrats and applied their insights to the social evidence before him in England, Franklin was especially struck by the devastating results of a mercantilist propensity to measure the wealth of nations in terms of a favorable balance of trade. According to Franklin and the physiocrats, this cast of mind produced a misguided obsession with cultivating manufactures for export to foreign markets. The politi-

8. On Franklin's contact with the physiocrats, see Alfred Owen Aldridge, *Franklin and His French Contemporaries* (New York, 1957), 23–30; Bernard Faÿ, *Franklin, The Apostle of Modern Times* (New York, 1929), 342–344; and Carl Van Doren, *Benjamin Franklin* (New York, 1938), 371–372.

cal system that artificially favored commerce and manufactures put a particularly high premium on this production for export, because it was erroneously thought that national wealth and greatness came from the sale of a country's most polished manufactures, or its luxuries, abroad. When Quesnay and his cohorts attempted to undermine the theoretical basis of the system of political economy that the hated Colbert had imposed on France, they insisted, on the contrary, that a natural export trade in agriculture was far more productive and valuable to a country than this forced trade in manufactures.[9] In this regard, Franklin was particularly concerned in his examination of the English case with the organization of its laboring classes according to the familiar mercantilist idea that national prosperity arose from exporting the cheap labor of working men, most often in the form of refined manufactures, to foreign countries.[10]

As Franklin described it, Britain's political economy was indeed marked by this emphasis on production for export and by the definition of the public good that such an emphasis entailed. Mercantilist spokesmen in Europe had long argued that an economy of this sort could be sustained only by a dense population with a large pool of "pauper" laborers who worked for extremely low wages. These wages had to remain low, it was generally believed, in order to keep down the costs of production, thereby permitting the manufacture of cheap products that could compete successfully in world markets. By these standards, a high density of population was a tremendous advantage to a country, because it forced numerous destitute and landless men, as Franklin suggested in his population essay, to compete with each other for employment and to accept the necessary low wages. Thus, the greater the population the better, for a large population offered the optimum basis for a successful

9. See especially Ronald L. Meek, *The Economics of Physiocracy: Essays and Translations* (Cambridge, Mass., 1963), 72–91, 231–262.

10. The most extensive discussion of this aspect of 18th-century mercantilist thought and policy is Edgar S. Furniss, *The Position of the Laborer in a System of Nationalism: A Study in the Labor Theories of the Later English Mercantilists* (Boston and New York, 1920). See also A. W. Coats, "Changing Attitudes to Labour in the Mid-Eighteenth Century," *Economic History Review*, 2d Ser., XI (1958–1959), 35–51; Coats, "The Relief of Poverty, Attitudes to Labour, and Economic Change in England, 1660–1782," *International Review of Social History*, XXI (1976), 98–115; and E.A.J. Johnson, *Predecessors of Adam Smith: The Growth of British Economic Thought* (New York, 1937).

export trade in manufactures. In this way, an old, densely populated country might even appear to profit from its demographic crisis. Writing in 1753, the Englishman William Horsley succinctly expressed this mercantilist point of view, when he observed that "herein consists the Marrow of that Maxim, *that Numbers of People are the Wealth of a Nation*: as where they are plenty, they must work cheap, and so Manufactures are encouraged for a foreign Market, and their Return is the Wealth of a Nation, which Numbers thus procure."[11]

Since the continued impoverishment of the "manufacturing poor" was thought necessary to underwrite national power and opulence, this mercantilist mentality sanctioned, and even demanded, a highly skewed distribution of wealth. It was a common belief of the time that society was composed of two broad and distinct groups—the propertied and respectable classes, on the one hand, and the great mass of unpropertied laborers who were condemned to lives of grinding poverty, on the other. As one popular eighteenth-century proverb put it, "The Labour of the Poor, is the Treasure of the Rich."[12] England's laboring poor were treated by their social betters as pliant, often troublesome tools, as an economic resource to be systematically organized and exploited; even the humane John Locke had regarded the propertyless poor as less than fully human and hardly entitled to complete political rights. Moreover, these indigent wretches, who by some contemporary estimates composed half of England's population, could never legitimately or realistically aspire to a higher station, but were always to be inured early to lives of menial labor and the strictest austerity. It was also not coincidental that the eighteenth century was the age of the workhouse, an institution designed to discipline and render fully productive the depressed masses of the population. By forcing paupers to labor in workhouses that prepared manufactures for export, it was hoped that these people could be molded into efficient but docile workers whose energy would promote England to a position

---

11. [William Horsley], *The Universal Merchant*... (London, 1753), XV. See also [George Whatley], *Principles of Trade*..., 2d ed. (London, 1774), 16–18, and Arthur Young, *Political Essays, Concerning the Present State of the British Empire*... (London, 1772), 193–199.

12. Dorothy Marshall, *The English Poor in the Eighteenth Century: A Study in Social and Administrative History* (London, 1926), 34. See also Jacob Viner, "Man's Economic Status," in James L. Clifford, ed., *Man versus Society in Eighteenth-Century Britain: Six Points of View* (Cambridge, 1968), 22–53.

of dominance in world markets. Some Englishmen even went so far as to suggest that if it were necessary to extract the labor of the incorrigibly idle and depraved among the laboring poor by more severe means, they should be enslaved.[13]

By the mid-eighteenth century, this mercantilist insistence on the need for subsistence wages and a poverty-stricken labor force to support a profitable foreign commerce was increasingly challenged by a wide range of writers. But even Franklin, in an essay of 1768, admitted that any law to ease the condition of the laboring poor by raising their wages might ironically, by raising production costs and the price of the finished product, result in an even worse dilemma: if England's manufactures "are too dear," he wrote, expressing a standard mercantilist argument, "they will not vent abroad, and all that part of employment will fail."[14] For Franklin, this was truly an unenviable position for a country to find itself in. A mercantilist political economy might be perversely appropriate for an old and populous society like England, but he could never forget that it perpetuated the misery and despair of millions of laboring men and their families. And to the extent that the system was created or directly encouraged by deliberate political choice, as many French writers claimed was the case in their country, it was particularly cruel and ill founded. As Franklin's friend the abbé Moréllet later noted, the rigid enforcement of low wages according to this mercantilist logic (in agriculture as well as in manufacturing) reflected a failure to comprehend the

13. For pertinent discussions of attitudes toward the "labouring poor" in the 17th and 18th centuries, see: Furniss, *Position of the Laborer*, chaps. 2, 4, and 8; Marshall, *English Poor*, chap. 1; Marshall, *English People in the Eighteenth Century* (London, 1956), chap. 5; Jacob Viner, *Studies in the Theory of International Trade* (New York, 1937), 51–57; Paschal Larkin, *Property in the Eighteenth Century, with Special Reference to England and Locke*, 2d ed. (New York, 1969), 106–112; C. B. Macpherson, *The Political Theory of Possessive Individualism: Hobbes to Locke* (Oxford, 1962), chap. 5; and Edmund S. Morgan, *American Slavery, American Freedom: The Ordeal of Colonial Virginia* (New York, 1975), esp. 381–387.

14. Franklin, "On the Labouring Poor," Labaree *et al.*, eds., *Franklin Papers*, XV, 106. In this essay Franklin deliberately attempted to put the most favorable possible light on the situation of England's laboring poor, perhaps because he wanted to convince British officials that he was not "too much of an American" to hold an office he was seeking. See Franklin to William Franklin, July 2, 1768, *ibid.*, 159–164. Later, when further alienated from British political economy, Franklin expressed much more sympathy for the laboring poor.

simple truth that the object of every political society ought to be the happiness of the greatest number of people. "Whatever may be the advantages of foreign commerce," Moréllet warned, "if in order to possess them, half the nation must languish in misery, we cannot without crime endeavor to obtain them."[15]

In a series of aphorisms written in 1769 for the consideration of his friend and correspondent, the Scottish philosopher Lord Kames, Franklin formalized his negative view of the British emphasis on gaining wealth by manufacturing for export. He asserted that "the Advantage of Manufactures is, that under their shape Provisions may be more easily carried to a foreign Market; and by their means our Traders may more easily cheat Strangers." "Few, where it is not made," he offered as an example, "are Judges of the Value of Lace," and "the importer may demand Forty, and perhaps get Thirty shillings for that which cost him but twenty." In a conclusion that reflected a classic physiocratic emphasis on agriculture as the only legitimate source of national wealth, Franklin again identified this type of "commerce" with fraudulence: "There seem to be but three Ways for a Nation to acquire Wealth. The first is by *War* as the Romans did in plundering their conquered Neighbours. This is *Robbery*. The second by *Commerce* which is generally Cheating. The third by *Agriculture* the only *honest Way*; wherein Man receives a real Increase of the Seed thrown into the Ground, in a kind of continual Miracle wrought by the Hand of God in his Favour, as a Reward for his innocent Life, and virtuous Industry."[16] It is important to understand that Franklin used the term "commerce" here to indict only mercantilist countries like England that were "fond of Manufactures beyond their real value." Any commerce that followed physiocratic guidelines and was more naturally tied

---

15. John Bigelow, ed., *The Works of Benjamin Franklin . . .* (New York, 1904), XII, 43. For the full text of a translation of Moréllet's essay, see *ibid.*, 41–54. The essay was printed in this edition of Franklin's writings because it had been mistakenly attributed to him, rather than Moréllet. The curious history of this piece has been sorted out by Alfred Owen Aldridge in *Franklin and His French Contemporaries*, 72–73.

16. "Positions to be Examined," Apr. 4, 1769, Labaree *et al.*, eds., *Franklin Papers*, XVI, 107–109. For further evidence of the physiocratic cast of Franklin's thinking, see: "Note Respecting Trade and Manufactures," July 7, 1767, *ibid.*, XIV, 211–212; Franklin to Cadwalader Evans, Feb. 20, 1768, *ibid.*, XV, 51–53; Franklin to Pierre Samuel du Pont de Nemours, July 28, 1768, *ibid.*, 181–182; Franklin to Lord Kames, Jan. 1769, *ibid.*, XVI, 1–4; Franklin to Jean-Baptiste LeRoy, Jan. 31, 1769, *ibid.*, 33–34; Franklin to Lord Kames, Feb. 21, 1769, *ibid.*, 46–47; and "Remarks on Agriculture and Manufacturing," 1771, *ibid.*, XVIII, 273–274.

to agriculture and the export of produce to foreign markets, as American commerce was, would clearly not warrant the label of "cheating."[17]

As the colonial crisis worsened, Franklin's alienation from the British system of political economy grew, and he often directed his attention to the regrettable consequences of a mercantilist tendency to sacrifice the comfort and security of England's common people to the interest of a profitable export trade. In late 1771 he made a fairly extensive tour of Ireland, Scotland, and the English textile-producing regions, where he found social conditions appalling. In a letter written in January 1772 to Dr. Joshua Babcock, Franklin commented at length on the great disparities of wealth that marked British society, and he contrasted the wretched condition of the common people there with the comfortable independence and self-sufficiency of New England freeholders. He expressed the hope that these New Englanders would long remain in their present condition; "but if they should ever envy the *Trade* of these Countries," Franklin continued in a bitterly sarcastic tone, "I can put them in a Way to obtain a Share of it. Let them with three fourths of the People of Ireland, live the Year round on Potatoes and Butter milk, without Shirts, then may their Merchants export Beef, Butter, and Linnen. Let them, with the Generality of the Common People of Scotland go Barefoot, then may they make large Exports in Shoes and Stockings: And if they will be content to wear Rags like the Spinners and Weavers of England, they may make Cloths and Stuffs for all Parts of the World."[18] Britain's exports, in short, were "pinch'd off the Backs and out of the Bellies of the miserable Inhabitants."[19]

Franklin was so disillusioned by the social consequences of British mercantilism that he barely stopped short of a wholesale indictment of advanced civilization and an endorsement of primitive simplicity. He ultimately recognized, however, that the British case represented only one type of civil society, a corrupt and degenerating species mired in the squalor and depravity of a mercantilist political economy that ironically produced "savages," the laboring poor who produced for the export trade, in the midst of an ostensibly advanced civilization. "Had I never been in the American Colonies," he wrote to Babcock, "but was to form my Judgment of Civil Society by what I have lately seen, I should never

17. Franklin to Cadwalader Evans, Feb. 20, 1768, *ibid.*, XV, 52.
18. Franklin to Joshua Babcock, Jan. 13, 1772, *ibid.*, XIX, 7.
19. Franklin to Thomas Cushing, Jan. 13, 1772, *ibid.*, 22–23.

advise a Nation of Savages to admit of Civilization: For I assure you, that in the Possession and Enjoyment of the various Comforts of Life, compar'd to these People every Indian is a Gentleman: And the Effect of this kind of Civil Society seems only to be, the depressing Multitudes below the Savage State that a few may be rais'd above it."[20] A year later, in the context of a discussion concerning the high death rate in industrial Manchester, Franklin excoriated "the Unwholesomeness of the Manufacturing Life" that typified England's political economy. "Farmers who manufacture in their own Families what they have occasion for and no more," he concluded, "are perhaps the happiest People and the healthiest."[21]

Franklin's disgust with British society was matched by his contempt for the corruption he saw in British political life, and he often connected the two problems. The absentee Scottish landlords who fleeced their miserable tenants, for example, had opted for lives of luxury in London "among the Dependants of a Court," prompting them to raise their rents "most grievously to support the Expence."[22] According to Franklin, Parliament was composed of these enervated tools of "the Court," men whose seduction by luxury had compromised their political integrity and made them dependent on the crown's ministers, who sold them the places and pensions that supported their expensive habits. One sad result of this corruption, which was tied to the British public debt and the bureaucracy that had grown up around it, was the dissipation of England's national wealth in supporting the idle, unproductive beneficiaries of the system. "Here Numberless and needless Places, enormous Salaries, Pensions, Perquisites, Bribes, groundless Quarrels, foolish Expeditions, false Accounts or no Accounts, Contracts and Jobbs," Franklin complained, "devour all Revenue, and produce continual Necessity in the Midst of natural Plenty."[23] In addition to supporting an economic order that brought so much misery to the laboring poor by relegating them to the position of pawns in the export trade, the political system in itself accounted for a devastating waste of resources.

20. Franklin to Joshua Babcock, Jan. 13, 1772, *ibid.*, 7. See also Franklin to Joseph Galloway, Feb. 6, 1772, *ibid.*, 71–72. For another example of Franklin's tendency to compare savage and civilized societies in a similar fashion, see "Marginalia in a Pamphlet by Matthew Wheelock," 1770, *ibid.*, XVII, 381–382.

21. Franklin to Thomas Percival, Oct. 14, 1773, *ibid.*, XX, 443.

22. Franklin, "On a Proposed Act to Prevent Emigration," Dec. 1773, *ibid.*, 523–524.

23. Franklin to Joseph Galloway, Feb. 25, 1775, Albert Henry Smyth, ed., *The Writings*

More important to Franklin, this thoroughly corrupted government also threatened to drain the colonists of their valuable wealth by molding them into passive consumers of England's luxury manufactures. As early as 1764 Franklin blasted the selfish desire, embodied in England's new colonial policies, "to manufacture and trade for all the world"—a desire that was particularly evident in the mother country's attempt to monopolize the American market.[24] From one perspective, the new colonial regulations of the 1760s and 1770s represented a sustained effort to integrate the colonies into a mercantilist system whose lifeblood was the exportation of manufactures. There was no doubt in Franklin's mind about the victims of this imperial arrangement. He only wished, in this regard, that Americans could see for themselves the merchants and shopkeepers who prepared wares for export to the colonies, "every one with his country-house and equipage, where they live like Princes on the sweat of our brows."[25] Summing up his contempt for the whole wretched system, Franklin sneered that "if America would save 3 or 4 Years the Money she spends in Fashions and Fineries and Fopperies of this Country, she might buy the whole Parliament, Minister and all."[26] By attempting to coerce the colonists into supporting the British system of political economy, he later charged, the English government behaved like "a mad Shopkeeper, who should attempt, by beating those that pass his Door, to make them come in and be his customers."[27] By 1775 Franklin suggested that the separation of the colonies from the cancerous corruption of "this old rotten State" had become necessary not only to preserve political

---

of Benjamin Franklin (New York, 1907), VI, 312. See also Franklin to Thomas Cushing, Oct. 10, 1774, *ibid.*, 251–252, and Franklin to Galloway, Oct. 12, 1774, *ibid.*, 253–254. Franklin had voiced his suspicions of ministerial corruption in British government earlier; see, for example, "On Sinecures," Sept. 28, 1768, Labaree *et al.*, eds., *Franklin Papers*, XV, 220–222. For similar expressions of concern by other colonial writers, see *The Power and Grandeur of Great-Britain . . .* (New York, 1768), 18–19, and Oliver Noble, *Some Strictures upon . . . the Book of Esther* (Newburyport, Mass., 1775), 9–11.

24. Franklin to Peter Collinson, Apr. 30, 1764, Labaree *et al.*, eds., *Franklin Papers*, XI, 182. For a similar expression of this complaint by another colonial writer, see *Observations on Several Acts of Parliament . . .* (Boston, 1769).

25. Franklin to Timothy Folger, Sept. 29, 1769, Labaree *et al.*, eds., *Franklin Papers*, XVI, 209.

26. Franklin to Thomas Cushing, Oct. 10, 1774, Smyth, ed., *Writings of Franklin*, VI, 251–252.

27. Franklin, "Comparison of Great Britain and the United States in Regard to the Basis of Credit in the Two Countries," 1777, *ibid.*, VII, 7.

liberty, but also, in a much broader sense, to secure the basis for a productive and prosperous republican political economy in America.[28]

Franklin's perception of English corruption thus culminated in the logic of American independence, and his view of England formed part of the comprehensive republican world view that the Revolutionaries embraced in their separation from the empire. Even the youthful Alexander Hamilton, who would later see England as a model of national power and greatness, rushed to adopt the general view of England's economy and society that Franklin articulated. Speaking of the mother country in 1774, Hamilton observed that "with respect to agriculture, the lands of Great Britain and Ireland have been long ago distributed and taken up," requiring no "additional labourers to till them." He went on to emphasize Britain's weakness as an old, overpopulated, luxury-ridden state that relied on a swollen foreign commerce to dispose of the manufactures necessary to keep its surplus inhabitants employed. In this regard, Samuel Seabury, Hamilton's adversary in public debate, accused the young incendiary of falsely portraying England as "an old, wrinkled, withered, worn-out hag."[29]

Along with the rest of the Revolutionaries, Franklin was greatly concerned with the ministerial corruption of Parliament and its perversion of England's precious balanced constitution. His understanding of the broader threat that this political corruption posed to the colonies was appropriately much informed by the opposition persuasion of the so-called "commonwealthmen" and "country" thinkers in England.[30] A

28. Franklin to Joseph Galloway, Feb. 25, 1775, *ibid.*, VI, 312. See also Franklin to Joseph Priestley, July 7, 1775, *ibid.*, 409; Franklin to Thomas Cushing, Oct. 10, 1774, *ibid.*, VI, 251–252; Franklin to Samuel Cooper, Apr. 27, 1769, Labaree *et al.*, eds., *Franklin Papers*, XVI, 118; and Franklin to Timothy Folger, Sept. 29, 1769, *ibid.*, 208–210.

29. "A Full Vindication of the Measures of the Congress . . . " (New York, 1774), and "The Farmer Refuted . . ." (New York, 1775), in Harold C. Syrett and Jacob E. Cooke, eds., *The Papers of Alexander Hamilton* (New York, 1961–), I, 59, 45–165; Bailyn, *Ideological Origins*, 137.

30. See Bailyn, *Ideological Origins*, chaps. 3 and 4; Caroline Robbins, *The Eighteenth-Century Commonwealthman: Studies in the Transmission, Development and Circumstance of English Liberal Thought from the Restoration of Charles II until the War with the Thirteen Colonies* (Cambridge, Mass., 1959); and J.G.A. Pocock's recent synthesis of his earlier writings in *The Machiavellian Moment: Florentine Political Thought and the Atlantic Republican Tradition* (Princeton, N.J., 1975). After the Revolution, Franklin often reflected on the corruption in English government and expressed doubts as to whether "a

central element of the republican ideology derived from this tradition was its emphasis on the sensitive interdependence of government and society, and Franklin's view of England reflected the common belief that political corruption and constitutional decay festered most readily in societies where individuals had lost their economic independence and moral integrity. To this extent, his sociological, anti-mercantilist perspective complemented well the more constitutionally oriented republicanism of the commonwealth tradition, for his analysis suggested quite clearly that England's political corruption grew out of, as well as exacerbated, the social evils of an old, highly developed, densely populated commercial society.[31]

Nation so long Corrupted" had enough "Public Spirit and Virtue" left to bring about the necessary reform. Franklin to Jonathan Shipley, Mar. 17, 1783, Smyth, ed., *Writings of Franklin*, IX, 23. See also Franklin to Henry Laurens, Feb. 12, 1784, *ibid.*, 169–170.

31. The influence of the "commonwealth" and "country" traditions on the development of America's Revolutionary ideology has been indisputably established. In the realm of political economy, the primary contribution to American thought came in the "country" thinkers' blistering indictment of England's new financial system and its many ramifications. I have not discussed this very important aspect of republican political economy because my purpose in this study is to explore other dimensions of the Revolutionary mind that have received comparatively little attention. The impact of the English opposition to the new fiscal system on American thought has been persuasively examined at some length by several historians, including Bailyn and Pocock. In addition to the seminal study by Lance Banning, *The Jeffersonian Persuasion: Evolution of a Party Ideology* (Ithaca, N.Y., 1978), see also Rodger D. Parker, "The Gospel of Opposition: A Study in Eighteenth-Century Anglo-American Ideology" (Ph.D. diss., Wayne State University, 1975). Despite the obvious continuities that these writers have established, it seems clear that, in the realm of political economy at least, American republican thought cannot be understood solely in terms of this commonwealth or country influence. The political economy of the commonwealthmen, in fact, was often at odds with the mainstream of American republicanism. John Trenchard and Thomas Gordon, authors of the popular *Cato's Letters*, for example, celebrated the virtues of a densely populated state that drew its wealth from commerce and manufactures rather than agriculture. For a discussion of the inadequacy of recent studies of the ideology of the Revolution that has implications somewhat different from those of my discussion, see Joseph Ernst's several articles: "Ideology and the Political Economy of Revolution," *Canadian Review of American Studies*, IV (1973), 137–148; "Political Economy and Reality: Problems in the Interpretation of the American Revolution," *ibid.*, VII (1976), 110–118; and "'Ideology' and an Economic Interpretation of the Revolution," in Alfred F. Young, ed., *The American Revolution: Explorations in the History of American Radicalism* (DeKalb, Ill., 1976), 161–185. See also, Joyce Appleby, "The Social Origins of American Revolutionary Ideology," *Journal of American History*, LXIV (1977–1978), 935–958.

By contrast, the republican view of America portrayed the New World as the theater for a dramatically different social and moral order. Here, men would be relatively equal in wealth and power, and, above all, independent and economically competent as individuals. Franklin's faith in such a prospect rested principally on his belief that America had not yet, and would not soon, reach that final corrupt stage of social development at which commerce and an advanced division of labor took their pernicious and debilitating toll. He believed that America was still at an essentially agricultural stage of social development; given the potential for a virtually limitless expansion of its burgeoning population across the North American continent, there was hope that it could remain so for ages to come. As long as the supply of open land kept abreast of population, Franklin believed, America would not be pushed into a higher, more precarious phase of development, and its reservoir of land would provide a welcome alternative to the manufacturing that might otherwise be necessary to employ its increasing numbers of people. The evils of a densely populated society, particularly the impetus created toward establishing an economy based on manufacturing for export, could be forestalled in America as long as its citizens were able to expand across space rather than develop through time. The rapid growth of population—unmistakable evidence of a young, healthy society—thus would not ironically create the conditions that undermined such youthful prosperity. In this sense, the Revolutionary dream was a bid for prolonged social youth, grounded in the faith that expansion across space might continuously offer the proper demographic basis for a republican social order.[32]

Franklin also believed that so long as America maintained its agricultural character, its republican government would not be tempted to subvert this flourishing natural order by imposing a corrupt social system through devious political means. The relationship between government and society, in America as in England, was reciprocal, and America's healthy republican society presented the proper framework for a free government that would in turn sustain the integrity of a republican society and economy. Franklin did not develop his conception of republican government in great detail. To the extent that his political vision had specificity, it listed the characteristics of European governments that had to be avoided. A virtuous and laborious people could always be "cheaply

32. For a fine discussion of Franklin's attention to the importance of westward expansion, see Stourzh, *Franklin and American Foreign Policy*, esp. 54–65 and 251–252.

governed" in a republican system, Franklin insisted, with "no offices of profit, nor any sinecures or useless appointments, so common in ancient and corrupted states." It was particularly important that American resources not be dissipated in the "vain, expensive Projects," especially wars, that corrupt governments in Europe habitually promoted. In this regard, Franklin was confident that an independent America would have no need of elaborate "fleets and standing armies," those wasteful and expensive "machines to be maintained for the pomp of princes."[33] The wars pursued by these governments, England's war against her former colonies being a case in point, represented a calamitous waste of natural and human resources that should be employed instead "in Works of public Utility."[34] The latter would always be the case, he hoped, in a young and predominantly agricultural America. Franklin believed, in short, that the combination of abundant land and the absence of a corrupt political system meant that America might be a "Land of Labour," where free men worked diligently on their farms to produce real wealth, in contrast to Europe, which was cursed with a plethora of men who, for demographic or political reasons, were mischievous sycophants or producers of frivolous "superfluities."[35]

Franklin often stated that as long as enough land existed in America, there would be no extensive manufacturing, and it is important to understand precisely what he and many of the Revolutionaries generally meant by this common assertion. As the prevailing eighteenth-century conceptualization of economic development suggested, men made a fundamental, often implicit distinction between the household manufacture of coarse "necessaries" and the more advanced, capitalized production of finer manufactures that were also frequently exported to foreign markets. Household manufactures were appropriate to an agricultural stage of social development when farmers produced within their own families the coarse clothing and utensils that suited their minimal needs and tastes. The production of finer manufactures outside the home was typical of older, more advanced, commercialized societies with large numbers of landless laborers. Adam Smith summarized this distinction in

33. Franklin to Charles de Weissenstein, July 1, 1778, Smyth, ed., *Writings of Franklin*, VII, 168, and Franklin, "Comparison of Great Britain and the United States," *ibid.*, 6.

34. Franklin to Sir Joseph Banks, July 27, 1783, *ibid.*, IX, 74.

35. Franklin, "Information to Those Who Would Remove to America," 1782, *ibid.*, VIII, 607, 603–614. See also Franklin to Benjamin Vaughan, July 26, 1784, *ibid.*, IX, 240–248.

the *Wealth of Nations* when he observed that "no large country . . . ever did or could subsist without some sort of manufactures being carried on in it; and when it is said of any such country that it has no manufactures, it must always be understood of the finer and more improved, or of such as are fit for distant sale. In every large country, both the clothing and household furniture of the far greater part of the people, are the produce of their own industry."[36]

The American commitment to manufacturing that took root during the non-importation movements of the 1760s and 1770s appropriately stressed the development of household and other predominantly small-scale manufactures. The moral thrust of this mania for manufacturing, which Franklin eagerly embraced, included the rejection of foreign luxury, a renewal of ancestral virtue, and the adoption of a simpler, "spartan" way of life.[37] Franklin very much wanted America to increase its produc-tion of these coarse, household manufactures. The advantages were several. Farmers were encouraged to be industrious in making productive use of their families' free time, and the money saved by substituting home manufactures for foreign goods became capital that could be used to improve their farms. These home manufactures were without exception useful necessaries, not frivolous luxuries, and to Franklin this made them quite different from so many of the manufactures that England produced for export to foreign (especially colonial) markets.[38] Even when Frank-

36. Adam Smith, *An Inquiry into the Nature and Causes of the Wealth of Nations*, ed. Edwin Cannan (New York, 1937 [orig. publ. London, 1776]), 381. For other examples of the customary 18th-century distinction between domestic (and other small-scale industries) and large-scale manufacturing, see the anonymous article "Manufactures" in the French Encyclopedia, Albert Soboul, ed., *Textes choisis de "l'Encyclopédie"* . . . (Paris, 1962), 158–165; and Arthur Young, *Political Essays, Concerning the Present State of the British Empire* (London, 1772), 174. See also the discussion in chap. 4 below.

37. See, for example, *The Commercial Conduct of the Province of New-York* . . . (New York, 1767), and "A Friend to the Colony," *Providence Gazette; and Country Journal* (R.I.), Nov. 14, 1767. For appropriate discussions of the non-importation movements, see: Rolla Milton Tryon, *Household Manufactures in the United States, 1640–1860* (Chicago, 1917), esp. 43–104; Victor S. Clark, *History of Manufactures in the United States*, I (New York, 1929), chap. 10; J. E. Crowley, *This Sheba, Self: The Conceptualization of Economic Life in Eighteenth-Century America* (Baltimore, 1974), chap. 5; and Edmund S. Morgan, "The Puritan Ethic and the American Revolution," *WMQ*, 3d Ser., XXIV (1967), 3–43. Morgan's superb article suffers from a failure to place American attitudes toward manufac-tures in a broader 18th-century context.

38. Franklin to Richard Jackson, Sept. 25, 1764, Labaree *et al.*, eds., *Franklin Papers*,

lin's view of American manufactures went beyond the simplest household types, he retained this emphasis on the production of necessaries. Always anticipating the prodigious growth of American population as it expanded westward, he became convinced that before long England would be unable to supply the full American demand, and that "Necessity therefore, as well as Prudence, will soon induce us to seek Resources in our own Industry."[39] Franklin had no difficulty integrating independent artisans and mechanics into his republican vision as long as they were "the necessary and useful kinds" who supplied the "Cultivators of the Earth with Houses, and with Furniture and Utensils of the grosser sorts." Often these artisans began as employees—journeymen—but the sober and industrious ones had an excellent chance in America of becoming masters of their own shops. These useful and respectable citizens, unlike the dependent laborers in larger European establishments, controlled their skill, labor, and tools; like the yeomen of the countryside, they had direct access to the means of production, which conferred upon them the independence that supported republican virtue. Since these artisans produced necessities that were in steady demand, they were also not dependent on the whim or fancy of fashion for their employment, a predicament that chronically plagued European workers in luxury trades. It was only the "Great Establishments of Manufactures" that had no place in republican America—establishments that employed poverty-stricken, landless laborers, and especially those that were dependent on government subsidy and promotion. In the early 1780s, Franklin discouraged European enterprisers with grandiose schemes of establishing such large manufactories from emigrating to America, where they were unneeded and unwelcome.[40] Just as America was not to be without all commerce,

---

XI, 359; Franklin to Cadwalader Evans, Feb. 20, 1768, *ibid.*, XV, 52; Franklin, "The State of the Trade with the Northern Colonies," Nov. 1–3, 1768, *ibid.*, 251; Franklin to Samuel Cooper, Apr. 27, 1769, *ibid.*, XVI, 118; Franklin to Cadwalader Evans, Sept. 7, 1769, *ibid.*, 200–201; Franklin to Timothy Folger, Sept. 29, 1769, *ibid.*, 209; Franklin to Humphrey Marshall, Mar. 18, 1770, *ibid.*, XVII, 109–110; Franklin, "The Rise and Present State of our Misunderstanding," Nov. 6–8, 1770, *ibid.*, 271–272; Franklin to Thomas Cushing, June 10, 1771, *ibid.*, XVIII, 126; Franklin to M. LeVeillard, Oct. 24, 1788, Smyth, ed., *Writings of Franklin*, IX, 674–675.

39. Franklin to Thomas Cushing, June 10, 1771, Labaree *et al.*, eds., *Franklin Papers*, XVIII, 126. See also Franklin to Peter Collinson, Apr. 30, 1764, *ibid.*, XI, 183.

40. Franklin, "Information to Those Who Would Remove to America," 1782, Smyth, ed., *Writings of Franklin*, VIII, 608, 611.

then, it was not to be without all manufactures; but it was to avoid the types of manufactures characteristic of more developed, commercialized, and generally corrupt societies.

"In our North American colonies, where uncultivated land is still to be had upon easy terms," wrote Adam Smith in 1776, "no manufactures for distant sale have ever yet been established in any of their towns."

> When an artificer has acquired a little more stock than is necessary for carrying on his own business in supplying the neighbouring country, he does not, in North America, attempt to establish with it a manufacture for more distant sale, but employs it in the purchase and improvement of uncultivated land. From artificer he becomes planter, and neither the large wages nor the easy subsistence which that country affords to artificers, can bribe him rather to work for other people than for himself. He feels that an artificer is the servant of his customers, from whom he derives his subsistence; but that a planter who cultivates his own land, and derives his necessary subsistence from the labour of his own family, is really a master, and independent of all the world.[41]

Here Smith identified the core of the republican vision of America that Franklin articulated so well: a society of independent, moderately prosperous, relatively self-sufficient producers who would succeed in staving off the dangers of an overly advanced, commercialized existence. In this society, there were to be none of Smith's wretched laborers who sold their labor for lives of drudgery and misery, no ignorant multitudes depressed, as Franklin had put it, "below the Savage State that a few may be rais'd above it." Republicans thus hoped and generally believed that America might remain for some time at what their English admirer Richard Price described as "that middle stage of civilization, between its first rude and its last refined and corrupt state."[42] American society was to be revolutionary, in short, precisely because it would not repeat the familiar eighteenth-century pattern of a stark and widening division between the propertied few and the masses of laboring, unpropertied poor. Smith's analysis of modern commercial society could lead only to a despairing acceptance of the unavoidable presence of a subhuman rabble

41. Smith, *Wealth of Nations*, ed. Cannan, 359.

42. Price, *Observations on Civil Liberty*, 70. For an interesting discussion of this idea of a "middle stage" of society, see Leo Marx, *The Machine in the Garden: Technology and the Pastoral Ideal in America* (New York, 1964).

in the advanced areas of Europe.[43] The republicans in the New World hoped that they had found an escape from this tragic fate in the wilderness that awaited them to the west.

[II]

At best, however, Franklin's vision of an expanding agricultural America provides only a general outline of the position taken by the republican Revolutionaries of 1776. All of them could agree that a republican form of government—without kings, nobles, and corrupted legislators, and thus dedicated to serving the public or common good—demanded a virtuous people and a social form that could sustain their virtue. But the republican ideology of the Revolution was fraught with tensions, ambiguities, paradoxes, and even contradictions, in large part because so much of it was derived from classical antiquity and therefore was in serious tension with a new age of growing commercial complexity. As Mandeville, Hume, and many other writers in Europe suggested, and as Americans quickly discovered, traditional social and moral formulas seemed increasingly incongruous in a rapidly changing eighteenth-century world.

In its purest form, classical republicanism stipulated that republics had to be rather rude, simple, pre-commercial societies free from any taint of luxury and corruption.[44] The essence of corruption was the encroachment of power on liberty, an insidious process most likely to occur in advanced, stratified societies where great wealth and inequality promoted avaricious behavior and dangerous dependencies among men. Writers in the republican tradition, most notably the seventeenth-century Englishman James Harrington, had convincingly shown, as John Adams put it, that "power always follows property," or, more specifically, that "the balance of power in a society" closely paralleled "the balance of property

43. For a discussion of Smith's alleged failure of imagination in this regard, which was characteristic of his age, see Robert L. Heilbroner, "The Paradox of Progress: Decline and Decay in *The Wealth of Nations*," Andrew S. Skinner and Thomas Watson, eds., *Essays on Adam Smith* (London, 1975), esp. 536–539.

44. See Wood, *Creation of the American Republic*, esp. 413–425. For a typical 18th-century explanation of the incompatibility of luxury and republicanism, see Adam Ferguson, *An Essay on the History of Civil Society* (Edinburgh, 1767), 381.

in land." The only possible way of preserving this balance "on the side of equal liberty and public virtue," Adams characteristically contended in 1776, was "to make the acquisition of land easy to every member of society," or "to make a division of land into small quantities, so that the multitude may be possessed of landed estates."[45] If the weak and unpropertied were indeed threatened with exploitation by the strong and privileged, as republican writers assumed, then Franklin's expanding society of relatively equal, independent landowners was the necessary antidote to corruption.

American republicans valued property in land primarily because it provided personal independence. The individual with direct access to the productive resources of nature need not rely on other men, or any man, for the basic means of existence. The Revolutionaries believed that every man had a natural right to this form of property, in the sense that he was entitled to autonomous control of the resources that were absolutely necessary for his subsistence. The personal independence that resulted from the ownership of land permitted a citizen to participate responsibly in the political process, for it allowed him to pursue spontaneously the common or public good, rather than the narrow interest of the men—or the government—on whom he depended for his support. Thus the Revolutionaries did not intend to provide men with property so that they might flee from public responsibility into a selfish privatism; property was rather the necessary basis for a committed republican citizenry.[46]

Property in land also served another crucial purpose in a republican society—it stimulated the productivity of an alert and active citizenry, and Americans rarely doubted, in this regard, that they were destined to be a peculiarly productive and prosperous people. They accepted "the well-known truth" that "the riches and strength of a free Country does not consist in property being vested in a few Individuals, but the more general it is distributed, the more it promotes industry, population and

45. John Adams to James Sullivan, May 26, 1776, Charles Francis Adams, ed., *The Works of John Adams* (Boston, 1850–1856), IX, 376–377. See also *ibid.*, V, 453–454. Probably the best discussion of Harrington's contribution to the republican tradition is Pocock, *Machiavellian Moment*, chap. 11.

46. My discussion here draws heavily on Pocock, *Machiavellian Moment*, chaps. 12 and 14, and the provocative suggestions in William B. Scott, *In Pursuit of Happiness: American Conceptions of Property from the Seventeenth to the Twentieth Century* (Bloomington, Ind., 1977), chaps. 1–4.

frugality, and even morality."[47] If expansion across space anchored Franklin's republican vision, it was his hope that this expansion would involve a special breed of virtuous and productive men. Back in the 1750s, when he had been zealously interested in settling the Ohio valley with the "many thousands of families" that were "ready to swarm" in search of fresh land, he had remarked to his friend, the evangelist George Whitefield, that it would be "a glorious Thing" for the crown to commission them jointly "to settle in that fine Country a large strong Body of Religious and Industrious People."[48] As Franklin then suggested, American expansion was to be carried out by a virtuous people whose industry would exploit the promise of America's bountiful resources. That such a people might produce great wealth was obvious. How they would cope with that wealth, and the effects it would have on American character, however, were not.

The classical republican heritage embraced by the Revolutionaries stressed the close relationship between public virtue—the austere and unselfish devotion to the common good that was on the lips of every patriot in 1776—and private virtue, which was exemplified by the character traits of frugality, temperance, and rigorous self-control. As John Adams explained a few months before the Declaration of Independence, "Public virtue cannot exist in a Nation without Private, and public Virtue is the only Foundation of Republics."[49] It was for this reason that so many republicans greatly feared both commerce and indulgence in wealth as dangerous threats to the success of the Revolution. In one sense, the Revolution can properly be viewed as a reactionary effort, as

47. Petition from Inhabitants of Kentucky, Jan. 2, 1784, Julian P. Boyd *et al.*, eds., *The Papers of Thomas Jefferson* (Princeton, N.J., 1950–), VI, 553. The importance of property as a necessary stimulant of industry and productivity was widely commented upon by 18th-century writers. See, for example, John Witherspoon, *Lectures on Moral Philosophy*, ed. Varnum Lansing Collins (Princeton, N.J., 1912), 74–79; Henry Home, Lord Kames, *Sketches of the History of Man* (Edinburgh, 1813 [orig. publ. 1774]), I, 91–100; and William Paley, *The Principles of Moral and Political Philosophy* (London, 1806 [orig. publ. 1785]), 121–125.

48. Franklin, "A Plan for Settling Two Western Colonies," 1754, Labaree *et al.*, eds., *Franklin Papers*, V, 462, and Franklin to George Whitefield, July 2, 1756, *ibid.*, VI, 468.

49. John Adams to Mercy Warren, Apr. 16, 1776, *Warren-Adams Letters* (Massachusetts Historical Society, *Collections*, LXXII–LXXIII [Boston, 1917–1925]), I, 222. See also Wood, *Creation of the American Republic*, 65–70, and Pocock, *Machiavellian Moment*, chaps. 14 and 15.

one historian has put it, "to bring under control the selfish and individualistic impulses of an emergent capitalistic society that could not be justified"—or at least that could not be justified by traditional moral standards.[50] In the flush years of 1775 and 1776, when thousands were swept up in the spirit of a "rage militaire," many of the Revolutionaries were inspired to hope that the American people might indeed conform to the classical notion of virtue and thus become the special kind of simple, austere, egalitarian, civic-minded people that intellectuals had dreamed about for centuries.[51] To these enthusiasts, the ancient republic of Sparta was an appropriate model for a new America, a rude but virtuous society of independent citizen-warriors who demonstrated an unselfish devotion to the collective good because they were shielded from the corrupting intrusion of commerce and luxury. This vision of America, in Samuel Adams's revealing words, as a "Christian Sparta," permeated the apocalyptic rhetoric that gave public expression to the spirit of the Revolution.[52]

But there was also an uneasy suspicion (and sometimes recognition) among the Revolutionaries that even predominantly agricultural America was already a relatively advanced commercial society, that Americans were to a great extent an ambitious commercial people with refined tastes and manners, and that under such conditions inflated expectations of classical public virtue might be unrealistic. Steeped in the patterns of classical literature and inspired by a real revolutionary fervor, educated and articulate Americans almost unthinkingly invoked the Spartan formula as an abstract ideal. When they confronted the sobering realities of eighteenth-century America, however, they invariably had nervous doubts about its republican potential.

John Adams probably best exemplifies this uneasy skepticism about the potential for classical virtue in America. By early 1776, Adams was thoroughly committed to both independence and republicanism. After admitting that "Virtue and Simplicity of Manners are indispensably necessary in a Republic among all orders and Degrees of Men," he added, however, that "there is so much Rascality, so much Venality and

---

50. Gordon S. Wood, ed., *The Rising Glory of America, 1760–1820* (New York, 1971), 5. This introductory essay contains a summary and extension of the argument presented in *The Creation of the American Republic*.

51. See also Charles Royster, *A Revolutionary People at War: The Continental Army and American Character, 1775–1783* (Chapel Hill, N.C., 1979), chap. 1.

52. Wood, *Creation of the American Republic*, 114–118.

Corruption, so much Avarice and Ambition such a rage for Profit and Commerce among all Ranks and Degree of Men even in America, that I sometimes doubt whether there is public Virtue enough to support a Republic."[53] The "Spirit of Commerce" was rampant in America, especially in Adams's own New England: since "even the Farmers and Tradesmen" were "addicted to Commerce," he seriously doubted if a positive passion for the public good could ever be superior to the indulgence of private and egoistic passions, especially the pursuit of wealth.[54] During the debates over non-importation in 1775, he was appropriately concerned with the question of just how long, realistically, his countrymen would tolerate a suppression of their foreign commerce:

How long will or can our People bear this? I say they can bear it forever. If Parliament should build a Wall of Brass, at low Water Mark, We might live and be happy; We must change our Habits, our Prejudices our Palates, our Taste in Dress, Furniture, Equipage, Architecture, etc., but We can live and be happy. But the question is whether our People have Virtue enough to be mere Husbandmen, Mechanicks, and Soldiers? That they have not Virtue enough to bear it always I take for granted. How long then will their Virtue last? till next Spring?[55]

Later, during the war, when his countrymen persistently demonstrated a want of classical forbearance, Adams similarly doubted if they would agree to the remedy of a public enforcement of republican austerity. "There is such a charm to the human heart in elegance," he sighed; "it is so flattering to our self-love to be distinguished from the world in general by extraordinary degrees of splendor in dress, in furniture, equipage, buildings, etc."[56] The psychological roots of the infatuation with luxury that eighteenth-century writers had examined at such length seemed to infect the souls of all men, even those of an agricultural people who aspired to emulate the ancient Spartans. Adams had ambivalent, at times contradictory, feelings about the character of the American people. In the final analysis, though, he saw clearly that they were not Spartans in any classical sense, and that American society was not as "young" and

53. Adams to Mercy Warren, Jan. 8, 1776, *Warren-Adams Letters*, I, 202.

54. Adams to Mercy Warren, Apr. 16, 1776, *ibid.*, 222–223.

55. Adams to James Warren, Oct. 19, 1775, *ibid.*, 146. See also Adams to Warren, Oct. 20, 1775, *ibid.*, 155–156.

56. John Adams to Ralph Izard, Oct. 2, 1778, Francis Wharton, ed., *The Revolutionary Diplomatic Correspondence of the United States* (Washington, D.C., 1889), II, 754.

primitive as traditional republicanism demanded it to be. If America was to be a republic, it appeared that commerce and its consequences would have to be integrated into a more relevant and realistic conception of republicanism.

Although the Spartan brand of virtue often seemed merely impractical in a relatively advanced commercial society, it could also, if viewed from another perspective, be regarded as wrong in principle and thus unrepublican as well. In a speech "On the Fall of Empires," delivered to the Continental Congress in May 1775, William Moore Smith noted that, ironically, the famed Lycurgus, ruler of ancient Sparta, had destroyed liberty in his attempt to prevent the accumulation of wealth and luxury that he thought would subvert it.[57] This tragedy brought to light a vexing dilemma, particularly relevant to the American situation. The crucial point, Smith asserted, was that true liberty was impossible without a security of property in its broadest sense. Smith's listeners hardly had to be reminded of this point, since the crux of the colonial dispute with England was an assertion of precisely this right to dispose freely of the fruits of one's industry. Even Samuel Adams, a leading promoter of the Spartan vision, had stated the matter quite clearly in 1768, speaking for the Massachusetts House of Representatives: "It is acknowledged to be an unalterable law in nature, that a man should have the free use and disposal of the fruit of his honest industry, subject to no controul."[58] Where property was thus secure in a republic, however, honest labor inevitably produced an accumulation of wealth, which too often brought with it the debilitating luxury and other evils destructive of virtue and liberty.

Preventing the completion of this vicious cycle by arbitrarily denying men the right to their property was patently unjust, so Smith looked for another way to resolve the dilemma. Wealth should not be excluded, but if the use of it was judiciously regulated perhaps it was not necessarily incompatible with republicanism after all. Speaking of Mandeville's well-known defense of commerce and luxury, Smith admitted that it could never justify vicious luxury or an insipid indulgence in sensual pleasure.

57. William Moore Smith, "On the Fall of Empires," *Dunlap's Pennsylvania Packet, or, the General Advertiser* (Philadelphia), May 29, 1775.

58. The House of Representatives of Massachusetts to Henry Seymour Conway, Feb. 13, 1768, in Harry Alonzo Cushing, ed., *The Writings of Samuel Adams*, I (New York and

Sounding a bit like David Hume, he went on to suggest that there was nevertheless "a certain degree of elegance, and a liberal consumption of the produce both of nature and art, which become those who are blest with affluence; and if such wish for true luxury," Smith continued, "we quarrel not with the name—Go! enjoy the luxury, not of mere animal pleasure, but the luxury of rational being, nay of Heaven itself—the luxury of *doing good*." "If the godlike use is made of our superfluities, after a decent provision for our families," he proclaimed, "we shall never have occasion to deem wealth incompatible with liberty." Fearing, perhaps, that even this limited acceptance of wealth and luxury might be misconstrued by an audience inured to classical formulas, Smith concluded with a ringing exhortation to his countrymen to avoid the gross, unbecoming Mandevillian luxury that had undermined the great empires of antiquity.[59] Indeed, the Revolutionaries did not seek to reject a proper degree of civilization in the name of republicanism; they wished only to stop at the point where refinement became corruption. By no means would they prohibit "the improvements which wealth and science are continually producing among mankind"; they advised only against "the love of useless show and pomp."[60]

Smith was not the only American to recognize the vexing problem of reconciling wealth and security of property with republicanism. Carter Braxton, a Virginia merchant, was decidedly hostile to the idea of establishing a traditionally pure republic in America, for he believed that the disinterested public virtue on which it depended was unnatural and impossible for the mass of the people in modern times. "To this species of Government," Braxton complained, "everything that looks like elegance and refinement is inimical." Pointing to "ancient Republicks" with "numberless sumptuary laws, which restrained men to plainness and

London, 1904), 190. See also "An Elector," *Pennsylvania Journal and the Weekly Advertiser* (Philadelphia), Oct. 3, 1781.

59. Smith, "On the Fall of Empires," *Pa. Packet*, May 29, 1775. Benjamin Rush expressed a similar hope in 1782 when he observed: "I do not think wealth acquired by commerce (provided that commerce is not in the souls of men) is necessarily fatal to liberty." Rush to Nathanael Greene, Sept. 16, 1782, L. H. Butterfield, ed., *Letters of Benjamin Rush* (Princeton, N.J., 1951), I, 285.

60. "Atticus," *Pennsylvania Chronicle, and Universal Advertiser* (Philadelphia), Dec. 14, 1767. See also David Rittenhouse, *An Oration, Delivered February 24, 1775 . . .* (Philadelphia, 1775), esp. 17–20.

familiarity in dress and diet," he ridiculed the idea that they offered a realistic and just model for contemporary America:

Schemes like these may be practicable in countries so sterile by nature as to afford a scanty supply of the necessaries, and none of the conveniences of life; but they can never meet with a favourable reception from people who inhabit a country to which Providence has been more bountiful. They will always claim a right of using and enjoying the fruits of their honest industry, unrestrained by any ideal principles of Government, and will gather estates for themselves and children without regarding the whimsical impropriety of being richer than their neighbours. These are rights which freemen will never consent to relinquish; and after fighting for deliverance from one species of tyranny, it would be unreasonable to expect they should tamely acquiesce under another.[61]

The American people, in short, would never deny themselves the fruits of the prosperity that their natural resources promised and that they were entitled to; nor should they permit any attempts to coerce them to do so. Republics based on the classical concept of virtue, Braxton concluded, were a just and feasible model only for naturally poor and very primitive societies, and not for the United States, where each individual possessed a fundamental right to property in his labor and where the potential for wealth was so great.

In one sense, Braxton was more honest than his countrymen whom he addressed. If Americans seriously intended to attain the classical standards of republicanism to which they were publicly committed, Braxton seemed to demand that they confront the momentous sacrifices that were necessarily involved. If they genuinely wished to embrace republicanism, they would have to defy every tendency in their nature, every aspect of their condition, and even the basic rights of free men in order to transform their character in the required manner. To Braxton, as to Hume, any endeavor of this sort was foolhardy, for it demanded that men renounce the polished refinement of a properly civilized and humane culture. Few Americans wished to make this sacrifice either. But most of the Revolutionaries, even with all their doubts and misgivings about themselves, seemed to hope that the spirit of classical republicanism could be

---

61. Carter Braxton, *An Address to the Convention of . . . Virginia; on the Subject of Government . . .* (Williamsburg, Va., 1776), in Peter Force, ed., *American Archives . . .* (Washington, D.C., 1837–1853), 4th Ser., VI, 752, 748–752. See also Wood, *Creation of the American Republic*, 96–97.

accommodated both to more modern republican principles and to a more complex social and economic environment. The answer, perhaps, was not to interpret republicanism as literally and stringently as Braxton had.

The intellectual dilemma such a challenge posed for American republicans was inescapable. The problem of finding a way to permit liberty, commerce, and prosperity and, at the same time, to deny their potentially corrupting effects was neither new in American history nor unusual in the context of the eighteenth century's poignant endeavor to bridge the growing gap between antiquity and modernity.[62] Most Americans had no choice but to adopt the deceptively simple and perhaps chimerical proposal that John Brown had offered in his widely read tract from the 1750s—"that Commerce and Wealth not be discouraged in their Growth; but checked and controuled in their Effects"—for very few of them, including Benjamin Franklin, ever seriously anticipated a republican America without commerce and the wealth and refinement it would inevitably bring.[63] Franklin's vision of an expanding agricultural republic was not a call for Americans to retreat to a social simplicity that was primitive or barbarous—indeed, no one appreciated more than he the advantages of Hume's version of civilized cultural progress. And above all, Franklin's republican vision was hardly that of a Spartan, self-contained society of hermit yeomen, for it was closely tied to a much broader international commercial vision.

62. Wood, *Creation of the American Republic*, 65. Most notably, of course, 17th-century New England Puritans had wrestled with this general dilemma. See Perry Miller, *The New England Mind: From Colony to Province* (Boston, 1953), esp. 40–52, and Stephen Foster, *Their Solitary Way: The Puritan Social Ethic in the First Century of Settlement in New England* (New Haven, Conn., 1971), chap. 4.

63. John Brown, *An Estimate of the Manners and Principles of the Times* (London, 1757), 217. See above, chap. 1.

CHAPTER THREE

COMMERCE AND THE

INDEPENDENT REPUBLIC

On April 6, 1776, the Continental Congress threw American ports open to all foreign vessels. Military necessity dictated this action, for if the colonies were to continue armed resistance they needed access to supplies from Europe. But beyond this element of wartime expediency, the opening of American ports to foreign commerce symbolized a vital dimension of Revolutionary aspiration: it expressed faith in the prospects for a revolution in international trade that would be initiated and guided by an independent, republican America. Paradoxically, in the midst of a lingering rhetorical attachment to the classical, anti-commercial ideal, many of the Revolutionaries embraced an ideology of "free trade" that tied their utopian vision to the hope of achieving a burgeoning and invigorating intercourse with the rest of the world. Few republicans denied the truth of the familiar axiom that foreign commerce posed the insidious danger of "vicious" luxury and corruption. But this fear was considerably assuaged by the vibrant faith that the Revolution would instigate the annihilation of a corrupting, mercantilist system of intercourse and replace it with a more natural and universally beneficent system of exchange. Since many of the Revolutionaries viewed traditional restraints on their trade as symptoms of British corruption, it is not surprising that their vision of a republican future encompassed vigorous commercial expansion.[1]

The initial burst of Revolutionary idealism was indeed international and commercial in scope; but, as with most forms of idealism, it was not divorced from more practical considerations of national interest. Many Americans understood quite clearly the crucial role that commerce could play in shaping a republican order in the New World. As always, they

1. See especially J. E. Crowley, *This Sheba, Self: The Conceptualization of Economic Life in Eighteenth-Century America* (Baltimore, 1974), 147–149.

were particularly concerned with their character as a people, and it was here that commerce might promise to underwrite, rather than to undermine, the success of the republican experiment. The commercial vision even appeared to turn the traditional Spartan formula on its head with the suggestion that foreign commerce was no longer to be considered antithetical to republicanism. As the necessary spur to industry, productivity, and virtue, commerce was instead the lifeblood of a republican system. During the initial trying years of independence, as the new nation struggled to achieve a satisfactory position in the international economy, it also struggled to secure the necessary social and economic basis for a viable republican culture. These two endeavors were closely interrelated, and the many frustrations and setbacks suffered by the Revolutionaries during these years triggered extensive controversy about the character of their society, the true meaning of republicanism, and the proper structure of a republican political economy in America.

[I]

To many Americans in 1776, the essence of republicanism was a heightened concern with the moral integrity of the individual. As Montesquieu had explained, there was a reciprocal relationship between the various forms of government and the manners and spirit, or character, of a people. Since the elimination of a king and his "court" removed the traditional restraints of force and fear, the citizens of a republic had to be "virtuous," or exhibit an extraordinary morality of self-control, in order to secure a stable and just polity.[2] In America, however, the purely classical conception of virtue—as consistently intense, disinterested self-abnegation on the part of austere Spartans—gradually merged into a more modern meaning that put a premium on the productive industry of the active citizen. Even Montesquieu had concluded that under proper circumstances the modern "spirit of commerce" might be an effective substitute for traditional civic virtue, for commerce was, to a point, "naturally attended with . . . frugality, economy, moderation, labour, prudence, tranquillity, order, and rule." Here he admitted what David

2. Gordon S. Wood, *The Creation of the American Republic, 1776–1787* (Chapel Hill, N.C., 1969), 65–70, and J.G.A. Pocock, *The Machiavellian Moment: Florentine Political Thought and the Atlantic Republican Tradition* (Princeton, N.J., 1975), chaps. 14 and 15.

Hume, Adam Smith, and other European thinkers who defended commerce as a predominantly civilizing agent suggested even more forcefully: by encouraging the development of disciplined and energetic individuals, commerce had the capacity to promote, rather than to destroy, virtue.[3]

Under the rubric of virtue, Revolutionary Americans always subsumed the vital character traits of diligence, industry, and frugality. More often than not, they placed their greatest emphasis on industry. Above all, a healthy republican citizen had to be active and industrious—what had to be avoided at all costs were idleness and the lethargic depravity it invariably bred. This fear of idleness was hardly a new concern in Revolutionary America, as it had been deeply woven into the original Puritan impulse. In addition to fearing debilitation from luxury, both Puritans and republicans habitually worried about the spiritual anarchy of indolence, which was synonymous with disorder, corruption, and sin.[4] If men were left to wander aimlessly in idle passivity, they would fall prey to the myriad temptations that enticed weak and undisciplined minds. It was the duty of the community and its elected leaders, therefore, to keep people as much as possible fully employed in useful and productive

3. Charles Secondat, Baron de Montesquieu, *The Spirit of the Laws*, trans. Thomas Nugent, 2 vols. (New York, 1900 [orig. publ. Paris, 1748]), I, Book V, chap. 6, 46. The changing meaning of virtue is an exceedingly complex subject worthy of a full-length study in itself. Several secondary studies offer a good introduction to the problem. See especially, J.G.A. Pocock, *Politics, Language, and Time: Essays on Political Thought and History* (New York, 1971), esp. 100–103; Pocock, "Virtue and Commerce in the Eighteenth Century," *Journal of Interdisciplinary History*, III (1972–1973), esp. 132–134; Gerald Stourzh, *Alexander Hamilton and the Idea of Republican Government* (Stanford, Calif., 1970), esp. 70–75; Melvin Richter, "The Uses of Theory: Tocqueville's Adaptation of Montesquieu," in Richter, ed., *Essays in Theory and History; An Approach to the Social Sciences* (Cambridge, Mass., 1970), 74–102; David Kettler, *The Social and Political Thought of Adam Ferguson* (Columbus, Ohio, 1965), chap. 6; John B. Stewart, *The Moral and Political Philosophy of David Hume* (New York, 1963), chap. 7; Thomas L. Pangle, *Montesquieu's Philosophy of Liberalism: A Commentary on* The Spirit of the Laws (Chicago and London, 1973); and Ralph Lerner, "Character and Commerce: The Anglo-American as New-Model Man," *William and Mary Quarterly*, 3d Ser., XXXVI (1979), 3–26. See also Edmund S. Morgan, "The Puritan Ethic and the American Revolution," *ibid.*, XXIV (1967), 3–43, and Max Weber's treatment of Franklin in his classic study, *The Protestant Ethic and the Spirit of Capitalism*, trans. Talcott Parsons (London, 1930 [orig. publ. Tübingen, 1904–1905]).

4. See Morgan, "Puritan Ethic and the American Revolution," *WMQ*, 3d Ser., XXIV (1967), 3–43; Crowley, *This Sheba, Self*, esp. chaps. 1–3; and David Bertelson, *The Lazy South* (New York, 1967), esp. 3–15.

activity. The authority of a republican government, the Massachusetts clergyman Zabdiel Adams asserted in 1782, "should be put forth to make the people industrious," for industry was "the life of all states."[5]

In the minds of an American people acutely attuned to the importance of social character, diligent labor in a calling was understood as the necessary means of warding off the physical and spiritual corruption that was antithetical to republicanism. John Witherspoon's lectures at Princeton on moral philosophy reminded his students of the important truth that "sobriety, industry, and public spirit are nearly allied, and have a reciprocal influence upon one another." Civil liberty in a republican state, he added, was especially useful "in its tendency to put in motion all the human powers," thus promoting industry, happiness, and the improvement of the mind.[6] When Benjamin Franklin remarked in the early 1780s that "industry and constant Employment are great preservatives of the Morals and Virtue of a Nation," he expressed a common theme of the Revolution.[7] American republicans readily agreed with Noah Webster's later observation that "virtue, health, the vigor of the mind, intellectual improvements, every thing that goes into the composition of happiness and greatness, seem to depend on active industry and employment."[8]

This American concern with molding an industrious people was obsessive at times, betraying the fear that even republicans were naturally prone to devastating lapses in the performance of their duty. Franklin's commitment to making this brand of virtue a habit among his countrymen was a dominant motif of his life and thought. From the early days of *Poor Richard's Almanack* to the writing of his *Autobiography* in later years, he marshaled his energy in the cause of inculcating industry and frugality in rural Americans, who apparently were in great need of exhortation as well as specific instructions on how to become virtuous. And to Franklin, this matter became intertwined with the success of the

5. Zabdiel Adams, *A Sermon Preached before His Excellency John Hancock* . . . (Boston, 1782), 37–38. See also Peletiah Webster, "A Fifth Essay on Free Trade and Finance" (Philadelphia, 1780), in Webster, *Political Essays on the Nature and Operation of Money, Public Finances and Other Subjects* (Philadelphia, 1791), 127.

6. John Witherspoon, *Lectures on Moral Philosophy*, ed. Varnum Lansing Collins (Princeton, N.J., 1912), 114, 99.

7. "Information to Those Who Would Remove to America," Albert Henry Smyth, ed., *The Writings of Benjamin Franklin* (New York, 1907), VIII, 613.

8. Noah Webster, *Ten Letters to Dr. Joseph Priestley* . . . (New Haven, Conn., 1800), 20.

republican experiment. As he characteristically remarked in 1787, "Only a virtuous people are capable of freedom. As nations become corrupt and vicious, they have more need of masters."[9]

There was little doubt among Americans that they would have to be a peculiarly active and industrious people in order to remain morally sound enough to secure their new system of government. But like most eighteenth-century writers, American thinkers regarded the maintenance of this virtue as no simple matter. It was generally accepted that, human nature being what it was, all but the most extraordinary individuals were notoriously averse to strenuous exertion and regular labor. Overcoming this "proneness of human Nature to a life of ease, of freedom from care and labour," as Franklin had put it, was a particularly vexing problem for a people who aspired to build a productive and prosperous republican civilization.[10] If the necessary stimulants to industry were not present, one American observer noted in 1779, man was naturally "one of the most indolent animals in creation." God had provided the most rudimentary sources of industry in the form of the omnipresent dangers of want and misery, but these incentives alone barely raised men above the level of savage subsistence. The primary "demands from appetite and the climate" were fairly "easily supplied," and if a man had "no further calls upon him," the result was both tragic and predictable: "he yawns, stretches himself in the sun, smokes his pipe, and remains a living proof, that man is, by nature, a lazy beast."[11]

As eighteenth-century thinkers wrestled with this thorny problem, they proposed, in essence, two methods of rescuing men from their customary lethargy. In his widely read essay, "Of Commerce," David Hume had first cited the familiar Spartan solution of converting a community into a fortified camp and infusing "into each breast so martial a genius, and such a passion for public good, as to make every one willing to undergo the greatest hardships for the sake of the public." In modern times, however, Hume argued, this method was an unrealistic, insufficient, and

9. Franklin to Messrs. The Abbes Chalut and Arnaud, Apr. 17, 1787, Smyth, ed., *Writings of Franklin*, IX, 659.

10. Franklin to Peter Collinson, May 9, 1753, Leonard W. Labaree *et al.*, eds., *The Papers of Benjamin Franklin* (New Haven, Conn., 1959–), IV, 481. See also Franklin, "On the Labouring Poor," 1768, *ibid.*, XV, 104.

11. John Sloss Hobart to Robert R. Livingston, Nov. 15, 1779, as quoted in James Louis Cooper, "Interests, Ideas, and Empires: The Roots of American Foreign Policy, 1763–1779" (Ph.D. diss., University of Wisconsin, 1964), 520–521.

if enforced coercively, unjust spur to industry. Commerce was the solution. Men had to be given voluntary incentives to labor, and Hume proposed the lure of increased pleasure and happiness as the best means of exciting human industry. If men were presented with the opportunity to exchange their surplus production (beyond what they needed to support themselves at the bare subsistence level) for the "conveniencies" and "luxuries" that commerce offered, they could be motivated to labor assiduously in their callings.[12]

Since Hume's perspective on this particular matter was part of his broader defense of modern commercial society, other writers who agreed with him commonly associated lethargy and indolence with the rude, primitive, and undifferentiated societies that classical republican theorists so lavishly praised. In the absence of commerce and the arts that commerce entailed, it was repeatedly argued, men were content to wallow in brutish indigence and dissipation, since they had no incentive to labor to acquire the amenities of a civilized existence. "If mankind confined themselves to the use of the bare necessaries of life," William Temple typically argued in 1758, "labouring one hour in a day in each family would procure them all: Where, then, and how could universal industry be excited?" The inescapable conclusion was that "a simplicity of living and universal industry are incompatible and repugnant to each other."[13] In other words, those people who lived by austere, Spartan standards could never form an industrious citizenry except under a coercive system that most eighteenth-century thinkers viewed as unjust.

This presumed incompatibility between simplicity and industry posed an especially disturbing dilemma for a predominantly agricultural society committed to republicanism. Hume was particularly concerned with the problem of maintaining industry in an entirely agricultural state, for he believed that in the absence of a more diversified economy there could be no incentive for farmers to produce beyond subsistence. "Where manufactures and mechanic arts are not cultivated," he contended, "the bulk of the people must apply themselves to agriculture; and if their skill and industry encrease, there must arise a great superfluity from their labour beyond what suffices to maintain them. They have no temptation, there-

12. David Hume, "Of Commerce," Eugene Rotwein, ed., *David Hume: Writings on Economics* (Madison, Wis., 1970 [orig. publ. 1955]), 12, 3–18.

13. [William Temple], "A Vindication of Commerce and the Arts . . ." (London, 1758), reprinted in John R. McCulloch, ed., *A Select Collection of Scarce and Valuable Tracts on Commerce . . .* (London, 1859), 503–504, 481–561.

fore, to encrease their skill and industry; since they cannot exchange that superfluity for any commodities which may serve either to their pleasure or vanity." As a result, he concluded, "a habit of indolence naturally prevails."[14] William Temple agreed that "if mankind employed themselves in nothing but the productions absolutely necessary to life, seven in eight must be idle, or all be idle seven-eighths of their time," which could only lead them to "indulge intemperance, and sink in the beastly vices of slovenly gluttony and drunkenness."[15] As James Anderson queried in the same vein, "Without commerce or arts, what inducement has the farmer to cultivate the soil?" "In this case," he argued, "every man will only wish to rear as much as is sufficient for his own sustenance, and no more. . . . For this reason a nation peopled only by farmers, must be a region of indolence and misery."[16]

The solution to this commonly debated problem, according to Hume, Temple, and Anderson, was to cultivate commerce and the arts. A lethargic subsistence farmer might thus be encouraged to produce the surplus that could be exchanged for conveniences and luxuries, thereby giving "spirit to his operations, and life and activity to his mind."[17] "A good market," Anderson concluded, "will always produce a spirited agriculture." He stipulated, moreover, that this market be a domestic, rather than a distant or foreign one, since an advanced division of labor within a country had definite advantages over a division of labor among different nations. In order to reap fully "the happy fruits that naturally result from the alliance of agriculture with manufactures and commerce," it was necessary, according to Anderson, to "place a manufacturer in the neighborhood."[18]

If Hume, Temple, and Anderson were correct in assuming that farmers would never produce more than a bare subsistence unless they were given compelling incentives to do so, the new republic in North America confronted a potentially serious dilemma. Ironically, the fecundity of the American soil only exacerbated the situation, for it appeared that men did not have to work particularly long or hard to gain "the bare necessaries of life" in the New World. Simply stated, the problem was this: in a

14. Rotwein, ed., *David Hume*, 10.

15. Temple, "Vindication," in McCulloch, ed., *Select Collection*, 539.

16. James Anderson, *Observations on the Means of Exciting a Spirit of National Industry* (Dublin, 1779), I, 88.

17. *Ibid.*, 89.

18. *Ibid.*, 95, 89–90, 88–95.

predominantly agricultural society like America, where subsistence was so easily procured, what would sustain industry, and hence virtue, among the people? American farmers might have the potential to be tremendously active and productive, but if markets were not available to absorb the surplus they were capable of producing, the basis of their republican industry would be lost. Colonial Americans had hardly been strangers to this problem. If agricultural production was so great "as to overstock all the Markets far and near," Jared Eliot had observed in 1762, the eventual consequence was that "the rich valuable Product of the Earth, lies upon the Hands of the Farmer." Such a situation was "of bad Tendency," for it served to "enervate and abate the Vigour and Zeal of the Farmer," rendering him indolent by blunting "the Edge of Industry."[19] The dilemma could not be evaded: if sufficient markets were not available to absorb their agricultural surpluses, how would American farmers achieve the necessary discipline to be energetic, fully productive, and hence republican?

For many reasons tied to their fear and distrust of an advanced division of labor in densely populated commercial societies, the Revolutionaries hesitated to embrace Hume's solution of fostering advanced manufactures at home. Adopting this familiar European remedy implied that America would be pushed ahead into a new, more complex, and politically dangerous stage of social development. For most Americans, a much better expedient was the opening of abundant foreign markets for the burgeoning surpluses that their farmers were peculiarly equipped to produce. In this way, it was hoped, the United States might secure the basis for a properly industrious and moral people but still remain the predominantly agricultural society that best supported republicanism. The Scottish writer Sir James Steuart had expressed a standard axiom of eighteenth-century political economy by noting that "when foreign demand begins to fail, so as not to be recalled, either industry must decline, or domestic luxury must begin."[20] Americans hoped to avoid this situation altogether, because both results of a failure of foreign demand mentioned by Steuart were dangerous to a republican people, who could afford neither a decline in industry nor a more advanced economy tied to the production of luxury manufactures. Only a vigorous foreign com-

19. Harry J. Carman and Rexford G. Tugwell, eds., *Essays Upon Field Husbandry in New England, and Other Papers 1748–1762, by Jared Eliot* (New York, 1934), 186–187.

20. Sir James Steuart, *An Inquiry into the Principles of Political Oeconomy*, ed. Andrew S. Skinner (Chicago, 1966 [orig. publ. London, 1767]), II, 237.

merce with plentiful markets and a highly developed international division of labor that would permit the United States to continue its specialization in agriculture could provide the necessary basis for a healthy society of active, enterprising, hence virtuous, republican farmers.

To this extent, however, an expanding American republic required more than merely a reservoir of virgin land in order to remain industrious and predominantly agricultural. It also demanded an open and unrestricted foreign commerce that offered rapidly expanding export markets. And given this formula, the fate of republicanism in America was tied in great measure to the vicissitudes of international trade. If agrarian republicans were viable only so long as there were adequate markets to absorb the fruits of their republican industry, it appeared that the rest of the world had to cooperate in creating the conditions that might permit America to remain a simple republic of virtuous farmers. The full employment and moral integrity of the mass of Americans thus depended on what was happening abroad. No foreign markets, no industrious republicans; it was that simple.

Americans had long recognized that agriculture and foreign commerce were partners in a marriage that promised individual as well as communal prosperity. It seemed that subsistence agriculture was fine for a primitive or barbarous people, but not for enterprising Americans. It was not enough to feed and clothe our bodies, Nathaniel Ames had advised readers of his almanac in 1767: "We must do more; we must raise something to sell for exportation, if we would increase in wealth." The expansion of "trade and commerce," therefore, was "as necessary to a state as wings to a bird."[21] In 1783, the Philadelphia merchant Peletiah Webster agreed that foreign commerce was of essential importance to all American interests, for "no sources of our wealth can flourish, and

21. Nathaniel Ames, *An Astronomical Diary; or, Almanack for . . . 1767* (Boston, 1766), 2. Benjamin Franklin had been made aware of the critical interdependence of American agriculture and commerce as early as 1729, when his first writing on economics explicitly made the point. See Franklin, "A Modest Inquiry into the Nature and Necessity of a Paper Currency," Labaree *et al.*, eds., *Franklin Papers*, I, 139–157. In the 17th century, New Englanders had discovered the importance of commerce to agricultural prosperity quite early. They also recognized that a vigorous overseas commerce was a necessary condition for colonial specialization in agriculture and cattle raising, since a decline in trade, they believed, always necessitated the development of native manufacturing. See E.A.J. Johnson, *American Economic Thought in the Seventeenth Century* (London, 1932), 139–140, and Richard L. Bushman, *From Puritan to Yankee: Character and the Social Order in Connecticut, 1690–1765* (Cambridge, Mass., 1967), 26–27.

operate to general benefit of the community, *without it*." This observation applied especially to "our *husbandry*, that grand staple of our country," which "can never exceed our home consumption" without a vigorous commerce. "It is plain at first sight," Webster observed, "that the *farmer* will not toil and sweat thro' the year to raise great plenty of the produce of the soil, if there is *no market* for his produce, when he has it ready for sale."[22]

The Revolutionaries almost unthinkingly absorbed into their republican outlook this logic of the importance of foreign markets and free trade to American agriculture. In so doing they embarked on a grand quest to achieve their vision of the good society—a society that would somehow reconcile their commitment to the cultivation of an active, industrious, enterprising, virtuous people with their commitment to the maintenance of a predominantly simple and agricultural social order. Their hope of success in this venture was pinned to the two forms of expansion, landed and commercial, that might enable them to defy the seemingly inexorable logic of social progress through time and remain at a middle stage of development, somewhere between the undesirable extremes of a rude and barbarous simplicity, on the one hand, and an overrefined and corrupt decadence, on the other. This vision could not eradicate completely the danger of corruption, for there was always the problem of wealth itself: might not an agricultural people succumb to the temptations of great wealth as readily as any other people? Americans could only hope that honest and steady labor in agriculture would successfully mold the kind of virtuous character that could sensibly and moderately absorb the undeniable rewards of industry. Perhaps wealth that accrued through the perseverance of habitual industry, unlike the sudden fortunes acquired through the manipulation and chicanery of speculators and stockjobbers in the old nations of Europe, would not necessarily undermine the integrity of a republican culture.[23]

22. Peletiah Webster, "A Dissertation on the Political Union and Constitution of the Thirteen United States of North-America" (Philadelphia, 1783), in Webster, *Political Essays*, 216. Benjamin Rush observed in 1782 that "America possesses immense resources for national importance which can only be brought forth with commerce, which in the present state of things can only be the offspring of peace." See Rush to Nathanael Greene, Sept. 16, 1782, L. H. Butterfield, ed., *Letters of Benjamin Rush* (Princeton, N.J., 1951), I, 285. See also *Pennsylvania Gazette* (Philadelphia), Nov. 17, 1784.

23. Peletiah Webster, for example, affirmed in 1779 the validity of the "very common observation" that "fortunes suddenly acquired without the *industry* of the possessor, rarely

[II]

The Revolutionaries' fundamental concern with sustaining their republican character was only part of their commitment to foreign commerce; they also believed that the expansion of American trade would have a missionary impact on the rest of the world. Many republicans eagerly embraced an eighteenth-century ideology of free trade, whose leading spokesmen included Montesquieu, Hume, Adam Smith, and the French physiocrats.[24] According to these writers, foreign as well as domestic commerce should be freed from all restraints so that it might flourish and, in the process, humanize men by refining their manners and morals. This vision extolled the civilizing virtues of an unfettered international commerce that would be liberated from outmoded and pernicious mercantilist restrictions. A system of free trade would soften the brutal tendencies of primitive men by bringing them into contact with other nations and cultures. The natural result of this familiarity and interdependence was the promotion of peace; by gently cementing reciprocal ties of dependence among different countries, free trade inevitably decreased the potential for war. To some thinkers, this arrangement was providentially ordained. "The creator of nature" intended "to make men dependent on each other through the diversity of this nature," and thus "the bonds of commerce" were forged "in order to incline the peoples of

---

ever increase his happiness and welfare, help his virtuous habits, or continue long with him; they must commonly ruin him." See Webster, "A Second Essay on Free Trade and Finance" (Philadelphia, 1779), in Webster, *Political Essays*, 37. Back in 1758 the New England clergyman Thomas Barnard had vividly stated the point: although "overgrown Wealth" had a tendency to poison men's manners and morals, "yet it may be remarked that where it is attained by a Course of Industry, it arrives more gradually, and is usually to be preserved by the same Means by which it was attained, and thereby the Body of a Community contract a Habit of Oeconomy; employ their Gains to the Ends they proposed in labouring for them; Temperance and Diligence, the Means of Wealth stick by them, and are impressed on their Posterity. Whereas Opulence derived from Rapine, coming without steady application, tempts Men to neglect the Occupations which maintain Firmness of Body and Sobriety of Mind, often intoxicates Men with Pride, or sinks them in Debauchery." See Barnard, *A Sermon Preached in Boston* . . . (Boston, 1758), 12.

24. See Nicos E. Devletoglou, "Montesquieu and the Wealth of Nations," *Canadian Journal of Economics and Political Science*, XXIX (1963), 1–25; Pangle, *Montesquieu's Philosophy of Liberalism*, chap. 7; and Stourzh, *Hamilton and Republican Government*, chap. 4.

the earth to keep peace with each other and to love each other."[25] "By commerce," Joseph Priestley argued in typical fashion,

we enlarge our acquaintance with the terraqueous globe and its inhabitants, which tends greatly to expand the mind, and to cure us of many hurtful prejudices, which we unavoidably contract in a confined situation at home. The exercise of commerce brings us into closer and more extensive connexions with our own species, which must, upon the whole, have a favourable influence upon benevolence; and no person can taste the sweets of commerce, which absolutely depends upon a free and undisturbed intercourse of different and remote nations, but must grow fond of peace, in which alone the advantages he enjoys can be had.[26]

Priestley's vision of peaceful intercourse expressed the idea, one familiar to the eighteenth century, that commerce elevated and expanded the human mind. To votaries of commerce, man had not been made to be shut up in his own country like a prisoner, for it was his business and duty to become acquainted with others of his species by opening a friendly intercourse with foreign peoples. This view of commerce as the necessary means of uniting the different nations of the world through bonds of mutual need and obligation was in sharp contrast to the older, mercantilist interpretation of commerce as strictly a means of plundering the wealth of other nations in order to amass riches and power at home. Instead of competition and war, the followers of Montesquieu proclaimed, commerce promoted cooperation and peace.[27]

Given their hostility to Britain and the mercantilist model, it is not surprising that many Americans in the early years of independence embraced this outlook and tied it directly to the spirit of their revolution.

25. The quote is from the article on "Commerce" in the French Encyclopedia, translated and printed in Nelly S. Hoyt and Thomas Cassirer, eds., *Encyclopedia: Selections* (Indianapolis, Ind., 1965), 49. This idea of the providential basis of commerce long predated the 18th century. See Jacob Viner, *The Role of Providence in the Social Order: An Essay in Intellectual History* (Philadelphia, 1972), 27–54, and Perry Miller, "The Religious Impulse in the Founding of Virginia: Religion and Society in the Early Literature," *WMQ*, 3d Ser., V (1948), 509–513.

26. Joseph Priestley, *Lectures on History and General Policy* . . . (Dublin, 1788), 327–328.

27. N. Webster, *Ten Letters*, 21. See also Benjamin Rush, *Essays, Literary, Moral, and Philosophical*, 2d ed. (Philadelphia, 1806), 17, and [James Chalmers], *Plain Truth; Addressed to the Inhabitants of America* . . . (Philadelphia, 1776), 46–47.

New Englanders, in particular, exulted at the prospect of an American commerce liberated from the shackles of British mercantilism. American merchants and sailors, Levi Frisbie asserted in 1783, could now rejoice in the liberty of the seas and look forward to "the enlargement and the prosperity of trade and commerce." Since Americans were "no longer harrassed with burdensome impositions, or unnecessary restrictions; no longer watched and pillaged by the mercenary tools of a tyrannical government," he announced, "they may waft their commodities to every climate, without molestation or disturbance;—the ports of every nation extend their arms to receive them, from whence they may import the various riches and treasures of the globe."[28] Other optimists, like John Warren, anticipated a new era of peace, since "commercial intercourse and connection have perhaps contributed more towards checking the effusion of blood, than all the obligations of morality and religion ... could ever have effected."[29] American clergymen were quick to point to the missionary power of this civilizing commerce. By humanizing men, Joseph Buckminster asserted, commerce ultimately molded minds that were receptive to spiritual grace. "The connections that may be formed by commercial intercourse, will not only be a source of wealth, and procure leisure for scientific pursuits," he predicted, "but a reciprocity of kind offices will expand and humanize the heart, soften the spirit of bigotry and superstition, and eradicate those rooted prejudices, that are the *jaundice* of the mind, the great obstacle to its improvement · in knowledge and virtue, and particularly to its reception of that grace of the gospel which maketh wise to eternal life."[30]

In his celebrated oration, *The United States Elevated to Glory and Honor*, delivered in 1783, Ezra Stiles aptly summarized this euphoric approach to the anticipated unleashing of American commerce. Commerce would bring wealth, of course, but to Stiles its importance far transcended any increase in comfort and prosperity, for the interchange of goods carried with it an interchange of knowledge, making men more civilized in both a material and an intellectual sense. "We shall have a communication with all nations in *commerce, manners* and *science*," Stiles predicted, "beyond any thing heretofore known in the world."[31]

28. Levi Frisbie, *An Oration, Delivered at Ipswich* . . . (Boston, 1783), 14–15.

29. John Warren, *An Oration, Delivered July 4th, 1783* . . . (Boston, 1783), 10.

30. Joseph Buckminster, *A Discourse Delivered in the First Church . . . December 11, 1783* (Portsmouth, N.H., 1784), 21–22.

31. Ezra Stiles, *The United States Elevated to Glory and Honor* . . . (New Haven, Conn., 1783), 50.

He never doubted for a moment that the United States would be the generating and refining force of this great reformation—American commerce would be the purveyor of American principles, which would be the distilled essence of wisdom imported from all corners of the globe. To Stiles and those of his commercial persuasion, the revolution in America was a missionary force that could not be contained. Through the expansion of American commerce, it would eventually become a movement of universal scope.

This great American revolution, this recent political phaenomenon of a new sovereignty arising among the sovereign powers of the earth, will be attended to and contemplated by all nations. Navigation will carry the american flag around the globe itself; and display the thirteen stripes and new constellation at *bengal* and *canton*, on the *indus* and *ganges*, on the *whang-ho* and the *yang-tse-kiang*; and with commerce will import the wisdom and literature of the east . . . there shall be an universal traveling *too* and *fro, and knowledge shall be increased.* This knowledge will be brought home and treasured up in america; and being here digested and carried to the highest perfection, may reblaze back from america to europe, asia and africa, and illumine the world with truth and liberty.[32]

American destiny and the republican revolution, in short, were inextricably bound to the civilizing influence of commercial expansion.[33]

For a variety of reasons, then, most Americans rarely doubted that foreign commerce was to play a central role in their revolution. As Thomas Paine wrote in *Common Sense,* "Our plan is commerce, and that, well attended to, will secure us the peace and friendship of all Europe."[34] There was tremendous confidence that the United States could indeed initiate a commercial revolution that would extend and reorganize international trade along liberal lines. To this extent, the publication in 1776 of the penultimate manifesto of free trade, Adam Smith's *Wealth of Nations,* seemed to be more than coincidence. If

32. *Ibid.*, 52.

33. See also Benjamin Hichborn, *An Oration, Delivered July 5th, 1784* . . . (Boston, 1784), 18–19; Samuel Macclintock, *A Sermon Preached before the Honorable the Council* . . . (Portsmouth, N.H., 1784), 26–27; and the *American Museum or Universal Magazine,* II (September 1787), 274. This last piece is an excerpt from an essay on encouraging American commerce, written by St. George Tucker, of Petersburg, Virginia, at the end of the war.

34. Philip S. Foner, ed., *The Complete Writings of Thomas Paine* (New York, 1945), I, 20.

commerce could be released from the mercantilist shackles that stifled and perverted it, the argument ran, it might become a predominantly civilizing, rather than a corrupting, force. Since America was the producer of necessaries that "will always have a market while eating is the custom of Europe" as well as a bountiful market for European manufactures, it was the natural catalyst for this commercial revolution. "It is the interest of all Europe," Paine boasted, "to have America as a free port."[35]

It was in this spirit of optimistic expectation that American ports were thrown open to world trade in April 1776, and the subsequent "plan of treaties" adopted by the Continental Congress in September.[36] Through the negotiation of new liberal trade agreements with the nations of the world, Americans could hope that their revolution would bring with it an end to mercantilism and the advent of a new era in international commerce and peace. In this new world, selfish, parochial, and unenlightened governments would no longer divert trade from the "natural," universally beneficial channels of which Adam Smith had spoken. And above all, Americans were confident of the prosperity and grandeur that this new order would bring to them. "We have laid the foundations of a new empire, which promises to enlarge itself to vast dimensions, and to give happiness to a great continent," David Ramsay proudly proclaimed in 1778. "It is now our turn to figure on the face of the earth, and in the annals of the world."[37]

[III]

The profound disillusionment that ensued is a familiar chapter in the history of the early years of independence. As American idealism confronted the harsh realities of the post-war era, the Revolutionaries encountered disturbing discrepancies between their vision of how the world should be and the way it actually was. Their response to this divergence

---

35. *Ibid.*

36. See especially Vernon G. Setser, *The Commercial Reciprocity Policy of the United States, 1774–1829* (Philadelphia, 1937), chap. 2; Felix Gilbert, *To the Farewell Address: Ideas of Early American Foreign Policy* (Princeton, N.J., 1961), chap. 3; and Paul A. Varg, *Foreign Policies of the Founding Fathers* (East Lansing, Mich., 1963), chaps. 1–3.

37. David Ramsay, *An Oration on the Advantages of American Independence* (Charleston, S.C., 1778), 20.

between expectations and experience was varied, and the resulting tensions in the republican mind surfaced in critical debates over a wide range of issues and problems. Since their approach to political economy was so closely tied to the sensitive matter of social character, the Revolutionaries were compelled to wrestle with much more than the rather straightforward question of how their economy should be organized. They were plunged into controversy over their character as a people and the nature of the republican experiment itself. As they endeavored to cope with the tensions and inconsistencies lurking in their vision, many Americans experienced an agonizing despair, prompting them to retreat toward traditional classical modes of expression that voiced serious doubts about the compatibility of commerce and republicanism. Others responded both to the post-war disillusionment and to the resurgence of classical-mindedness with a reaffirmation of the centrality of commerce, and even luxury, to the shaping of a republican culture. Within this controversy over social character and classical models, only its relevance to the more practical issues of political economy did not require debate. Some of the problems that arose during this trying period of adjustment were never resolved, others were tentatively resolved, and many were evaded or left to resolve themselves in what was hoped would be a brighter future.

The Revolution unequivocally failed to produce a new world of free trade.[38] American efforts to negotiate the system of treaties envisioned in the plan of 1776 met with very limited success. Most significant was the failure to induce England at the end of the war to move in the direction of American desires. As early as July 1783, Parliament moved to exploit the feebleness of the American confederacy and to keep the former colonies in a position of commercial dependency. The crucial measure in this policy was an exclusion of American ships from the British West Indies, a measure that promised to impede critically an important and very profitable branch of American commerce. In addition to undercutting American shipping and the carrying trade, British orders-in-council created serious problems for American farmers tied to the export trade. The West Indian market for American salted meat, fish, and dairy products was

---

38. See, in addition to the works cited in n. 36 above, Merrill D. Peterson, "Thomas Jefferson and Commercial Policy, 1783–1793," *WMQ*, 3d Ser., XXII (1965), 584–610, and Frederick W. Marks III, *Independence on Trial: Foreign Affairs and the Making of the Constitution* (Baton Rouge, La., 1973), chap. 2.

severely limited, and American wheat was virtually excluded from the British home market by Corn Law restrictions. Other European nations failed to compensate for this British intransigence by accepting American overtures for free trade and opening substitute markets. To compound the new republic's difficulties even further, American trade with Spain, southern Europe, and the Mediterranean also declined as a result of extensive harassment from the Barbary pirates of that region.[39]

Initially, most Americans discovered a convenient scapegoat for their frustrations in the policies of incorrigibly unenlightened European governments. By the fall of 1783 congressional reports began to voice despair at the growing influence of the "forces of reaction" across the Atlantic. Too many nations, jealous of the new republic's potential for commercial greatness, had not yet perceived "this important truth, that the sphere of their own Commerce will be eventually enlarged by the growth of America."[40] "Altho' it might in general be considered as most wise for them to aid our progress in the acquisition of wealth, seeing that by such means their own Commerce with us would become more lucrative, extensive, and secure," one report complained, "yet it is not uncommon for those who manage the affairs of nations, to pursue a course inconsistent with the prosperity of the people subjected to their authority; political interests sometimes really differ from those of Commerce, and in many cases, they appear to differ, where they are the same."[41] Americans discovered, in short, that mercantilism was far from moribund, and their response was to charge perverse and misguided European governments with foolishly subverting the commercial ideals of the Revolution by engaging in traditional practices—practices that violated not only the spirit of enlightened natural law, but even the true interests of their own constituents.

39. Marks, *Independence on Trial*, 36–45, 52–66. See also Gordon C. Bjork, "The Weaning of the American Economy: Independence, Market Changes, and Economic Development," *Journal of Economic History*, XXIV (1964), 541–560, and Robert Bruce Bittner, "The Definition of Economic Independence and the New Nation" (Ph.D. diss., University of Wisconsin, 1970), esp. the introduction and chap. 1.

40. Committee report on restrictions on commerce, Worthington Chauncey Ford *et al.*, eds., *Journals of the Continental Congress, 1774–1789* (Washington, D.C., 1904–1937), XXV, 618.

41. *Ibid.*, 662. See also Richard Henry Lee to Lafayette, June 11, 1785, and to John Adams, Oct. 23, 1785, in James Curtis Ballagh, ed., *The Letters of Richard Henry Lee*, II (New York, 1914), 369–370, 399.

This post-war American outlook was best summarized in the draft of a congressional committee report of April 1784. The committee on commercial matters began by affirming unequivocally the crucial importance of commerce to the United States as a necessary stimulant of the industry that produced both wealth and virtue: "The delicate situation of commerce at this time, claims the attention of the several States, and it will be admitted that few objects of greater importance can present themselves to their notice. The fortune of every Citizen is interested in the fate of commerce: for it is the constant source of industry and wealth; and the value of our produce and our land must ever rise or fall in proportion to the prosperous or adverse state of trade." Already, the report continued, Great Britain had "attempted a monopoly which is destructive of our trade with her West-India Islands." Although there was little reason "to expect that a measure so unequal, and so little calculated to promote mercantile intercourse" would be "persevered in by an enlightened nation," the measure seemed to be "growing into a system, and if it should be attended with success, there is too much reason to apprehend other nations might follow the example, and the commerce of America become the victim of illiberal policy." Should this tendency indeed take firm hold in European governments, the committee concluded, the United States might "never command reciprocal advantages in trade; and without such reciprocity, our foreign commerce must decline and eventually be annihilated."[42]

This stunning defeat of the Revolutionaries' commercial aspirations was especially galling because it was accompanied by the immediate reappearance of an unfavorable balance of trade. Americans had rather naively hoped that independence from the empire would automatically alleviate this familiar and dangerous problem, since their commerce, as David Ramsay had put it, would "no longer be confined by the selfish regulations of an avaricious stepdame" but instead would "follow wherever Interest leads the way." "Our great object, as a trading people," Ramsay had commented in 1778, "should be to procure the best prices for our commodities, and foreign articles at the most reasonable rates," and it required "but a moment's recollection" to realize "that as we now have a free trade with all the world, we shall obtain a more generous price for our produce, and foreign goods on easier terms, than we ever could, while we were subject to a British monopoly." The Navigation

42. Ford *et al.*, eds., *Journals of Continental Congress*, XXVI, 269–270.

Acts—"a glaring monument of the all-grasping nature of unlimited power"—had unjustly restrained American trade from flowing in its natural and most profitable channels, which explained why it had chronically suffered unfavorable balances. Now that the formal imperial basis for the artificial profits of British merchants and middlemen was being destroyed, Americans would be able to engage in a more flourishing direct trade with European markets, which would bring higher prices for their exports and also lower the price of imports.[43] Benjamin Franklin agreed that an unrestricted foreign demand for American produce would be a boon to the republic's farmers, and he added that another of the many "happy consequences of our commerce being open to all the world, and no longer a monopoly to Britain" would be a new competition among foreign countries for the vast American market in manufactures, resulting, he claimed, in lowered prices for the imports that the United States had to buy.[44]

As early as 1784, however, the Revolutionaries discovered that independence alone had not brought about the kind of free trade that would eliminate the unfavorable balances of trade that had plagued them as colonists. Importations once again considerably exceeded exportations, contributing to a distressing drain of specie, extensive indebtedness, and an ominous social malaise. Since most of the republic's excessive importation came in the familiar form of England's finer manufactures, or luxuries, some commentators looked beyond the faults of European governments and pointed an accusing finger at the American people themselves, complaining that an old species of corruption was flourishing under the new guise of freedom. It was necessary to remember, one critic remarked, that "however necessary and advantageous a free trade may

43. Ramsay, *Oration on Advantages of Independence,* 8, 9.

44. Franklin to Richard Price, Feb. 1, 1785, Smyth, ed., *Writings of Franklin,* IX, 286. See also Franklin to M. LeVeillard, Mar. 16, 1786, *ibid.,* 495–496; Franklin to William Hunter, Nov. 24, 1786, *ibid.,* 548; Franklin to Dupont de Nemours, June 9, 1788, *ibid.,* 659–660; Franklin to Benjamin Vaughan, Nov. 2, 1789, *ibid.,* X, 52; and Franklin to Alexander Small, Nov. 5, 1789, *ibid.,* 66. The best introduction to the pre-Revolutionary balance of trade predicament and its impact on American political economy is Joseph Albert Ernst, *Money and Politics in America, 1755–1775: A Study in the Currency Act of 1764 and the Political Economy of Revolution* (Chapel Hill, N.C., 1973). For a discussion of the problem as it affected the Chesapeake economy, see also Ronald Hoffman, *A Spirit of Dissension: Economics, Politics, and the Revolution in Maryland* (Baltimore, 1973), chap. 1, esp. 18.

be to a nation, it should not be a licentious one."[45] Americans were simply overextending themselves by importing more than they could pay for. They were not forced to buy foreign luxuries; indeed, if they were a properly moral people, they would resist the temptation to indulge in this frivolous consumption. But instead of becoming an industrious and frugal people, Americans were being seduced by the lure of this licentious foreign commerce—a spurious form of "free trade"—and the fictitious prosperity it offered. Thus the moral weakness of the American citizenry, it seemed to many observers, might be the primary cause of the republic's predicament.[46]

By the mid-1780s, as the commercial situation continued to deteriorate, this concern with American manners, morals, and character, and hence with the fate of the republican experiment, grew more intense. The despair that followed repeated failures to make progress toward a new world of open commerce induced among some republicans an obsessive fear of luxury and a suspicious distrust of foreign commerce in general. This disillusionment, fueled by economic hard times and the distressing social consequences of an unfavorable balance of trade, was frequently characterized by the resurgence of a rhetorical commitment to a traditional, anti-commercial conception of republicanism. As many perturbed Americans fretted over the mounting evidence that their countrymen were a corrupt and extravagant people incapable of sustaining a republican system, they bemoaned, often in shrill and hysterical tones, their country's falling away from the republican standards of classical antiquity.[47]

45. *The Political Establishments of the United States . . .* (Philadelphia, 1784), 8. See also the *Massachusetts Centinel: and the Republican Journal* (Boston), June 12, 1784. For a discussion of the commercial situation in Virginia at the end of the war, see Drew R. McCoy, "The Virginia Port Bill of 1784," *Virginia Magazine of History and Biography*, LXXXIII (1975), 288–303.

46. See especially, Wood, *Creation of the American Republic*, chap. 10, and Morgan, "Puritan Ethic and the American Revolution," *WMQ*, 3d Ser., XXIV (1967), 34–40.

47. Above all, see Wood, *Creation of the American Republic*, esp. 413–425. To many Americans the Revolution had indeed run amok, and they expressed their profound disillusionment by comparing their country's predicament to the tragic fate of the ancient republics that had succumbed to luxury and corruption. Most of these republics had at least gone through the customary cycle of "growth, perfection, and decay," Aedanus Burke commented, but America, "like an untimely birth, suffered an abortion before it was in maturity fit to come into the world." See [Burke], *Consideration on the Society or Order of Cincinnati . . .* (Charleston, S.C., 1783), 28.

This reactionary republicanism, which reasserted the applicability of the Spartan model to the American experience, did not go unchallenged, however. Other republicans explicitly denied the relevance of classical models, reaffirmed a commitment to modern commercial society, and even attempted a coherent defense of luxury in response to those who were obsessed with its alleged dangers. Concern about the character of American society and its suitability for republicanism was widespread during the 1780s, but not all disappointed Americans retreated to the familiar and comfortable ideological mold of classical analogies and primitivist anxieties.[48]

Indeed, some observers had never doubted that Americans were a commercial people whose virtue could not be measured in classical terms. In the early 1780s Gouverneur Morris had frankly described his countrymen as "highly commercial, being as it were the first born children of extended Commerce in modern Times."[49] Alexander Hamilton's prose reeked of disgust and impatience toward the end of the war as he, too, tried to impress upon his readers that their fixation on classical antiquity was misguided. "We may preach till we are tired of the theme," he wrote in *The Continentalist*, "the necessity of disinterestedness in republics, without making a single proselyte."

The virtuous declaimer will neither persuade himself nor any other person to be content with a double mess of porridge, instead of a reasonable stipend for his services. We might as soon reconcile ourselves to the Spartan community of goods and wives, to their iron coin, their long beards, or their black cloth. There is a total dissimulation in the circumstances, as well as the manners, of society among us; and it is as ridiculous to seek for models in the simple ages of Greece and Rome, as it would be to go in quest of them among the Hottentots and Laplanders.[50]

As another writer, "Philaeni," similarly argued, the practices of ancient Greece and Rome were in "no ways adapted to the modern Christian

48. In *Creation of the American Republic*, Wood fails to discuss in sufficient depth the challenges to this reactionary republicanism, the extent and influence of which he probably overemphasizes. Surprisingly, Wood completely ignores the "free trade" element of American republicanism.

49. Morris to Matthew Ridley, Aug. 6, 1782, quoted in Clarence Ver Steeg, *Robert Morris, Revolutionary Financier* (Philadelphia, 1954), 166–167.

50. *The Continentalist*, No. VI, July 4, 1782, Harold C. Syrett and Jacob E. Cooke, eds., *The Papers of Alexander Hamilton* (New York, 1961–), III, 103.

world," and he derided those Americans who preached "preposterous ideas derived from Antique histories of barbarous ages, no how reduceable to practice in the modern world of commerce."[51]

By the mid-1780s, when both the commercial crisis and the outpouring of Spartan lamentations were at their peak, these "modern" republican spokesmen found an even more pressing need to assert their point of view. James Warren had written to John Adams in Europe about the decline and ruin of America, ascribing it to a sudden decay of manners and morals brought about by a frivolous infatuation with foreign commerce and luxury. In reply, Adams expressed doubt that his countrymen's character could have changed so quickly. If Americans were now corrupt, then they had probably always been so, even in the halcyon days of the Revolution. Adams continued by asserting that this lack of "virtue" was not altogether to be regretted. "It is most certain that our Countrymen," he wrote, "are not and never were, Spartans in their Contempt of Wealth, and I will go further and say they ought not to be. Such a Trait in their Character would render them lazy Drones, unfit for Agriculture Manufactures Fisheries, and Commerce, and Population of their Country."[52] Thus the lure of commerce and luxury, in Adams's opinion, played a critical role in exciting the industry and productive labor that made Americans a properly civilized people. As Benjamin Franklin wrote to a friend in 1784, "Is not the Hope of one day being able to purchase and enjoy Luxuries a great Spur to Labour and Industry? May not Luxury, therefore, produce more than it consumes, if without such a Spur People would be, as they are naturally enough inclined to be, lazy and indolent?" Franklin confessed that he had no remedy for the luxury people complained of in America, and he was not even sure "that in a great State it is capable of a Remedy" or, indeed, that "the Evil is in itself always so great as it is represented."[53] Above all, luxury was valued

51. "Philaeni," *Strictures on the Landed and Commercial Interest of the United States, for 1786* (New York, 1786), 20.

52. John Adams to James Warren, July 4, 1786, *Warren-Adams Letters* (Massachusetts Historical Society, *Collections*, LXXII–LXXIII [Boston, 1917–1925]), II, 277. For expressions of concern similar to Warren's, see Mercy Warren to Adams, Apr. 27, 1785, *ibid.*, 252; Samuel Wales, *The Dangers of our National Prosperity . . .* (Hartford, Conn., 1785); and James Swan, *National Arithmetick: or, Observations on the Finances of the Commonwealth of Massachusetts . . .* (Boston, 1786), esp. 13–21.

53. Franklin to Benjamin Vaughan, July 26, 1784, Smyth, ed., *Writings of Franklin*, IX, 243. See also Franklin, "The Internal State of America," *ibid.*, X, 122.

by these Americans as a solvent of idleness. Although neither Adams nor Franklin followed the drift of his argument to its inevitable conclusion, both verged on contending that some degree of luxury was indispensable in a republican society.

In response to a spectacular display of anti-luxury hysteria in 1785 and 1786, others did not hesitate to go beyond Adams and Franklin. The establishment in Boston in 1785 of a Tea Assembly, the so-called "Sans Souci Club," provoked a howling debate over the manners and morals of Bostonians that quickly zeroed in on the more fundamental question of the nature of American society and the character of its people.[54] Those who defended the club's gatherings for conversation and polite amusement did so by developing the themes Hamilton, Franklin, and Adams had touched on, all of which were grounded in the basic contention that civilized life in modern commercial society was different from, and infinitely superior to, the republicanism of antiquity. Luxury, they argued, was both inevitable and desirable in civilized nations, as it was a sign of the liberty and humanity that had been lacking in the primitive, barbarian societies that the club's opponents so foolishly pointed to as models for America. "Roman virtue," one defender of the Sans Souci concluded, "scrutinized to its motive, and measured by the standards of humanity and reason, will be found seldom to rise above senseless ferocity." American goals, on the contrary, were civilized: peace, liberty, and safety.[55] Another writer ridiculed the pretensions of the club's enemies by sketching the logical outcome of their republicanism: "Let us break the bands of society, refuse all connection with the arts and sciences which live under the patronage of commerce and retire to the woods; let us learn of the savages *simplicity* of life, to forget humanity, and cut each other's throats without remorse, and even with satisfaction, for the inestimable reward of a garland of parsley, or a wreath of pine." In reply to those who attacked the members of the club for indulging their propensity for amusement, this writer could only ask: "To what end do we toil, if not to promote our ease and to procure an exemption from labour?"[56]

---

54. For a fuller description and analysis of the Sans Souci imbroglio, see Wood, *Creation of the American Republic*, 422–425.

55. "Crito," *Independent Chronicle. And the Universal Advertiser* (Boston), Jan. 20, 1785.

56. *Mass. Centinel* (Boston), Jan. 19, 1785.

Perhaps the most interesting clash of opinion on these matters came in Connecticut, during a debate in October 1786, over the desirability of sumptuary or anti-luxury laws in the United States. Jedediah Morse, who argued for the laws, based his discussion on the question: "How exactly does the situation of the United States compare with that of ancient Sparta?" His opponent, David Daggett, could only argue that Morse drew all the wrong conclusions from his comparison. Sumptuary laws in America would be a mark of tyranny in an enlightened age, a throwback to those antediluvian times when the state saw fit to limit the citizen in the use of his property. In addition to violating this sacred right of property, such legislation would be a foolish and quixotic attempt to arrest the progress of American civilization. Luxury was inevitable in mature societies, and it brought with it a refinement of the arts and a culture in its "meridian splendor." To those who argued that America was a young society falling prematurely prey to the evils of an old and corrupt empire, Daggett responded in the following terms:

We are a young nation, it is true, but we sprang from an old one: our situation is different from that of other empires at their infancy; a more polished, a more learned, a more commercial people, at the same period of our national existence, we must be a more luxurious people. And as soon as you can cause us to exchange our refinement for barbarity, our learning for ignorance, and our liberty for servitude, then may we see parsimony take the place of luxury, and I may add too misery and wretchedness triumphing over happiness.[57]

Daggett thus reaffirmed the ideological basis for a more modern conception of republicanism than that of his antagonists, modern in the sense that it explicitly and unflinchingly rejected the traditional anti-commercial dimension of the classical paradigm. In the late 1780s William Vans Murray, in his *Political Sketches*, aggressively attacked the still prevalent—but in his eyes fallacious—idea that republican government "required a tone of manners unattainable and unpreservable in a society where commerce, luxury, and the arts, have disposed the public mind to the gratification of refinement."[58] In the preface to his *Defence of the*

57. *New-Haven Gazette, and the Connecticut Magazine*, Oct. 12, 1786. See also "An Essay on American Genius," *Mass. Centinel*, Feb. 10, 1787.

58. *American Museum*, II (September 1787), 220. See Alexander DeConde, "William Vans Murray's *Political Sketches*: A Defense of the American Experiment," *Mississippi Valley Historical Review*, XLI (1954–1955), 623–640.

Constitutions of America, John Adams stressed the tremendous changes that had overtaken the Western world in the previous few centuries, making explicit the significant discontinuity he saw between the ancient and modern experiences. "The arts and sciences in general, during the three or four last centuries," he argued, "have had a regular course of progressive improvement. The inventions in mechanic arts, the discoveries in natural philosophy, navigation, and commerce, and the advancement of civilization and humanity, have occasioned changes in the condition of the world, and the human character, which would have astonished the most refined nations of antiquity."[59] Adams thus accepted luxury as part of the modern condition and, in reference to his own country, asserted that "a free people are the most addicted to luxury of any." "In a country like America," he concluded, "where the means and opportunities for luxury are so easy and so plenty, it would be madness not to expect it, be prepared for it, and provide against the dangers of it in the constitution."[60] To these republicans, in short, the aim of instilling a Spartan creed in modern commercial America, despite the current sad state of affairs, was nonsensical and misguided. Americans were, and had to continue to be, a properly refined people. If they wanted to be free, they would have to accept luxury and seek only to contain and regulate its potentially dangerous consequences.

[IV]

The renewal of this debate over the relationship between commerce, luxury, and the American commitment to republicanism closely paralleled a simultaneous debate over the proper structure of the American economy. The nagging despair of anguished Spartans, who asserted that foreign commerce did more to undermine than to support a republican order, suggested a vision of America's political economy different from the one based on free trade. This alternative vision caught the spirit of the English observer Richard Price's contention that the American states were "spread over a great continent, and make a world within them-

---

59. John Adams, *A Defence of the Constitutions of Government of the United States of America* . . . (London, 1787), I, A2.
60. *Ibid.*, III, 336–337.

selves."[61] Since Americans were capable of producing everything they needed at home, Price remarked in 1784, they had no need of foreign commerce, which too often brought with it luxury, corruption, debauchery, and the constant risk of war. All the United States could draw from intercourse with Europe, according to Price, was "INFECTION."[62] Many Americans agreed that the vices of an excessive commerce were contagious, debilitating, and "highly detrimental to an infant country" like the United States, and even commercial republicans like Thomas Paine acknowledged the potentially enervating influence of foreign commerce on America's social character.[63] As frustration mounted during the 1780s, expressions of this anti-commercial sentiment became extreme and insistent enough to imply that the United States, in order to establish its republican character, would have to isolate itself completely from European corruption by renouncing all foreign commerce. "Foreign trade," one such orator charged, "is in its very nature subversive of the spirit of pure liberty and independence, as it destroys that simplicity of manners, native manliness of soul, and equality of station, which is the spring and peculiar excellence of a free government." There was no better evidence of this truism, he asserted, than the pathetic condition of the fledgling republics in North America.[64]

Price's model of an isolated and self-sufficient republic was thus an appealing vision, particularly when Americans were caught in the throes of economic depression and moral despair. Yet many Americans seemed to recognize that an insular political economy of this sort would require either the introduction of new forms of manufacturing with a forced and dangerous de-emphasis of agriculture and westward expansion, or the acceptance of a very primitive, Spartan way of life that could easily degenerate into barbaric savagery. Moreover, Price's insular vision

---

61. Richard Price, *Observations on the Importance of the American Revolution . . .* (London, 1784), 62.

62. *Ibid.*, 63.

63. Zabdiel Adams, *The Evil Designs of Men . . .* (Boston, 1783), 26, and Foner, ed., *Writings of Paine*, I, 36. For a brilliant discussion and analysis of Paine's commercial republicanism, see Eric Foner, *Tom Paine and Revolutionary America* (New York, 1976), esp. 98–106.

64. "An Oration Delivered at Petersburgh, Virginia on the 4th of July, 1787 . . . ,"*American Museum*, II (November 1787), 421. The American attachment to the spirit of Price's insular vision had initially taken root during the resistance movement of the 1760s and

seemed hopelessly at odds with the realities of American life. The young republic lacked the necessary infrastructure for the highly developed internal commerce that would necessarily anchor his vision, and too many Americans already had a vested interest in and a taste for foreign commerce to give it up. "It has long been a speculative question among Philosophers and wise men," George Washington commented in 1785, "whether foreign Commerce is of real advantage to any Country; that is, whether the luxury, effeminacy, and corruptions which are introduced along with it; are counterbalanced by the convenience and wealth which it brings with it." But "the decision of this question" was "of very little importance" to American public officials, who had "abundant reason to be convinced, that the spirit for Trade which pervades these States is not to be restrained." Since the American people were irrevocably committed to the pursuit of foreign commerce, the only practical course of action, Washington concluded, was to endeavor "to establish just principles" for its conduct.[65]

Eventually, the barrage of anti-commercial outbursts that permeated the public rhetoric of the 1780s provoked other, more theoretical defenses of foreign commerce from Americans who feared that Price's "world within itself" model of political economy, as impractical as it might seem, would be seriously pursued by desperate republicans. "The absurdity of this idea," fumed the Massachusetts merchant Stephen Higginson, referring to the notion of Americans attempting to produce everything they consumed, "will be greatly increased when applied to a commercial people, as the attempting to practice upon it, would be in effect to attempt the destruction of all Commerce; for it is by the exchange only of superfluous Articles between Nations, that Commerce can be supported, or rather it is this exchange which constitutes Commerce."[66] Another critic asserted that "a civilized nation, without com-

---

1770s. For a vivid expression of this anti-commercial outlook, see *The Commercial Conduct of the Province of New-York . . .* (New York, 1767), esp. 18–19.

65. Washington to James Warren, Oct. 7, 1785, John C. Fitzpatrick, ed., *The Writings of George Washington* (Washington, D.C., 1931–1944), XXVIII, 290–291. See also, Washington to Benjamin Harrison, Oct. 10, 1784, *ibid.*, XXVII, 473–474. For a similar statement from Thomas Jefferson at about the same time, see Jefferson to G. K. van Hogendorp, Oct. 13, 1785, Julian P. Boyd *et al.*, eds., *The Papers of Thomas Jefferson* (Princeton, N.J., 1950–), VIII, 633. See also, Jefferson to John Jay, Aug. 23, 1785, *ibid.*, 426–427, and Jefferson to Washington, Mar. 15, 1784, *ibid.*, VII, 26.

66. Higginson to John Adams, Dec. 30, 1785, J. Franklin Jameson, ed., "Letters of

merce, is a solecism in politics," for it was "in the rudest state of mankind only, that a people can exist, without any communication with other societies."[67] Defenders of commerce also hastened to remind its detractors that it was a source of industry and other virtue-sustaining character traits. "By restricting commerce," William Hillhouse argued near the end of the decade, "we should cut off the life and source of industry; and pave the way for indolence, and a train of vices more destructive to community, than those arts of elegance and refinement (which it is said, and justly said) are the concomitants of commerce." Noting that "no people will raise more than is sufficient for their own consumption, and to supply the demands of foreign markets," Hillhouse reminded his fellow republicans that any nation precluded from an invigorating foreign commerce, including America, would inevitably be "sunk in ignorance, effeminacy, and vice."[68]

Nevertheless, defenders of commerce could not deny that something was seriously wrong with America in the 1780s. Nor could they deny that some kind of readjustment of the nation's political economy was in order. It was one thing to defend commerce as an abstraction, quite another to defend the post-war pattern of American commerce. No one questioned the need to overcome an unfavorable balance of trade and its adverse social consequences. But Americans differed greatly in their approaches to rectifying the problems of the 1780s. Some of them stressed the paramount need for immediate action in order to realize the noble dream of free trade and thereby fulfill the commercial promise of the Revolution. What was needed, they argued, was a stronger national government in America that would be capable of pressuring foreign governments into giving up their mercantilist ways and lowering barriers to the republic's commerce. Such a course of action seemed particularly appropriate in light of the need to assure adequate markets for the surplus productivity of American farmers. Perhaps the world of free trade that had so inspired the Revolutionaries was not a futile chimera, despite initial disappointments. With a reformed and more competent political system, it might yet be made to work.

Stephen Higginson, 1783–1804," *Annual Report of the American Historical Association for the Year 1896* (Washington, D.C., 1897), I, 731.

67. *American Museum*, II (July 1787), 23.

68. William Hillhouse, *A Dissertation, in Answer to a late Lecture . . .* (New Haven, Conn., 1789), 4–5. See also, Enos Hitchcock, *An Oration: Delivered July 4, 1788 . . .* (Providence, R.I., 1788), 21–23.

Other observers reacted to the crisis of the 1780s by stressing the need to reorient the traditional American emphasis on agriculture by developing manufactures on a more extensive scale. Probably the most significant debate of the decade concerned this question of manufactures and their relation to republicanism in America, a debate that had crucial implications for the decisions that policymakers would face for decades to come. The burgeoning interest in manufactures during the 1780s was clearly a response to the commercial crisis of the period, and it is important to recognize that this interest arose from a fear among many Americans that commerce, and more specifically the exportation of agricultural surpluses abroad, was no longer capable of sustaining either prosperity or a viable basis for republicanism. As the Scottish political economist Sir James Steuart had warned, agricultural surpluses that outran the capacity of available markets to absorb them created a dangerous situation; "for if the whole be not consumed," he noted, "the regorging plenty will discourage the industry of the farmer."[69] By the mid-1780s, as many Americans saw enough idleness and unemployment in their midst to sense the cogency of Steuart's warning, they were prompted to explore more closely the traditional Old World emphasis on the importance of domestic manufactures.

69. Steuart, *Inquiry into Principles of Political Oeconomy*, ed. Skinner, I, 41.

CHAPTER FOUR

AN UNEASY ADOLESCENCE:
MANUFACTURES AND THE
CRISIS OF THE EIGHTIES

The actual extent and severity of the economic depression of the 1780s has remained a matter of dispute among the many historians who have surveyed the period. There is little doubt, however, that the commercial crisis had a profoundly unsettling effect on the way in which Americans viewed themselves and their society. The dislocations it caused, especially in urban areas where the labor force was largely tied to maritime commerce, contributed to a growing anxiety that America was not the "young," vibrant society that Franklin and others had assumed it to be. Widespread unemployment, swelling poor relief rolls, an upsurge in crime and immorality—there was apparently no end to the signs of decay and old age. The new nation seemed to be afflicted by the very symptoms of the British political and moral economy that the Revolutionaries had risked their lives to escape. Some still spoke with confidence of America's "juvenile vigour," but many more were terrified by the specter of a new country that had prematurely taken on the characteristics of an ancient and corrupt society. Even Franklin, who ever remained the optimist, had to concede that America, too, had its "labouring Poor," even if they were better fed, clothed, lodged, and paid than anywhere in the Old World.[1]

1. The reference to America's "juvenile vigour" is from the *Pennsylvania Gazette* (Philadelphia), Aug. 10, 1785. Franklin's comments may be found in his essay "The Internal State of America," in Albert Henry Smyth, ed., *The Writings of Benjamin Franklin* (New York, 1907), X, 118. This essay is also printed in the *Pa. Gazette*, May 17, 1786. A good example of the growing sense among Americans that they lived in a fairly complex, stratified society may be found in "the Free Republican #5," *Independent Chronicle* (Boston), Dec. 22, 1785. For a discussion of urban laborers and the problem of unemployment, see David Montgomery, "The Working Classes of the Pre-Industrial American City, 1780–1830," *Labor History*, IX (1968), 3–22.

Not even the United States seemed able to escape the curses of idleness and poverty, and the moral turpitude they spawned. As inevitably as "dead puddles soon become foul and putrid," wrote one disconsolate Massachusetts observer in 1785, "so the indolent and inactive soon contract diseases," diseases that were making the republican dream in America seem nothing more than a cruel delusion.[2]

As Americans came to doubt the reality of their country's social youth, many became increasingly disillusioned and skeptical of the potential for a revolution in international commerce that would permit the United States to remain predominantly agricultural.[3] The American commitment to "free trade" was principled and tenacious, but the commercial crisis of the 1780s made inevitable a reexamination of the assumptions and beliefs that guided American political economy, especially ideas about the proper place of manufactures in American life. Since conditions had changed so drastically, many republicans now contended, so too must American habits of thought and action. "During our existence as a dependent people," one pro-manufacturing group argued, "the extension of manufactures in this country, was of less importance than at present" since "the various markets then open to its commerce, afforded a sure demand for its exportations: and the inhabitants of it found constant employment, in the production and transportation of its commodities." But the United States had assumed "a new political station," and experience demonstrated that it had to adopt "a correspondent alteration" in its "internal economy" as "the markets for our produce are reduced in number; and certainly our navigation is depressed."[4] Above all, to more and more Americans the traditional mercantilist assumption that manufactures were necessary to maintain industry and full employment, heretofore

2. *Massachusetts Centinel* (Boston), Aug. 20, 1785.

3. See above, chap. 3, esp. 82–85.

4. Address of the board of managers of the Pennsylvania Society for the Promotion of Manufactures and the Useful Arts, *American Museum*, II (October 1787), 360. See also, "On American Commerce," the Boston *Independent Chronicle*, Apr. 21, 1785. For useful secondary discussions of the American economic scene in the 1780s relative to these matters, see: Robert Bruce Bittner, "The Definition of Economic Independence and the New Nation" (Ph.D. diss., University of Wisconsin, 1970); Gordon C. Bjork, "The Weaning of the American Economy: Independence, Market Changes, and Economic Development," *Journal of Economic History*, XXIV (1964), 541–560; Frederick W. Marks III, *Independence on Trial: Foreign Affairs and the Making of the Constitution* (Baton Rouge, La., 1973), chap. 2; and Merrill Jensen, "The American Revolution and American Agriculture," *Agricultural History*, XLIII (1969), 107–124.

considered relevant only to Europe, seemed suddenly and ominously relevant to the republican experience in the New World.

[I]

When Americans spoke of "manufactures" they could mean quite different things. Eighteenth-century commentators often made unexpressed or implicit distinctions and associations that are lost upon the modern observer. As we have seen in the case of Franklin, Americans rarely questioned the need or advantage of coarse, household manufactures that were the natural ally of agriculture and befitted a republican condition. The infatuation with "homespun" that had accompanied the non-importation movements before the war continued into the 1780s and prompted Americans to cry out for the development of "domestic manufactures." If Americans could learn to substitute household manufactures for the foreign frippery they foolishly rushed to purchase, it was hoped that their balance of trade, as well as their manners and morals, would inevitably improve. Few Americans seriously objected to such small-scale manufactures as those practiced in workshops by independent craftsmen and artisans, for these "urban yeomen" were the fitting counterparts to the industrious republicans of the countryside. Only the most complex, advanced forms of manufacturing evoked serious doubts and anxieties; forms of industry, as Franklin had typically argued, appropriate only for "old," fully peopled, and corrupt societies. Such manufacturing had no place in a young republic.[5]

In order to understand the debate over manufactures in the 1780s, it is absolutely essential to realize that Americans usually made several crucial associations when they contemplated manufactures beyond the simple household or small workshop scale. The first and most fundamental association was with the problem of overpopulation and poverty. It was a common idea that the development of large-scale manufactures became necessary when the pressure of population growth on a limited supply of land created large numbers of people who could not gain useful employment from agriculture. These landless poor, the surplus population of "old" societies, represented a potentially catastrophic social problem unless employment was created for them, and they generally formed the

5. See above, chap. 2.

class of dependent wage-laborers who worked for a master in the many manufacturing houses (or "manufactories") that typified Old World political economy.

There was, moreover, a specific institution—the workhouse—that was intimately associated with this whole process. Since Elizabethan times the Poor Law authorities in England had assembled groups of paupers in "houses of industry" and set them to spinning and other similar tasks. It was only natural and logical, therefore, that the new factories of the eighteenth century were often thought of as workhouses and were shunned particularly by those laborers who prided themselves on their independence. These workhouses, which had been designed to provide compulsory labor for those "without a calling," were among the first to practice the custom of gathering large groups of destitute workers in one room or building to carry on a process of manufacture. Consequently, the large-scale factory form of production tended to be associated with the need to provide menial employment for the idle, abjectly dependent poor.[6] To this extent, public "manufactories" were thought to be peculiarly appropriate for old, "crowded" societies that were plagued by idleness and poverty.

A second association, related to the first, tied large-scale manufacturing to "luxury." Historians generally agree that the birth of the modern factory system did not actually occur until the technological revolution of the middle and late eighteenth century. However, earlier, state-subsidized, proto-factory forms of production in seventeenth-century Europe had gathered together large groups of workers to engage in the production of luxury goods, often for the direct use of the king and his court. France had led the way in the creation of an elaborate system of "manufactures d'Etat," including the famous Gobelins establishment, which produced the ornate tapestries that embellished Versailles and other palaces. In addition to these state-owned "factories," there were other "manufactures royales"—privately owned concerns that were encouraged and supported by government grants, loans, contracts, and privileges. These establishments, which catered exclusively to the needs of the state and

6. Thomas Jefferson, *Notes on the State of Virginia*, ed. William Peden (Chapel Hill, N.C., 1955), 164. See T. S. Ashton, *The Industrial Revolution, 1760–1830* (London, 1948), 78; Victor S. Clark, *History of Manufactures in the United States*, I (New York, 1929), 188–193; and Richard B. Morris, *Government and Labor in Early America* (New York, 1946), introduction.

the extravagant way of life that characterized royal courts, contributed to a frequent association, beginning in the seventeenth century, of state-subsidized luxury production with large-scale manufacturing in general.[7] Indeed, luxuries (or the "finer" manufactures) were always associated with an advanced division of labor, the advantages of which could best be secured in large establishments where groups of specialized laborers could work in close conjunction with one another. For these reasons, it was not unusual for men in the eighteenth century to connect manufacturing beyond the simple household scale with the concept of "luxury" and everything luxury implied. To those American republicans who associated the luxury and "fashion" of European courts with effeminacy and corruption, these connotations were automatically pejorative.

Poverty and luxury, the two concepts most often associated with large-scale manufactures, were frequently seen to be interrelated. In the late 1780s, two Frenchmen, Etienne Claviére and J. P. Brissot de Warville, introduced their *Considerations on France and America*, an examination of the possibility of economic intercourse between their country and the United States, with a general discussion of the advanced manufactures appropriate to populous countries.[8] Significantly, they argued that large-

7. See Paul Mantoux, *The Industrial Revolution in the Eighteenth Century: An Outline of the Beginnings of the Modern Factory System in England*, trans. Marjorie Vernon, rev. ed. (New York, 1961 [orig. publ. New York, 1928]), introduction, esp. 28–33; Witt Bowden, *Industrial Society in England towards the End of the Eighteenth Century*, 2d ed. (London, 1965 [orig. publ. 1925]), chaps. 1, 2, and 4; Joseph J. Spengler, *French Predecessors of Malthus: A Study in Eighteenth-Century Wage and Population Theory* (Durham, N.C., 1942), 110; Tom Kemp, *Economic Forces in French History* (London, 1971), chap. 2; and Werner Sombart, *Luxury and Capitalism*, trans. W. R. Dittmar (New York, 1938 [orig. publ. Munich and Leipzig, 1913]), chap. 4. As late as 1772, Arthur Young, the English writer, noted that the simplest manufactures—of blacksmiths, carpenters, masons, brewers, and the like—were often not even referred to as "manufactures," as the term was frequently reserved to apply to only the more advanced forms of industry. Young hoped to discourage this tendency. "In common conversation," he explained, "these artificers, etc. are not included under the expression of manufacturers, but that is a mere inaccuracy, for they are as much so as the costly establishment of the Gobelins itself: they are found so extremely necessary to every movement in common life, and so scattered about the kingdom that we naturally call them by a different name from such as work for foreign exportation, and are established in a particular spot or town." Young, *Political Essays, Concerning the Present State of the British Empire* . . . (London, 1772), 174.

8. Etienne Claviére and J. P. Brissot de Warville, *Considerations on the Relative Situations of France and the United States of America* . . . , translated from the French (London, 1788).

scale manufacturing was not always the result of population pressure on a limited supply of land, but might also be brought about by a corrupt social order with an extreme and unjust inequality of wealth. The type of political economy that incorporated "Old World" manufacturing establishments could, in other words, be produced by artificial as well as by natural means. "These manufactures ought," they wrote, "to be the productions of an excess of population only, which cannot give its industry to agriculture or simple manufactures; but in general they are the result of the gathering together of the poor and wretched, in great cities." This "gathering together," a condition usually imposed by devious political means, forced unfortunate and exploited laborers to work for subsistence wages in the production of luxuries that catered to "the fancies of the rich." Such a situation was hardly a sign of a nation's prosperity; it was "the result and proof of a bad social organization, of too unequal a division of property, and consequently of an unjust distribution of necessary employments, which forces industry to change, from the fabrication of what is necessary and useful, to that which is fantastic, forced, and pernicious." The production of luxuries in such an ill-constituted society relegated the poverty-stricken to lives of drudgery in factories that were "so many tombs which swallow up generations entire."[9] This tragedy was the unmistakable sign of a corrupt society, much like the England that American radicals had envisioned during the Revolutionary crisis, in which the idle, luxurious, and privileged few exploited the labor of their social inferiors to underwrite an effeminate and decadent style of life. All good republicans shuddered at the thought of such a system extending itself to the New World. Above all, Americans usually associated large-scale manufacturing with poverty, luxury, propertyless dependence, and the Old World system of political and social inequality.

For such reasons, most Americans in the 1780s were predisposed to believe that the extensive development of large-scale manufactures in the republic was inappropriate and unnecessary. This did not mean, of course, that America should not have any manufactures of its own but only that it would be foolish and perhaps dangerous, as one member of the Connecticut General Assembly put it, to "attempt great establishments, or finer fabricks." "So long as we continue an agricultural people, (and such we shall be while lands are so plenty and cheap), we cannot expect to carry out manufactures to any high degree of perfection." "It is

9. *Ibid.*, 5–6, 34, 56.

certainly well worth our while, however," he added, "to promote those of nails, cordage, coarse woollens, linens, etc."[10] A writer in the *Massachusetts Centinel* similarly asserted that the traditional arguments against American manufactures extended "so far only as respects great manufactures in general, which cannot be carried on, but by rigid system, and immense capitals; but by no means concludes against all manufactures universally."[11] Americans could have their simpler manufactures, in short, but they should not be converted into a manufacturing people, since "the remains of that feudal system, which are yet to be traced in the policy of European governments, enables the rich individuals to immerse in the deadly shades of their manufacturing houses, many thousands of miserable slaves."[12]

That such a political economy was anathema in a society of free and independent republicans was never questioned. In celebrating that Americans were not forced to engage in the production of finer manufactures, Noah Webster even echoed Adam Smith's concern with the effects of an advanced division of labor on the mental and spiritual health of working men. Because Americans were a young, relatively unspecialized, and undifferentiated people, Webster argued in 1785, they were naturally suited to be good republicans.

The people in America are necessitated, by their local, situation, to be more sensible and discerning, than nations which are limited in territory and confined to the arts of manufacture. In a populous country, where arts are carried to great perfection, the mechanics are obliged to labour constantly upon a single article. Every art has its several branches, one of which employs a man all his life. A man who makes heads of pins or springs of watches, spends his days in that manufacture and never looks beyond it. This manner of fabricating things for the use and convenience of life is the means of perfecting the arts; but it cramps the human mind, by confining all its faculties to a point. In countries thinly inhabited, or where people live principally by agriculture, as in America, every man is in some measure an artist—he makes a variety of utensils, rough indeed, but such as will answer his purpose—he is a husbandman in summer and a mechanic in winter— he travels about the country—he converses with a variety of professions—he

10. *Mass. Centinel* (Boston), Nov. 1, 1786.

11. *Ibid.*, Feb. 14, 1787.

12. *Independent Chronicle* (Boston), Oct. 13, 1785. For an illuminating discussion of the persistence of many of these fears about industrial life into the 19th century, see Herbert G. Gutman, "Work, Culture, and Society in Industrializing America, 1815–1919," *American Historical Review*, LXXVIII (1973), 531–588, esp. 568–569.

reads public papers—he has access to a parish library and thus becomes acquainted with history and politics, and every man in New England is a theologian. This will always be the case in America, so long as there is a vast tract of fertile land to be cultivated, which will occasion emigrations from the states already settled. Knowledge is diffused and genius roused by the very situation of America.[13]

Webster's outlook reflected quite well the prevailing consensus that Americans should only manufacture "necessaries," or those articles that were relatively simple and, for the most part, capable of being produced within the household or small workshop. These manufactured necessities were easily produced by an agricultural people, whereas the more complicated, finer manufactures grew up only when natural social development had been carried to an unhealthy extreme, or when they were forced by a corrupt, mercantilist social and political system.[14] By the mid-1780s, however, the disquieting impact of the commercial crisis provoked a new outpouring of support for the development of American manufactures, and in the midst of these cries for native industry, some commentators appeared either to ignore or to question explicitly the relevance of several prevailing beliefs and assumptions. By 1788, Claviére and Warville, who were anxious to convince the United States that it should remain a simple agricultural society, complained that too many Americans had lost sight of necessary and crucial distinctions in their haste to advocate the promotion of manufactures. "The same arguments which prove the necessity of making stockings, family linen, etc. at home," they grumbled, "are applied without distinction to cloths, silks, and the most complicated and pernicious manufactures." The two Frenchmen even accused Americans of aspiring to imitate the faulty model of England, a country whose situation, they insisted, was "absolutely different."[15] Although in reality very few Americans publicly argued that the

13. Noah Webster, *Sketches of American Policy*, ed. Harry R. Warfel (New York, 1937 [orig. publ. 1785]), 29. See above, chap. 1, for the reference to Adam Smith.

14. Most southerners, and indeed many Americans, clung to such an outlook for years to come. In 1795, for example, Samuel E. M'Corkle, a North Carolina minister, argued that the mechanic arts were "Honourable" only when connected with agriculture. See *A Sermon, on the Comparative Happiness and Duty of the United States . . .* (Halifax, N.C., 1795).

15. Claviére and Warville, *Considerations*, 65, 158. For a typical pro-manufacturing reaction to the commercial crisis, see *The Commercial Conduct of the United States of America Considered* (New York, 1786).

United States should imitate the British system of political economy, serious cracks in the original consensus were appearing as increasingly sustained and vocal efforts emerged to make a case for the development of more extensive and more advanced manufactures in the young republic.[16]

[II]

The basic rationale for the promotion of American manufactures was pithily stated in the June 1785 resolution of a Philadelphia committee in the midst of the commercial crisis: "That as agriculture and manufactures are the great employment of the people, and constitute the wealth of the country; and that as the former must decline with our export trade, it becomes necessary to extend the latter."[17] To many observers, America's problem seemed to be that it could no longer profitably dispose of its agricultural surplus abroad, which resulted in stagnation, idleness, and serious unemployment at home. Since "we have already glutted every foreign market," one analyst concluded, "let us turn our attention to manufactures."[18] The American agricultural surplus was too large, and much of it had to be disposed of on unprofitable terms; America would thus be better off if some of its farmers devoted themselves to manufactures instead.[19] If America actually had a surplus of farmers with no available markets to consume the commodities they produced, the development of manufactures might convey a double benefit: manufactures would employ those who could no longer make a living in agriculture and the export trade and at the same time would create a market for surplus American produce that could not be exported. Above all, social conditions in the United States seemed to indicate that America was ripe for just such an alteration in its political economy.

"Whenever a country is fully stocked with inhabitants, it is then in a situation to require and encourage manufactures, beyond what is prac-

---

16. See especially Edmund S. Morgan, "The Puritan Ethic and the American Revolution," *William and Mary Quarterly*, 3d Ser., XXIV (1967), 3–43. My analysis is intended to supplement Morgan's by considering certain aspects of the pro-manufacturing movement that he chose not to discuss.

17. *Pa. Gazette* (Philadelphia), June 22, 1785.

18. *American Museum*, II (August 1787), 117.

19. *New-Haven Gazette*, Nov. 23, 1786.

ticable or prudent to attempt, in its early state."[20] Such was the conventional wisdom, always assumed to be the basis of an argument against, and not for, the development of manufactures in America. But in the midst of the turbulence of the 1780s some writers began to suggest that America was not so young, and that the population density of the United States, especially in its coastal areas, was greater than everyone had assumed. Franklin had celebrated the rapid rate of population growth in the New World; now some observers began to wonder if this phenomenon had implications and ramifications quite different from those Franklin had suggested.[21] Indeed, the pressure of population growth on a limited supply of land in some eastern areas of the United States, especially in New England, seems actually to have created by the 1780s a situation of "crowding," with an increase in social stratification, a growing concentration of wealth, and the development of a more visible and mobile class of poor people.[22] This "Anglicization" of American society, a designation that the eighteenth-century republicans would have appreciated, implied that for more and more Americans in the 1780s the United States was indeed coming to resemble corrupt and overcrowded England. If many areas of New England had actually reached a stage of demographic and social crisis by the mid-1780s, changing social realities created an appropriate context for changes in political-economic thought.

The 1780s may well have been the decade with the fastest rate of population growth in American history.[23] Appropriately, this trend im-

20. Discourse by John Morgan, Mar. 15, 1789, in New Bern, North Carolina, in *American Museum*, VI (July 1789), 74.

21. See J. J. Spengler, "Malthusianism in Late Eighteenth Century America," *American Economic Review*, XXV (1935), 691–707.

22. The secondary literature on the "Anglicization" of 18th-century America is voluminous. Kenneth Lockridge summarizes the argument in his article, "Land, Population and the Evolution of New England Society, 1630–1790," *Past and Present*, No. 39 (1968), 62–80; his own monograph on Dedham, Massachusetts—*A New England Town: The First Hundred Years* (New York, 1970)—is one of many local studies that suggest the trend. See also Allan Kulikoff, "The Progress of Inequality in Revolutionary Boston," *WMQ*, 3d Ser., XXVIII (1971), 375–412, and Raymond A. Mohl, *Poverty in New York, 1783–1825* (New York, 1971). In a more recent article, "Social Change and the Meaning of the American Revolution," *Journal of Social History*, VI (1973), 403–439, Lockridge has brilliantly opened the question of the extent to which contemporaries perceived and reacted to these social changes.

23. J. Potter, "The Growth of Population in America, 1700–1860," in D. V. Glass and D.E.C. Eversley, eds., *Population in History: Essays in Historical Demography* (London, 1965), 631–638.

pressed many votaries of manufactures. "The inhabitants of America are supposed to double their numbers every twenty years," William Barton reminded his countrymen in 1785. "What, then, is to become of this vast increase of the inhabitants of our towns? They cannot be all laborers; and but a small part can engage in husbandry, the learned professions, or merchandize: consequently, the greater part must apply to trades and manufactures, or starve." It was true that manufactures could not succeed on a large scale without a high density of population and relatively low wages, but the rapid rate of population growth in America promised soon to provide these conditions. Citing a treatise on the employment of the poor in workhouses, Barton suggested that manufactures would be a useful way of employing the industrious poor of America.[24] Other commentators approached the matter of rapid population growth from a somewhat different perspective. They argued that since fathers no longer had it in their power to give every son a suitable tract of land, many young Americans were forced to move prematurely and unprofitably west into uncivilized subsistence areas. Unless alternative employment in manufacturing was provided, one analyst asserted, America would continue to leave its "own poor to wander in the woods and wilds of the back countries, to live like Indians, and to be useless to our governments."[25] Similarly, other Americans bemoaned the increasing emigration of the unemployed to foreign lands in search of a better life. There were reports of three vessels loaded with such passengers departing Philadelphia for Cartagena, and Phineas Bond, the British consul in Philadelphia, informed correspondents that he was besieged with applications from frustrated English laborers who wished to return home.[26] The irony could hardly have been greater: these desperate men were abandoning the young republic, the supposed land of opportunity, because it was too crowded to afford them a decent living.

By the late 1780s more and more Americans were jolted into the recognition that idleness and poverty, as serious social problems, were

---

24. William Barton, "Essay on the Promotion of American Manufactures," *American Museum*, II (September 1787), 258–259. This essay had appeared in newspapers in the fall of 1785. See the Boston *Independent Chronicle*, Sept. 22, 1785.

25. *Pennsylvania Packet* (Philadelphia), Aug. 26, 1785.

26. *American Museum*, V (May 1789), 494–495; Bond to Lord Carmarthen, June 28, 1788, and Bond to Evan Nepean, Nov. 16, 1788, in J. Franklin Jameson, ed., "Letters of Phineas Bond . . . ," *Annual Report of the American Historical Association for the Year 1896* (Washington, D.C., 1897), I, 568, 587.

hardly peculiar to the Old World. Some vented their frustrations on the poor themselves by insisting that the poverty-stricken were victims only of their own lethargy and depravity, but even such observers had to admit that "there can be little hope of their reformation, without the compulsory interposition of government."[27] In Philadelphia, despite the persistence of a traditional belief that the poor were always responsible for their plight, there was a grudging recognition of the existence of imposing barriers to full and constant employment that were beyond individual moral control.[28] Most commentators agreed that a substitution of native manufactures for the foreign products Americans currently imported was needed to provide employment for American rather than foreign laborers. It was utterly insane, one analyst suggested, for Americans to "continue to employ manufacturers at several thousand miles distance, while a great part of our own people are idle, or employed to very little purpose—and another very considerable part likely to become bankrupts, if not beggars."[29] The promotion of domestic manufactures, in short, was the necessary means of making Americans into an active, industrious, republican people, since "by manufacturing ourselves, and employing our own people, we shall deliver them from the curse of idleness. We shall hold out to them a new stimulus and encouragement to industry and every useful art."[30]

The idea of manufacturing as a palliative for idleness and poverty was far from new in the 1780s. Such an idea had been present during every serious commercial crisis the colonies had experienced in the eighteenth century. In particular, the movement for home manufactures during the 1760s and 1770s had been inextricably tied to this goal of providing employment for the poor. By the eve of the Revolution, most of the larger colonial towns had set up establishments ("manufactories") for this purpose. Usually privately operated, these projects drew upon local work-

27. *Pennsylvania Mercury and Universal Advertiser* (Philadelphia), June 29, 1787. The literature on poverty in 18th-century America is scanty but growing. See John K. Alexander, "The City of Brotherly Fear: The Poor in Late Eighteenth-Century Philadelphia," in Kenneth T. Jackson and Stanley K. Schultz, eds., *Cities in American History* (New York, 1972), 79–97, and Gary B. Nash, "Poverty and Poor Relief in Pre-Revolutionary Philadelphia," *WMQ*, 3d Ser., XXXIII (1976), 3–30.

28. John K. Alexander, "Philadelphia's 'Other Half': Attitudes toward Poverty and the Meaning of Poverty in Philadelphia, 1760–1800" (Ph.D. diss., University of Chicago, 1973), 22–39.

29. *American Museum*, I (February 1787), 116.

30. *Ibid.*, 119.

houses, helping to lighten the community's poor relief burden while at the same time taking advantage of a cheap labor supply.[31] Whether in Boston, New York, or Philadelphia, the pattern was generally the same: "Our design in pursuing this Business," a Boston committee had insisted in 1768, "is not to enrich ourselves, but for employing the many Poor we have in the Town and giving them a Livelihood." In New York, advocates of manufactures talked of overcoming the idleness of those "pests of society" who were driven to crime and dissipation. And in Philadelphia, where the "United Company of Philadelphia for Promoting American Manufactures" had established a manufactory that employed over five hundred people, supporters of the company considered the institution "a providential work, intended by the Almighty as a means of subsistence of such of his creatures among us as are not qualified to gain a livelihood any other way."[32] No one familiar with the European experience denied that "in all old countries where there are no considerable manufactures, the inhabitants in general are wretched"; the question now arose, however, whether the same insight applied to the older colonies of America where, some observers argued, there were already many who either could not get land or were unsuited for labor in agriculture.[33] Thus, by the 1780s, when similar organizations were once again established, there was already a native tradition of associating large-scale or "public" manufactures with the alleviation of poverty.[34]

Renewed interest in public, non-household manufactures centered precisely in those areas of New England and the Middle Atlantic states where population density was highest and the problem of poverty most visibly severe. A petition to the Massachusetts legislature in June 1788 argued forcefully that the commonwealth had reached a point in population and agriculture at which it became absolutely necessary to establish manufactures. In Boston, several manufactories designed to employ va-

31. Morris, *Government and Labor*, 13; Mohl, *Poverty in New York*, 46–51; J. Leander Bishop, *A History of American Manufactures, from 1608–1860 . . .* (Philadelphia, 1868), 333–387.

32. *Report of the Record Commissioners of the City of Boston, Containing the Boston Town Records, 1758–1769* (Boston, 1886), XVI, 250; *New-York Journal; or, the General Advertiser*, Dec. 24, 1767; and *Pa. Packet* (Philadelphia), Oct. 16, 1775.

33. "The North American, No. II," *Boston-Gazette*, Jan. 9, 1769.

34. For a fairly complete discussion of these and the earlier groups, see Frank Warren Crow, "The Age of Promise: Societies for Social and Economic Improvement in the United States, 1783–1815" (Ph.D. diss., University of Wisconsin, 1952), chap. 10.

grants, beggars, and others who "eat the bread of idleness" were set up. New York and Philadelphia societies also established similar factories in the late 1780s.[35] Writing to the duke of Leeds from Philadelphia in November 1789, Phineas Bond confidently predicted that although the United States was making great progress in the production of coarse manufactures, only "thickly-settled" New England was at all close to being able to compete with the highly capitalized, finer manufactures of Europe.[36] Bond's judgment was undoubtedly accurate, but it failed to capture the intensity of the commitment that some Americans were developing to all kinds of manufactures, including those large-scale public enterprises that could produce "finer" manufactures and employ the labor surplus that was increasingly evident in many areas of the country. If America was becoming more like England, perhaps it would be necessary, as well as wise, to adopt a more appropriate political economy.

The economic and social dislocations of the 1780s seemed to indicate to more and more Americans, in short, that the United States was not going to be the kind of society Franklin had envisioned. "Old age" was coming on much more rapidly than he and the Revolutionaries had ever expected. One writer even advocated the introduction of luxury manufactures in America by arguing that "the extravagance of the rich will clothe and feed the poor"; if advanced manufactures were established in America, "the luxury of individuals, so much complained of in the present day, will be then a public benefit." Private vices, public benefits; there was now at least one unabashed Mandevillian in the American midst. This argument was, indeed, a radical defense of luxury that had traditionally been applied only to Europe.[37] Some Americans were coming to suspect that the Revolutionary vision of a republican society in which there would be no "labouring poor"—where everyone would be indepen-

35. Robert S. Rantoul, "The First Cotton Mill in America," Essex Institute, *Historical Collections*, XXXIII (1897), 1–43; *Mass. Centinel* (Boston), Sept. 6, 1788, and July 29, 1789; and *American Museum*, V (April 1789), 325. There was also much pro-manufacturing sentiment in densely populated Connecticut and Rhode Island; see Harry R. Warfel, *Noah Webster: Schoolmaster to America* (New York, 1936), 209, and Peter J. Coleman, *The Transformation of Rhode Island, 1790–1860* (Providence, R.I., 1963), chaps. 1 and 2.

36. Jameson, ed., "Letters of Phineas Bond," *Annual Report of the AHA for . . . 1896*, I, 630–635, 654.

37. *American Museum*, V (March 1789), 256. For expressions of the traditional view, see *ibid.*, II (September 1787), 218. Franklin, in his 1784 "luxury" letter to Benjamin Vaughan, had alluded to this defense of luxury without fully endorsing it. Smyth, ed., *Writings of Franklin*, IX, 244.

dent and economically secure—was a chimera. As one writer who noted the "present numbers unemployed in America" put it, "In all civilized states, an excess of poverty will be the inevitable lot of some," and "it may therefore naturally be expected, that the poor in general will experience a certain degree of dependence, and servility."[38] Perhaps advanced, large-scale manufactures were now appropriate and even necessary in a not-so-young republic. Promoting new forms of industry was one way of coping with the social malaise of the 1780s, for it promised at least to alleviate the chronic idleness and unemployment that made a mockery of the republican vision of an industrious citizenry. Such a solution also portended, however, the decline of the ideal of a universally propertied people that had been central to the Revolutionary spirit of 1776.

38. *Gazette of the United States* (New York), May 2, 1789. The context of these remarks was a defense of black slavery, and one of the writer's arguments was that "all Europe evinces, that where there are no *black slaves*, there must be *white slaves*." He was referring, of course, to the "labouring poor."

CHAPTER FIVE

THE CONSTITUTION:

TWO VISIONS

While speaking in January 1811 in defense of the constitutionality of the Bank of the United States, a Virginia congressman rhetorically asked his colleagues if the authors of the Constitution had not wisely anticipated the irrepressible consequences of social development in America:

Is it in the least probable that the men selected for their wisdom, perfectly acquainted with the progress of man in every age; who foresaw the changes which the state of society must undergo in this country from the increase of population, commerce, and the arts, could act so absurdly, as to prescribe a certain set of means to carry on the operations of a Government intended not only for the present but for future generations?[1]

No doubt the framers would have been pleased with this assessment of their prescience. By the summer of 1787 most of them were acutely aware that America was maturing rapidly and that the future promised the development of an even more complex and sophisticated society. Not all of them found it easy to confront the implications of this promise, but very few refused to accept its inevitability. Even those who had not lost faith in Franklin's original vision of a youthful republic recognized more clearly than ever that they could hope only to forestall for as long as possible the unavoidable ramifications of social development.

"Civilization and corruption have generally been found," noted one of the more pessimistic American observers in 1785, "to advance with equal steps." Ultimately, the United States would become as corrupt as the most advanced areas of Europe; yet it was undoubtedly within the power

1. Daniel Sheffey in U.S. Congress, Joseph Gales, comp., *The Debates and Proceedings in the Congress of the United States . . .* (Washington, D.C., 1834–1856), 11th Cong., 3d sess., XXII, 734, hereafter cited as *Annals of Congress*.

of its citizens to place this "sad catastrophe at a distance."² Perhaps more than any other prominent American of the 1780s, James Madison thought precisely in these terms. Like most supporters of the new Constitution, this astute young Virginian believed that a reorganization of American government was the necessary prerequisite to the establishment of a republican political economy. Madison later discovered, however, that not all of his Federalist colleagues shared his particular conception of a republican America; some of them, he was appalled to learn, even thought in terms of deliberately promoting what he thought it necessary to forestall. Different men were developing quite different solutions to the persistent problem of adapting the traditional republican impulse to modern commercial America. Although the ideological flux of the 1780s created the basis for the Federalist consensus of 1787, it also assured future controversy about the precise meaning of American republicanism and the role of the new federal government in securing it.

[I]

Madison's initial post-war vision of a republican America was quite similar in its general outline to Franklin's, for above all Madison thought in terms of developing across space rather than through time. Westward expansion was central to Madison's outlook, but equally important were his commitments to the principles of commercial liberalism and to the promise of a new, more open international commercial order. The dynamics of the Virginian's vision were straightforward. If Americans could continue to resort to virgin lands while opening adequate foreign markets for their produce, the United States would remain a nation of industrious farmers who marketed their surpluses abroad and purchased the "finer" manufactures they desired in return. Household industry would be relied upon to supply the coarser manufactures that were necessary to prevent a dangerously unfavorable balance of trade. Like Adam Smith, Madison believed this brand of social "development" proper because it comported with natural law.³ America could remain young and

2. *Independent Chronicle* (Boston), Nov. 24, 1785.
3. Smith usually discussed America's economic development in the context of his "natural" sequence for the employment of capital; see especially Book II, chap. 5, and Book III,

virtuous, while offering both a haven for the landless poor of Europe and a bountiful market for the advanced manufactures that a fully peopled Europe was forced to produce. Indeed, Madison's commitment to westward expansion and "free trade" put him in the mainstream of republican thought at the end of the war.

Like most Americans, however, Madison always realized that the viability of landed expansion in America was contingent on the ability of new settlers to get their surpluses to market. If frontier farmers had no way of marketing what they produced, there was little incentive to emigrate to the West at all. A non-existent or inaccessible market would turn those who did settle the frontier into lethargic subsistence farmers instead of industrious republicans. This perception of the importance of commerce to the settlement of the frontier had always carried serious implications for the character of American society. If the men and women who emigrated to the West were not properly tied to a commercial nexus, various commentators had long suggested, they would degenerate into a socially and politically dangerous form of savagery. Expressions of this concern often accompanied appeals for the construction of "internal improvements"—roads and canals—that would rescue the fringes of American settlement from this danger by integrating them into a commercial economy. As early as 1770, for example, Pennsylvanians anxious to promote a canal in their state had typically cited the "complicated and numerous" mischiefs that arose from the isolation of their western settlements. "It is from hence," one writer asserted, "that many of the distant back inhabitants are become uncivilized, and little better than barbarians.—They are lazy, licentious, and lawless—and, instead of being useful members of society, are become seditious, and dangerous to the community." Once these settlers were drawn into the civilizing orbit of commerce, however, a dramatic transformation in their character would occur: "The uncivilized will, by a communication with the civilized, lose their ignorance and barbarism. They will learn industry from the industrious, virtue from the virtuous, loyalty from the loyal; and thereby become useful members of society, and good subjects." Most important, they would be molded into productive citizens: "Render it practicable for them to gain by their industry, and they will be industrious, and, by their

---

chap. 1, of the *Wealth of Nations*, ed. Edwin Cannan. This subject will be discussed at some length in chapter 7 of the present study.

industry, add to the surplus of our foreign exportation."⁴ This matter of civilizing the West had seemed particularly pressing before the Revolution to eastern Pennsylvanians who were disturbed by the chronic political turmoil on their frontier, but the content and wide-ranging implications of their concern were of continuing relevance to all American republicans who worried about the character of their landed expansion.

As America looked westward in the 1780s, control of the Mississippi River to its mouth became an essential goal of national policy, for this river was the necessary avenue to foreign markets for those who were settling the immediate frontier. This concern drew the United States into an inevitable confrontation with the Spanish, who in early 1784 formally denied Americans the right to navigate the Mississippi and to deposit their goods at New Orleans.⁵ The problem of gaining uncontested American control of the Mississippi River arose from disputes over the boundary settlements of the peace treaties that ended the Revolution and would not be fully resolved until the Louisiana Purchase of 1803. During the initial decade of independence, control of the Mississippi posed an especially disturbing dilemma for Madison and other American republicans.

Madison was both outraged and perplexed by the unexpected display of Spanish arrogance, and he insisted that it was not in the interests of either Spain or the United States to deny Americans use of the Mississippi. Writing to Jefferson in the summer of 1784, Madison argued that American settlement of the backcountry, which only a free use of the Mississippi could promote, would benefit all European nations who traded with the United States by delaying the establishment of competitive American manufactures for many years and by increasing the consumption of foreign manufactures. If Americans were kept profitably occupied in agriculture, in other words, there would be no "supernumerary hands" to produce manufactures who might compete with foreign producers for the American market. In a passage that reflected many of the traditional assumptions of eighteenth-century political economy, Madison sketched two possible scenarios for American development:

4. *Pennsylvania Chronicle* (Philadelphia), Jan. 1–8, 1770.

5. For brief secondary accounts of the crisis with Spain over the West, see, among many, Merrill Jensen, *The New Nation: A History of the United States during the Confederation, 1781–1789* (New York, 1950), 170–173, and Frederick W. Marks III, *Independence on Trial: Foreign Affairs and the Making of the Constitution* (Baton Rouge, La., 1973), 21–25.

The vacant land of the U.S. lying on the waters of the Mississippi is perhaps equal in extent to the land actually settled. If no check be given to emigrations from the latter to the former, they will probably keep pace at least with the increase of people, till the population of both become nearly equal. For 20 or 25 years we shall consequently have few internal manufactures in proportion to our numbers as at present, and at the end of that period our imported manufactures will be doubled. . . . Reverse the case and suppose the use of the Miss: denied to us, and the consequence is that many of our supernumerary hands who in the former case would [be] husbandmen on the waters of the Missipi will on this other supposition be manufacturers on this [side] of the Atlantic: and even those who may not be discouraged from seating the vacant lands will be obliged by the want of vent for the produce of the soil and of the means of purchasing foreign manufactures, to manufacture in a great measure for themselves.[6]

The thrust of Madison's analysis was clear; in order to remain predominantly agricultural, America needed to combine landed and commercial expansion. If, on the contrary, Americans were denied access to export markets for their produce, a fundamental reorientation of their political economy in the direction of increased manufacturing was inevitable.

The diplomatic crisis in the West neatly fused the issues of western expansion and foreign trade, but Madison's concern with the latter issue extended far beyond the question of the Mississippi River. By the mid-1780s the commercial crisis afflicting the United States was wreaking havoc in virtually all areas of the country. This commercial problem, according to Madison, spawned the political and moral chaos that threatened the republican character of America. "Most of our political evils," he wrote in March 1786, "may be traced up to our commercial ones, as most of our moral may to our political."[7] Like most Americans, Madison was particularly concerned with the restrictions Britain placed on American trade with its West Indian islands. Many Americans argued that the interest of every state was involved with this trade and, in a broader sense, that American commerce as a whole was dependent on it, since without a prosperous intercourse with these islands the balance of American trade with Great Britain would inevitably be unfavorable. "Access to

6. Madison to Jefferson, Aug. 30, 1784, Robert A. Rutland *et al.*, eds., *The Papers of James Madison* (Chicago, 1962–   ), VIII, 107–108. See also Madison to Lafayette, Mar. 20, 1785, *ibid.*, 250–254, and John Jay to Florida Blanca, Apr. 25, 1780, Henry P. Johnston, ed., *The Correspondence and Public Papers of John Jay*, I (New York and London, 1890), 295–297.

7. Madison to Jefferson, Mar. 18, 1786, Rutland *et al.*, eds., *Madison Papers*, VIII, 502.

the West Indies," as Jefferson put it in 1785, "is indispensably necessary to us."[8] Several ways existed to improve the unfavorable balance of American trade, including the exercise of self-restraint on the part of those citizens who overindulged in their consumption of foreign luxuries. The key for Madison, however, was to liberate American trade from the shackles of British mercantilism. Above all, the United States had to break down the barriers that confined its commerce to "artificial" channels and denied it full access to "natural" markets like those in the West Indies.

By 1786 many Americans had decided that a policy of commercial retaliation against restrictions on their trade was mandatory.[9] Few of them, however, could match Madison's faith in the efficacy of such a policy. His confidence in the ability of the United States to coerce Britain and other foreign countries into lowering barriers to American commerce was predicated on several key assumptions, the primary belief being that a young, virile society had natural advantages in its intercourse with older, fully peopled, more complex societies. Due to its highly advanced, luxury-ridden condition, for instance, Britain depended on foreign demand to employ its surplus inhabitants. "It is universally agreed," wrote one American of England, "that no country is more dependent on foreign demand, for the superfluous produce of art and industry;—and that the luxury and extravagance of her inhabitants, have already advanced to the ultimate point of abuse, and cannot be so increased, as to augment the home consumption, in proportion to the decrease that will take place on a diminution of foreign trade."[10] The prosperity of the British economy was thus contingent on access to the rich American market. Should the United States ever restrict this market for British manufactures in retaliation for restraints on its export trade, the "manufacturing poor" in England would be thrown out of work and perhaps even starve. Such were

---

8. Jefferson to Monroe, June 17, 1785, Julian P. Boyd *et al.*, eds., *The Papers of Thomas Jefferson* (Princeton, N.J., 1950–), VIII, 232. See also Madison to Monroe, Aug. 7, 1785, Rutland *et al.*, eds., *Madison Papers*, VIII, 333–336. In their analysis of American colonial commerce, James F. Shepherd and Gary M. Walton stress the importance of the West Indies trade to the mainland colonies, especially the "invisible earnings" from native shipping that helped pay deficits in other areas of trade. See *Shipping, Maritime Trade, and the Economic Development of Colonial North America* (Cambridge, 1972), esp. chap. 9.

9. See especially Robert Bruce Bittner, "The Definition of Economic Independence and the New Nation" (Ph.D. diss., University of Wisconsin, 1970), chaps. 2 and 3.

10. William Bingham, *A Letter from an American* . . . (Philadelphia, 1784), 13.

the pitfalls, Franklin and Madison would have reminded the British, of a mercantilist political economy geared to the exportation of finer manufactures and luxuries.[11]

By 1786 Madison thought it obvious that the implementation of an effective commercial policy, as well as the resolution of the crisis in the West, required a national government stronger than the Continental Congress. In a broader sense, this reorganization of the American political system was necessary to create the basis for a republican political economy. Madison feared, as did many other members of the American elite, that the disorder and unrest of the 1780s signified the decay of industry, diligence, frugality, and other republican character traits among the American people. The task at hand was to form a national political economy capable of permitting and encouraging Americans to engage industriously in virtue-sustaining occupations. To Madison this task entailed the creation of a central political authority able to reverse the dangerous trends of the decade and to stave off, for as long as possible, the advance of America into a more complicated and dangerous stage of social development. Because social conditions in the United States encouraged such reflection, Madison entered the constitutional convention in the spring of 1787 having already given much serious thought to the problems of poverty and unemployment in advanced, densely populated societies.[12]

Of particular interest in this regard is an exchange of letters between Madison and Jefferson in late 1785 and early 1786. Writing from France, Jefferson pondered the plight of the laboring and idle poor of Europe. He blamed their wretchedness on an unequal division of property and entrenched feudal privilege, then further observed that "whenever there is in any country, uncultivated lands and unemployed poor, it is clear that the laws of property have been so far extended as to violate natural right." The earth had been given as a common stock for all men to labor and live on, and "if, for the encouragement of industry we allow it to be appropriated, we must take care that other employment be furnished to

11. See above, chap. 2. Madison developed more fully the logic of commercial coercion in the early 1790s, when he tied it to his policy of commercial discrimination. This will be discussed in further depth in the next chapter.

12. A superb secondary discussion of this aspect of Madison's outlook can be found in Douglass G. Adair, "The Intellectual Origins of Jeffersonian Democracy: Republicanism, the Class Struggle, and the Virtuous Farmer" (Ph.D. diss., Yale University, 1943), esp. 280–295. My discussion builds on Adair's analysis.

those excluded from the appropriation." Jefferson extended this analysis of the situation in France to his native land. Although it was "too soon yet in our country to say that every man who cannot find employment but who can find uncultivated land, shall be at liberty to cultivate it, paying a moderate rent," it was "not too soon to provide by every possible means that as few as possible shall be without a little portion of land." Indeed, Jefferson's sobering contact with the landless poor in Europe made him all the more anxious to prevent the development of a similar class in America.[13]

Madison agreed that Jefferson's reflections formed "a valuable lesson to the Legislators of every Country, and particularly of a new one." However, in assessing the causes of the comparative comfort of the people in the United States, at least for the present, he asserted that more was involved than the absence of entrenched feudal privileges. "Our limited population," Madison argued, "has probably as large a share in producing this effect as the political advantages which distinguish us." "A certain degree of misery," he stated, as a general rule "seems inseparable from a high degree of populousness." This rule had profoundly disturbing implications for Madison, because it meant that even if a nation's land was equitably distributed and its laws thoroughly liberal and republican, a large population in itself might still create dangerous social problems. "No problem in political Œconomy has appeared to me more puzzling," he wrote,

than that which relates to the most proper distribution of the inhabitants of a Country fully peopled. Let the lands be shared among them ever so wisely, and let them be supplied with labourers ever so plentifully; as there must be a great surplus of subsistence, there will also remain a great surplus of inhabitants, a greater by far than will be employed in cloathing both themselves and those who feed them, and in administering to both, every other necessary and even comfort of life. What is to be done with this surplus? Hitherto we have seen them distributed into manufacturers of superfluities, idle proprietors of productive funds, domestics, soldiers, merchants, mariners, and a few other less numerous classes. All these classes notwithstanding have been found insufficient to absorb the redundant members of a populous society.[14]

13. Jefferson to Madison, Oct. 28, 1785, Boyd *et al.*, eds., *Jefferson Papers*, VIII, 681–682.

14. Madison to Jefferson, June 19, 1786, *ibid.*, IX, 659–660. For a fuller discussion of this passage in a somewhat different context, see Drew R. McCoy, "Jefferson and Madison

Madison thus wrestled with the familiar problem of securing viable and sufficient sources of employment for the landless human surplus characteristic of the highly developed, old countries of Europe. He was struck, furthermore, by a depressing irony. Referring to the "manufacturers of superfluities, idle proprietors of productive funds, domestics, soldiers, merchants, mariners," and the like, he observed that "a reduction of most of those classes enters into the very reform which appears so necessary and desirable." The equal, more republican division of landed property that Jefferson espoused, he explained, would inevitably lead to "a greater simplicity of manners, consequently a less consumption of manufactured superfluities, and a less proportion of idle proprietors and domestics," while a "juster government" would also occasion "less need of soldiers either for defence against dangers from without, or disturbances from within."[15] Republican reforms thus eventually compounded rather than ameliorated the problem, since they closed off the customary avenues of escape for an idle, surplus population. For this reason, Madison implied, the dilemma in a "fully-peopled" republic would ironically be even worse than in a corrupt, luxury-ridden society.

As always, Madison had one eye on the American future. During the constitutional convention, Charles Pinckney of South Carolina chastised his countrymen for considering themselves "the inhabitants of an old instead of a new country," and Madison's response to this charge is revealing. Pinckney made the traditional argument for America's youthfulness by pointing to the West: "In a new Country, possessing immense tracts of uncultivated lands, where every temptation is offered to emigration and where industry must be rewarded with competency, there will be few poor, and few dependent." Indeed, Pinckney concluded, "that vast extent of unpeopled territory which opens to the frugal and industrious a sure road to competency and independence will effectually prevent for a considerable time the increase of the poor or discontented, and be the means of preserving that equality of condition which so eminently distinguishes us."[16]

Madison was not convinced by Pinckney's analysis of American so-

---

on Malthus: Population Growth in Jeffersonian Political Economy," *Virginia Magazine of History and Biography*, forthcoming.

15. Madison to Jefferson, June 18, 1786, Boyd *et al.*, eds., *Jefferson Papers*, IX, 660.

16. Max Farrand, ed., *The Records of the Federal Convention of 1787*, rev. ed. (New Haven, Conn., 1966), I, 401, 398, 400.

ciety. "In all civilized Countries," he observed, "the people fall into different classes havg. a real or supposed difference of interests." In addition to creditors and debtors, farmers, merchants, and manufacturers, there "will be particularly the distinction of rich and poor." Madison agreed with Pinckney that America had neither the hereditary distinctions of rank nor the horrendous extremes of wealth and poverty that characterized Europe, but he quickly added that "we cannot however be regarded even at this time, as one homogeneous mass, in which every thing that affects a part will affect in the same manner the whole."[17] Indeed, America was already a fairly complex, stratified society. "The man who is possessed of wealth, who lolls on his sofa or rolls in his carriage," Madison was reported to have argued, "cannot judge of the wants or feelings of the day laborer."[18] And when Madison looked at the inevitable ramifications of continued population growth in America, he became even more pessimistic. "In framing a system which we wish to last for ages, we shd. not lose sight of the changes which ages will produce. An increase of population will of necessity increase the proportion of those who will labour under all the hardships of life, and secretly sigh for a more equal distribution of its blessings." When in time such men would outnumber "those who are placed above the feelings of indigence," there would be a serious danger of social upheaval and of radical attacks on property. Referring to the Shays uprising in Massachusetts, Madison remarked that although "no agrarian attempts have yet been made in this Country, . . . symptoms of a leveling spirit . . . have sufficiently appeared in a certain quarters to give notice of the future danger."[19]

Madison returned to this general theme again and again during the course of the convention. "In future times," he predicted of the United States, "a great majority of the people will not only be without landed, but any other sort of property."[20] As the population of America increased, its political economy would inevitably become more complex. Although the relative proportion between the commercial and manufacturing classes and the agricultural was yet small, Madison contended that it would daily increase. "We see in the populous Countries in Europe

17. *Ibid.*, 422.
18. *Ibid.*, 431. This quotation is from Robert Yates's transcription of Madison's speech.
19. *Ibid.*, 422–423.
20. *Ibid.*, II, 203–204.

now," he declared, "what we shall be hereafter."[21] And in the Virginia ratifying convention of 1788, Madison hinted strongly that the day when "population becomes so great as to compel us to recur to manufactures" lay not very far in the future: "At the expiration of twenty-five years hence, I conceive that in every part of the United States, there will be as great a population as there is now in the settled parts. We see already, that in the most populous parts of the Union, and where there is but a medium, manufactures are beginning to be established."[22]

The profound impact of the economic and social dislocations of the 1780s on Madison's vision of America is perhaps best revealed in his correspondence with John Brown in 1788 concerning a constitution for the prospective state of Kentucky. Madison argued strongly that property be made a qualification for suffrage, and that there be a dual suffrage for the upper and lower houses of the legislature in order to protect both "the rights of persons" and "the rights of property." His reasoning here was that both the indigent and the rich, who invariably formed classes in any civilized society, had each to be given its proper share in government. Madison reminded Brown that although the specific need to protect property rights had not been given much attention at the commencement of the Revolution, subsequent experience had demonstrated the naiveté of the assumption that the United States was a peculiarly undifferentiated society in which "the rights of property" and "the rights of persons" were synonymous.

In the existing state of American population, and American property[,] the two classes of rights were so little discriminated [at the commencement of the Revolution] that a provision for the rights of persons was supposed to include of itself those of property, and it was natural to infer from the tendency of republican laws, that these different interests would be more and more identified. Experience and investigation have however produced more correct ideas on this subject. It is now observed that in all populous countries, the smaller part only can be interested in preserving the rights of property. It must be foreseen that America, and Kentucky itself will by degrees arrive at this state of Society; that in some parts of the Union a very great advance is already made towards it.[23]

21. *Ibid.*, 124.

22. Rutland *et al.*, eds., *Madison Papers*, XI, 125.

23. Observations on Jefferson's Draft of a Constitution for Virginia, ca. Oct. 15, 1788, *ibid.*, 287.

Prudence thus demanded that the Kentucky constitution, as well as the United States Constitution, allow for the changes that the future would inevitably bring.

While Madison always worried about the political implications of these future developments, he never really resolved his underlying dilemma: once the inevitable pressure of population increase had created large numbers of propertyless indigents in America, what would sustain the republican character of the United States? At the core of republicanism was an intense concern with the autonomy or "independence" of the individual, and particularly with the material or economic basis for that autonomy. Since the abject dependence of the landless or laboring poor rendered them vulnerable to bribery, corruption, and factious dissension, a society with large numbers of these dependents was hardly suited to the republican form. Although Madison evinced a fatalistic acceptance of the future as he envisioned it, always urging that the new Constitution be so drawn that it could accommodate these social changes, he seemed unable to escape the traditional fear that all republics, including the one in America, were necessarily short-lived.[24] It was wise to anticipate and provide for future changes; it was even wiser to forestall their development for as long as possible. Madison's republic was in a race against time.

The new Constitution promised to create a government equal to the task of forestalling, if not of preventing, these adverse developments. A stronger national government with the power to raise revenue and regulate commerce would ideally be capable of resolving the foreign policy problems that threatened to prematurely age the country. Such a government could pave the way for westward expansion by dealing forcefully with threatening foreign powers like Spain, but even more important, it could fulfill the commercial promise of the Revolution by forcing the dismantling of the restrictive mercantilist systems that obstructed the marketing of American agricultural surpluses. As Oliver Ellsworth of Connecticut argued in defense of the Constitution, American farmers suffered because American merchants were "shut out from nine-tenths of

24. This concern with the fragility of republican government was widespread in America at the time of the constitutional convention, usually surfacing in the fear that some form of monarchy was inevitable in the American future. See, for example, Hugh Williamson's and Benjamin Franklin's statements in the convention. Farrand, ed., *Records of the Federal Convention*, II, 101, and I, 83.

the ports in the world" and forced to sell at low prices in the "few foreign ports" that were open to them. Addressing the farmers of America, he asserted that "you are oppressed for the want of power which can protect commerce, encourage business, and create a ready demand for the productions of your farms."[25] Thomas Jefferson, writing in early 1789, agreed that the American system should be to "pursue agriculture, and open all the foreign markets possible to our produce."[26]

Continued westward expansion would ease the impact of a rapidly increasing population in the United States, and the opening of foreign markets for American produce would further ensure that Americans not be forced into occupations detrimental to the republican character of their society. It could be hoped, then, that Madison's human "surplus" in America might continue to produce "necessaries" required by foreigners for as long as possible rather than be forced by adverse circumstances like those of the 1780s to become manufacturers of superfluities, idle proprietors of productive funds, soldiers, or the like. In short, the exportation of American agricultural surpluses appeared to offer a tentative republican solution to the "problem in political economy" that had so puzzled the young Virginian. America needed open markets as well as open space to make republicanism work. Perhaps a government strong enough to encourage the proper form of westward expansion and to force free trade could answer the dilemma of population growth in an agricultural and republican nation—at least for the foreseeable future.

[I I]

One of Madison's closest allies in the struggle to ratify the Constitution was a brilliant lawyer from New York, Alexander Hamilton, who several years earlier in *The Continentalist* had warned his countrymen against their obsession with classical republicanism.[27] In many respects Hamilton was an anomaly; perhaps more than any of his countrymen, he had succeeded in discarding the traditional republican heritage that had so heavily influenced the Revolutionary mind. He was particularly receptive

25. Paul Leicester Ford, ed., *Essays on the Constitution of the United States* . . . (Brooklyn, N.Y., 1892), 140, 149.
26. Jefferson to Charles Lilburne Lewis, Jan. 10, 1789, Boyd *et al.*, eds., *Jefferson Papers*, XIV, 428.
27. See above, chap. 3.

in this regard to the writings of David Hume as they applied both to political economy and to constitutional thought. Indeed, it seems clear that Hamilton's introduction to many of Hume's works during the course of the Revolution had greatly influenced the development of his social and political outlook.[28] He came to accept the commercialization of society as not only inevitable but fundamentally salutary as well, and he never doubted that the real disposition of human nature was toward luxury and away from classical virtue. Such a condition, he concluded, made traditional or classical republicanism hopelessly irrelevant to the American experience. Any talk either of Spartan equality and virtuous agrarianism, or of fear of commercial corruption, was nothing more than sententious cant that evaded the necessary realities of life in modern commercial society. In this connection, his reaction to Pinckney's speech in the constitutional convention was even more incisive than Madison's. "It was certainly true," Hamilton remarked, "that nothing like an equality of property existed: that an inequality would exist as long as liberty existed, and that it would unavoidably result from that very liberty itself." The "difference of property" in America was already great, and "commerce and industry" would inevitably increase it still further.[29]

Hamilton's commitment to constitutional revision long predated the convention of 1787. He subscribed to the formula for reform that Robert Morris and other nationalists had established at the end of the war, a formula that integrated constitutional change with the funding of the Revolutionary debt and a vigorous program of economic expansion tied to the consolidation and mobilization of mercantile capital.[30] Hamilton envisioned America not as a virtuous agrarian republic, but as a powerful, economically advanced modern state much like Great Britain—a state that would stand squarely on the worldly foundations of "corruption" that Bernard Mandeville had spoken of in *The Fable of the Bees*.[31] Thus Hamilton's vision of the future was not clouded by the traditional

28. See especially John C. Miller, *Alexander Hamilton: Portrait in Paradox* (New York, 1959), 46–51, and Gerald Stourzh, *Alexander Hamilton and the Idea of Republican Government* (Stanford, Calif., 1970), esp. 70–75. See also Lance Banning, *The Jeffersonian Persuasion: Evolution of a Party Ideology* (Ithaca, N.Y., 1978), 133–136.

29. Farrand, ed., *Records of the Federal Convention*, I, 424, 432.

30. See the superb discussion in E. James Ferguson, "The Nationalists of 1781–1783 and the Economic Interpretation of the Constitution," *Journal of American History*, LVI (1969–1970), 241–261.

31. See above, chap. 1.

republican fears that continued to plague Madison and much of agrarian America. He simply accepted social inequality, propertyless dependence, and virtually unbridled avarice as the necessary and inevitable concomitants of a powerful and prosperous modern society. In one sense, Madison was still caught between the conflicting claims of classical republicanism and modern commercial society, struggling to define and implement a viable synthesis that was relevant to the American experience. Hamilton had stepped confidently and unequivocally into modernity.

On a very general but significant level, therefore, Hamilton supported the new Constitution for reasons quite different from Madison's. He did not intend to use the new government as a means of promoting the conditions that would stabilize America at a predominantly agricultural stage of development; he wanted instead to use that new government to push the United States as rapidly as possible into a higher stage of development, for he interpreted this change as progress, not decay. Unlike Madison, in other words, Hamilton had an unabashedly positive sense of development through time. As his famous economic reports of the next decade revealed, he looked forward to the establishment of advanced, highly capitalized manufactures in the United States and did everything he could within the constraints of his fiscal system to promote them. An anonymous pamphleteer caught the spirit of Hamilton's vision in 1789 when, after praising England as "the most opulent and powerful nation in Europe," he urged the new national government to give every possible encouragement to large-scale manufactures, the hallmark of British greatness.[32] To men of this stripe, England offered a positive rather than a negative model for American development. Both Madison and Hamilton had abandoned the idea of perpetual youth for the republic; both accepted the inevitability of social complexity and the futility of the purely classical vision. Nevertheless, they brought very different attitudes and expectations to bear on their incipient careers as national political leaders.

The new American government thus began its operations in April 1789 in an ideological environment that can best be described as confused and transitional. The dislocations of the 1780s had raised complex

32. *Observations on the Agriculture, Manufacture and Commerce of the United States* (New York, 1789), 27–28. This essay has usually been attributed to Tench Coxe, although Joseph Dorfman, in *The Economic Mind in American Civilization* (New York, 1946–1959), I, xvii, 277–279, argues convincingly against Coxe and suggests James Swan, a Boston merchant and pamphleteer, instead.

questions and problems about the nature of American society and its republican potential. Caught between ancient and modern ways of thinking, most Americans came to realize that there could be no simple formula for a republican America. Perhaps no better evidence of the recognition of this new complexity can be found than in two premiums offered by the *American Museum* in 1789. The first was for "the best essay on the proper policy to be pursued in America, with respect to manufactures—and on the extent to which they may be carried, so as to avoid, on the one hand, the poverty attendant on an injurious balance of trade—and, on the other, the vices—the misery—and the obstruction of population, arising from assembling multitudes of workmen together in large cities or towns." The second premium was for "the best essay on the influence of luxury upon morals—and the most proper mode, consistent with republican freedom, to restrain the pomp and extravagance of ambitious or vain individuals."[33]

These premiums reflected an ideological universe in flux. No single individual, however, could possibly have done more to draw and harden the lines of ideological combat among Americans than Alexander Hamilton who, as the first secretary of the Treasury, quickly seized the policy-making initiative in the new federal government.

33. *American Museum*, VI (July 1789), preface.

CHAPTER SIX

THE SPECTER OF WALPOLE:

REPUBLICANISM AT BAY

When the First Congress of the United States assembled in the spring of 1789, the establishment of a national commercial policy was an urgent item on its agenda. As the central figure in the House debates, James Madison quickly proposed three purposes that commercial regulations might serve: to provide revenue to reestablish the public credit; to encourage the development of American shipping and navigation; and, most important, to use a program of discrimination against England to press for reciprocity in Anglo-American trade. This third goal was to become both the linchpin of Madison's program for an independent, republican America and a focus of conflict between two rival systems of political economy. One system, advocated by Madison, sustained a vision of social and economic development across space, whereas the other system, advanced by Madison's former nationalist ally of the "critical period," Alexander Hamilton, supported an alternative vision of development through time.[1]

The sudden collapse after 1789 of the personal and political friendship between Madison and Hamilton was as portentous as it was unexpected. The coherence of Hamilton's "system," in which domestic and foreign policies were integrated in a plan to foster a specific pattern of social and economic development in America, has long been recognized. That the Virginian had a comparable "system" of his own, however, has not. Hamilton's system is more familiar because it was more explicit, but Madison's is no less significant, especially since it was embraced in most

---

1. This chapter is an elaboration of my research note, "Republicanism and American Foreign Policy: James Madison and the Political Economy of Commercial Discrimination, 1789 to 1794," *William and Mary Quarterly*, 3d Ser., XXXI (1974), 633–646. For a brief but suggestive discussion of the concepts of development across space and through time, see Major L. Wilson, "The Concept of Time and the Political Dialogue in the United States, 1828–48," *American Quarterly*, XIX (1967), 619–644, esp. 623.

of its particulars by his compatriot Thomas Jefferson.[2] To identify the elements of each system and, above all, to analyze the assumptions, values, and expectations that shaped these two competing conceptions of an American republic, early American policies and programs must be placed in their appropriate context. The clash of these two systems of political economy can be neither understood nor properly appreciated unless it is examined in the light of eighteenth-century perceptions of social progress, decay, corruption, and the like.[3] Such an examination, focusing on the public debates over Madison's commercial discrimination policy and Hamilton's Report on Manufactures, underlines the coherence of each system as well as their fundamental incompatibility.

[I]

As one of the most influential members of the First Congress, Madison moved immediately in April 1789 to implement his program for an economically viable and independent republican America.[4] The cornerstone

2. For a concise description and explanation of the Hamiltonian "system" and its incompatibility with Madison's commercial policy, see Paul A. Varg, *Foreign Policies of the Founding Fathers* (East Lansing, Mich., 1963), 77–78, and Joseph Charles, *The Origins of the American Party System: Three Essays* (Chapel Hill, N.C., 1956), 13, 30–31. In his analysis of Jefferson's commercial policy, Merrill Peterson has advanced the idea of a contrasting Jeffersonian "system" without exploring in much detail the crucial connections between commercial and foreign policy, on the one hand, and the Jeffersonian approach to internal economic development, on the other. See "Thomas Jefferson and Commercial Policy, 1783–1793," *WMQ*, 3d Ser., XXII (1965), 584–610.

3. Only recently have historians begun to appreciate the intensely ideological character of political conflict in these years, and as yet they have not exploited fully the insights that flow from an appreciation of "republicanism" as a distinctively 18th-century political culture. Perhaps the best discussions of the Jeffersonian side of the ideological struggle of the 1790s are Douglass G. Adair, "The Intellectual Origins of Jeffersonian Democracy: Republicanism, the Class Struggle, and the Virtuous Farmer" (Ph.D. diss., Yale University, 1943), and Lance Banning, *The Jeffersonian Persuasion: Evolution of a Party Ideology* (Ithaca, N.Y., 1978). See also John Zvesper, *Political Philosophy and Rhetoric: A Study of the Origins of American Party Politics* (Cambridge, 1977). Richard Buel, Jr., *Securing the Revolution: Ideology in American Politics, 1789–1815* (Ithaca, N.Y., 1972), fails to exploit fully the ideological depth of the "republican" opposition to Hamilton's system.

4. The proceedings and debates may be found in *Annals of Congress*, 1st Cong., 1st sess., I, 102ff. Volumes I and II, containing the First Congress, were published in two editions, both with the 1834 imprint, but with differences in running heads and pagination (see Marion Tinling, "Thomas Lloyd's Reports of the First Federal Congress," *WMQ*, 3d Ser.,

of that program was commercial discrimination, a policy that called for a distinction in tonnage and tariff duties favoring nations that had entered into commercial treaty with the United States over those that had not. Countries that had spurned the terms of the "plan of 1776" (and its successors) and refused to negotiate reciprocity treaties with the new republic would be put at a disadvantage in their intercourse with America and thus given an incentive to come to terms. The primary target of discrimination was Great Britain, which had refused since the peace of 1783 to enter into mutually acceptable commercial arrangements with its former colonies. As befitted a staunch republican and a Virginia planter, Madison bemoaned the existing structural ties between the American and British economies. He saw the liberal extension of credit, in particular, to be a curse, since it was used by experienced British merchants to divert American commerce from its "natural channels." Despite formal independence, Madison argued, Americans were still chained to the shackles of British mercantilism; not only did British merchants and capital dominate American trade, thereby restricting foreign markets for American exports, but they also diverted it into "artificial" and politically dangerous channels of dependence that ultimately threatened the republican character of the United States.[5] Madison characteristically complained in May 1789 that England "has bound us in commercial manacles, and very nearly defeated the object of our independence."[6] By early 1794, when his push for a retaliatory commercial policy reached its crest, he was tremendously concerned with the influence that could be "conveyed into the public counsels by a nation directing the course of our trade by her capital, and holding so great a share in our pecuniary institutions." Such an influence, he feared, would eventually affect "our taste, our manners, and our form of Government itself."[7] Madison's overriding aim throughout this period was to remove the British manacles on American commerce, and his vehicle was always retaliatory commercial legislation in the form of discrimination.

According to Madison, discrimination could not fail to accomplish

---

XVIII [1961], 520n). The citations in my research note, "Republicanism and American Foreign Policy," *ibid.*, XXXI (1974), 633–646, are to the other edition (running heads, "Gales and Seaton's History of Debates in Congress").

5. *Annals of Congress*, 1st Cong., 1st sess., I, 185–186, 204–206.
6. *Ibid.*, 238.
7. *Ibid.*, 3d Cong., 1st sess., IV, 215.

two basic purposes. First, it would encourage the development of native American shipping, an objective dearer to him than to most of his fellow southerners. Proclaiming to Congress that he was "a friend to the navigation of America" who would always "be as ready to go as great lengths in favor of that interest, as any gentleman on this floor," Madison insisted that an independent navigation industry was indispensable both for naval defense and for easy, dependable access to foreign markets for American produce.[8] The development of American shipping would directly benefit agriculture, he explained, since "by encouraging the means of transporting our productions with facility, we encourage the raising them."[9] Substituting native for British shipping was also a crucial means of releasing American trade from the long-standing pattern of English control. Second, and more important, discrimination would coerce the British into granting America a just reciprocity in commerce. It would force the relaxation (and perhaps destruction) of the British Navigation Acts, thereby loosening the deadly grip of British credit and redirecting American commerce into more "natural" channels. Madison was particularly interested in promoting direct trade with France, a nation in commercial treaty with the United States, by reducing the lucrative (and unnatural) British re-export trade of American produce to markets on the Continent. The other primary target was, of course, the British West Indies. Madison referred specifically to this branch of American commerce when he wrote to Jefferson in June 1789 that "our trade at present entirely contradicted the advantages expected from the Revolution, no new channels being opened with other European nations, and the British channels being narrowed by a refusal of the most natural and valuable one to the U.S."[10] Through his policy of discrimination, he hoped to force open this critical branch of the republic's commerce that the British had closed to American vessels in 1783.[11]

Few of Madison's fellow congressmen failed to see the value and importance of his objectives. What some of them questioned was his fervent conviction that the young republic had the power to achieve them through his policy of commercial coercion. To understand why Madison was so convinced that an "infant country" could coerce the predomi-

8. *Ibid.*, 1st Cong., 1st sess., I, 237. See also 189–190, 285–286.

9. *Ibid.*, 112.

10. Madison to Jefferson, June 30, 1789, Julian P. Boyd *et al.*, eds., *The Papers of Thomas Jefferson* (Princeton, N.J., 1950–), XV, 226.

11. *Annals of Congress*, 1st Cong., 1st sess., I, 182–183. See also above, chaps. 3 and 5.

nant naval power in Europe, it is necessary to examine in further depth the eighteenth-century assumptions that supported his commitment to discrimination.

From a twentieth-century perspective, Madison's analysis of the comparative nature and strength of the American and British economies was a peculiar one. Great Britain was in a precarious position. "Her dependence, as a commercial and manufacturing nation," he argued, "is so absolutely upon us that it gives a moral certainty that her restrictions will not, for her own sake, be prejudicial to our trade."[12] Since the United States produced "necessaries" for export—food and raw materials—and in return imported "superfluities" in the form of British manufactures, Britain was "under a double dependence on the commerce of the United States." Her West Indies could not subsist without American supplies, particularly lumber and grain, and her hordes of indigent manufacturers could not subsist without American customers. Madison and his supporters usually emphasized the latter form of dependence, proposing the general rule that "in proportion as a nation manufactures luxuries must be its disadvantage in contests of every sort with its customers."[13] The United States had no such problem, as it was blessed with an economy that provided a unique and relatively untapped source of natural power. Since "the produce of this country is more necessary to the rest of the world than that of other countries is to America," Madison contended, "we possess natural advantages which no other nation does." Therefore, "if we have the disposition, we have abundantly the power to vindicate our cause."[14]

Several of Madison's fellow congressmen were at a loss to penetrate this logic and rejected his evaluation both of the latent strength of an undeveloped American economy and of Britain's dependence on it. They did not understand how Madison could regard British clothing and hardware as "superfluities," and unlike Madison, they very much feared the dire consequences of British economic power should discrimination provoke a full-scale commercial war with that nation.[15] Madison's categori-

12. *Annals of Congress*, 1st Cong., 1st sess., I, 246. See also 205–206, 238–240.

13. *Ibid.*, 3d Cong., 1st sess., IV, 157, 216.

14. *Ibid.*, 1st Cong., 1st sess., I, 205–206.

15. Representative John Lawrence of New York led the opposition to discrimination in Congress. *Ibid.*, 177, 202–204, 234–236. In private correspondence Congressman Fisher Ames of Massachusetts proved to be a determined foe of Madison's policy. See letters from Ames to George Richards Minot, May 27, 29, and July 2, 1789, in Seth Ames, ed., *Works*

zation of American imports from Britain as "superfluities" and "luxuries" stemmed in part from his belief that the United States had the potential to manufacture any "necessaries" it currently imported. He was confident that the young republic could, in the unlikely event of a commercial war with England, be converted very quickly into a society of self-sufficient yeomen who spun all their clothing at home. But Madison's faith in the ability of Americans to subsist on their own cannot fully explain his extreme view of British weakness and dependence on America, a view disputed by several of his contemporaries and, most important, unequivocally rejected by the secretary of the Treasury.[16]

The rationale for Madison's discrimination policy was closely tied to the traditional "country" image of eighteenth-century England that was pervasive in America before the Revolution. The England that Madison and many of his supporters described in the early 1790s closely resembled the England that Franklin had come to loathe in the 1770s; an unhealthy, debauched, densely populated society, mired in the depravity of a mercantilist political economy that embodied the miseries of national "old age."[17] The British system of public finance, with its funded debt, privileged corporations, paper money, "stockjobbers," and all the attendant moral evils, epitomized for many proponents of discrimination England's fundamental social decay. As William Branch Giles argued in defense of Madison's discrimination policy, Great Britain was "tottering under the weight of a King, a Court, a nobility, a priesthood, armies, navies, debts, and all the complicated machinery of oppression" that demonstrated "the debility of the system, and the decrepitude of old age."[18] Madison himself paid closest attention to the group on which Franklin had so often focused his concern—the manufacturing or "labouring" poor, who were the victims of both a redundant population and a corrupt social and political system. As Giles asserted, and Madison agreed, "In Great Brit-

---

of Fisher Ames (Boston, 1854), I, 45–46, 48–50, 59. See also Samuel Higginson to John Adams, Dec. 21, 1789, in J. Franklin Jameson, ed., "Letters of Samuel Higginson, 1783–1804," *Annual Report of the American Historical Association for the Year 1896* (Washington, D.C., 1897), I, 771–772.

16. *Annals of Congress,* 1st Cong., 1st sess., I, 237–240. See also *ibid.,* 3d Cong., 1st sess., IV, 215, 382. For a detailed discussion of Hamilton's initial opposition to "Jeffersonian" commercial policy, see the editorial note in Boyd *et al.,* eds., *Jefferson Papers,* XVIII, 516–558.

17. See above, chap. 2.

18. *Annals of Congress,* 3d Cong., 1st sess., IV, 284, 281–285.

ain, every species of occupation and employment is not only filled, but surcharged," and "her subjects . . . were compelled to plough the ocean for subsistence." As an old and fully peopled society suffering under the burden of a mercantilist political economy, England was shackled by its hordes of dependent wage-laborers whose very existence rested on a chronically precarious and fluctuating foreign vent for their manufactures.[19]

Great Britain was economically "dependent" on the United States, in short, precisely because so many of its citizens were not free; that is, independent in either an economic or a political sense. In particular, the thousands of Englishmen who had been forced into the manufacturing of luxuries and frivolous "superfluities" could never be independent, since they depended for subsistence on a capricious, often transient demand for their products. In his essay, "Fashion," published March 20, 1792, in Philip Freneau's *National Gazette*, and later in congressional debates on commercial discrimination, Madison pointed to the pathetic plight of twenty thousand English buckle manufacturers and their employees who had been ruined by a sudden preference for shoestrings and slippers. These victims of the "mutability of fashion," who offered a disgusting example of "the lowest point of servility," were the unfortunately typical victims of an old, morally corrupt society in which, as Claviére and Warville had put it, industry had changed "from the fabrication of what is necessary and useful, to that which is fantastic, forced, and pernicious."[20] Referring to these dependent indigents, Madison advanced the general rule that "in proportion as a nation consists of that description of citizens, and depends on external commerce, it is dependent on the consumption and caprice of other nations." In this case, the ruined buckle manufacturers who exported their wares to America were as dependent on the arbiters of fashion in the United States as they were on those in England.[21] Because of this situation, Madison insisted, an American policy of discrimination could not fail to succeed, for an economy characterized by industries of this nature was particularly vulnerable to pressure from customers who exported in return "necessaries" that would always command a "sure Market." Blessed with plentiful natural re-

19. *Ibid.*, 283–284. See also above, chap. 2.

20. Gaillard Hunt, ed., *The Writings of James Madison* (New York, 1900–1910), VI, 99–101; *Annals of Congress*, 3d Cong., 1st sess., IV, 216. For the reference to and quotation of Claviére and Warville, see above, chap. 4.

21. "Fashion," in Hunt, ed., *Writings of Madison*, VI, 100–101.

sources (primarily an abundance of open land) and a healthy political culture, the United States was, by comparison with England, a young and virile society of independent republicans who would be the inevitable victors in any test of commercial strength.[22] Indeed, Madison never doubted that America's latent "natural" power was fully capable of shattering the British restrictions on American commerce that threatened the virtue and autonomy of the new republic.[23]

Although commercial restrictions were to be Madison's vehicle for securing an independent republican America, it is important to understand that his intention was not to raise semi-permanent tariff walls that might encourage industrial growth, a balanced internal economy, and an isolated self-sufficiency. His conception of economic independence did not necessarily include extensive domestic manufactures, the development of a great home market, or a diminishing reliance on foreign markets for the absorption of American agricultural surpluses. The retaliatory duties in Madison's discrimination program were a temporary means to an end—the realization of an international economic order in which all such restrictions would be unnecessary because commerce would finally be free to flow in its "natural" channels.[24] In a new world of free trade, Americans would not have to worry about being dependent on foreign markets as long as they continued to export the right kind of products, "necessaries." Unless the United States began producing

22. *Annals of Congress*, 3d Cong., 1st sess., IV, 212.

23. Madison could have found confirmation both of his comparative view of the American and British economies and of the potential viability of commercial coercion in Adam Smith's *Wealth of Nations* (1776). See especially Book IV, chap. 7, pt. 3, in which Smith portrays the British economy as unbalanced and dangerously precarious, particularly vulnerable to the very type of scheme Madison was advancing 15 years later. Adam Smith, *An Inquiry into the Nature and Causes of the Wealth of Nations*, ed. Edwin Cannan (New York, 1937 [orig. publ. London, 1776]), 590–593.

24. Madison repeatedly professed his adherence to "a very free system of commerce," in which "industry and labor are left to take their own course," free from "unjust, oppressive, and impolitic" commercial shackles. *Annals of Congress*, 1st Cong., 1st sess., I, 111. For the system to function properly between nations, however, all nations had to comply, and Madison was determined to induce compliance from Great Britain. Some scholars, particularly William Appleman Williams, have portrayed Madison as a "mercantilist" whose commercial discrimination policy was consciously designed to promote the extensive development of American manufactures. See *The Contours of American History* (Cleveland, Ohio, 1961), 111–223. This point of view misinterprets Madison's fundamental motives and the thrust of his system, while often failing to make necessary distinctions between different types of manufacturing.

whimsical "superfluities" or "luxuries," it would never become dependent on foreign customers or nations. For this reason Madison particularly dreaded the day when an old, corrupt America would resort to the production of articles like brass buckles for export. His discrimination policy was in one sense designed to forestall this unhappy development for as long as possible by securing the open international order that would preserve America's social youth. If such a policy could drive open the necessary foreign markets for America's burgeoning agricultural surpluses, it was possible that Americans would not be forced into the manufacturing of luxuries for export, as the English had been, in order to employ their expanding population.[25]

Opponents of discrimination did not share Madison's fervent conviction that the policy would succeed rather quickly in destroying the pernicious web of British mercantilist restrictions. Failing to share his confidence, they painted a dreary and quite different picture of the policy's probable ramifications. Many of them argued that discrimination would, in fact, provoke the British into even more devastating restrictions on American commerce, threatening the basis of America's prosperous agricultural export trade and forcing the premature development of manufactures. John Lawrence, a New York congressman who was a leading opponent of discrimination, asserted that a commercial war with England might even shake the moral foundations of the republic. The resulting loss of foreign markets for American farmers, he explained, "must unavoidably check domestic industry, the sole foundation of national welfare and importance." "For what stimulus will the farmer have to raise more produce than is necessary for his own support?" he asked. "Will he toil in cultivating the earth, in gathering in its increase, to have the fruits of his labor perish in his granaries? Once destroy this spring of industry, and your country totters to ruin."[26]

Lawrence's suggestion that commercial discrimination would succeed only in annihilating American foreign commerce and thereby would "destroy the soul of the nation, the ardent industry of the people" expressed a profound concern with the moral importance of commerce and foreign markets in sustaining republican industry.[27] Madison certainly

25. See above, chaps. 3 and 5.

26. *Annals of Congress*, 1st Cong., 1st sess., I, 177.

27. *Ibid.*, 235. For an excellent example of the attention many Americans paid to the importance of foreign commerce in this regard, see Hugh Williamson's speech in Congress in Nov. 1792, *ibid.*, 2d Cong., 2d sess., II, 693–694.

shared this concern, for his advocacy of discrimination was to a great extent based on it. He was unequivocally convinced, however, that his policy would extend and liberalize, rather than cramp and confine, America's intercourse with the rest of the world and thus enhance "the soul of the nation" instead of destroying it. Because of America's youthful vigor and the decrepitude of Britain's old age, the republic had the power to overcome any barriers to its virtuous character. A successful program of commercial discrimination would, he believed, soon prove the truth of this argument. Since the British could not afford any interruption of their commerce with America, according to Madison they would never engage in the massive retaliation that Lawrence feared would force a major reorientation of America's political economy in the direction of increased manufacturing.[28]

It seems clear that Madison never expected discrimination to seriously alter the predominantly agricultural character of American society by forcing the extensive development of manufactures. He had no aversion to household manufactures, which constituted "the natural ally of agriculture," but he never intended to encourage large-scale manufacturing enterprises appropriate to older, fully peopled societies. To the limited extent that he expected discrimination to foster manufactures, Madison spoke explicitly of those "carried on, not in public factories, but in the household or family way, which he regarded as the most important way."[29] His commitment to manufactures was thus limited to those that could, as he emphasized, be carried on as well in the southern states as in the densely populated North or East.[30] And from a broader perspective, of course, he hoped that the triumph of commercial discrimination, by assuring Americans open access to the foreign markets that would sustain their full industry in agriculture, would discourage any impetus toward the development of large-scale, public manufacturing.

28. *Ibid.*, 3d Cong., 1st sess., IV, 157, 215, 274, 382.

29. Hunt, ed., *Writings of Madison*, VI, 99; *Annals of Congress*, 3d Cong., 1st sess., IV, 221.

30. *Ibid.*, 221–222. See also John C. Miller, *The Federalist Era, 1789–1801* (New York, 1960), 144n.

[II]

Madison had rather naively assumed that the implementation of his discrimination policy would come as a matter of course once the new Constitution was put into practice. He had not anticipated much opposition to the policy, believing its acceptance to have been implicit in the adoption of the new government.[31] By August 1789, when discrimination had first failed to pass Congress, however, Madison began to sense the unexpected magnitude of his undertaking. His failure to secure adoption of discrimination was to be repeated several times in the course of the Washington administrations and was finally sealed in the Jay Treaty of 1795, which prohibited for ten years the type of anti-British commercial program he had championed. What must have shocked Madison most was that the leading opponent of discrimination turned out to be Hamilton, his former nationalist ally. Ironically, a few years earlier Hamilton had argued in *Federalist* number eleven that one virtue of the proposed government would be its ability to pursue just such a policy and thereby secure American commercial independence. But by the summer of 1789, as the New Yorker was about to launch his career as the first secretary of the Treasury, he had become a determined and implacable foe of Madison's program and would remain one until his retirement in 1795.[32]

Influenced strongly by David Hume's defense of modern commercial society, Hamilton's cast of mind by the 1790s was much closer to the English "court" mainstream than to the "country" opposition that had predominated in Revolutionary America and that continued to shape the perceptions of republicans like Madison.[33] Hamilton's economic system, tied to a funded debt, a national bank, and the mobilization of mercantile capital, was based on assumptions and beliefs that not only offended

31. Madison had some justification for his belief that the idea of commercial retaliation against Great Britain had been part of the general thrust behind ratification of the Constitution. For discussions of this point, see Vernon G. Setser, *The Commercial Reciprocity Policy of the United States, 1774–1829* (Philadelphia, 1937), 102, and Jerald A. Combs, *The Jay Treaty: Political Battleground of the Founding Fathers* (Berkeley, Calif., 1970), 27–28.

32. See especially Samuel Flagg Bemis, *Jay's Treaty: A Study in Commerce and Diplomacy*, rev. ed. (New Haven, Conn., 1962), 55–66.

33. Gerald Stourzh, *Alexander Hamilton and the Idea of Republican Government* (Stanford, Calif., 1970); J.G.A. Pocock, "Virtue and Commerce in the Eighteenth Century," *Journal of Interdisciplinary History*, III (1972–1973), 130–131; and Banning, *Jeffersonian Persuasion*, esp. chap. 5. See also above, chap. 5.

"country" ideologues but also explicitly denied the efficacy and wisdom of commercial discrimination. Since Hamilton's view of England was not formed according to the assumptions of classical republicanism or country ideology, Madison's idea of American "necessaries" and British "superfluities" was thoroughly alien to his way of thinking. The secretary of the Treasury vigorously denied that the fledgling republic, because of the nature of its economy, had the power necessary to destroy or to alter significantly the prevailing European system of commercial intercourse. Such an idea was patent nonsense, according to Hamilton, who carefully developed the alternative theory that nations with extensive manufactures, like Britain, had overwhelming advantages in their intercourse with predominantly agricultural countries like America.[34] Indeed, from Hamilton's point of view, Britain's prolific production of advanced manufactures and "luxuries" was a sign of national maturity and strength, not of senility and decay.

Because the secretary was convinced that discrimination would be a foolishly reckless ploy on the part of a weak and undeveloped America, he shuddered at the prospect of its implementation. Like Lawrence, he assumed that it could lead only to a disastrous commercial war with Britain that would endanger the security and even the very existence of the new nation. Most ominously, such a contest threatened to diminish and perhaps destroy Anglo-American trade, a calamity that would seal the doom of the secretary's ambitious program for economic development in the young republic. Hamilton's system was predicated on the concept that revenue from Anglo-American trade would bolster the funded national debt; in order to work it required warm commercial relations with Great Britain or, in blunter terms, a temporary acquiescence to British maritime domination. Furthermore, close commercial ties to that country were necessary to supply the United States with the credit and capital that could ignite the kind of economic growth Hamilton desired.[35] For both ideological and practical reasons, therefore, Hamilton's "system" was incompatible with Madison's commercial discrimination.

Hamilton's primary purpose in funding the national debt and incorporating the first Bank of the United States was to stabilize the new national

---

34. See especially, the Report on Manufactures, in Harold C. Syrett and Jacob E. Cooke, eds., *The Papers of Alexander Hamilton* (New York, 1961–), X, 230–340, esp. 287–290.

35. Merrill D. Peterson, *Thomas Jefferson and the New Nation: A Biography* (New York, 1970), 423–424.

government and establish its credit. Beyond that, he aimed to facilitate the organization and investment of private capital. The proper operation of the funding system and the Bank, he hoped, would draw both foreign and domestic capital into the hands of ambitious entrepreneurs who would invest wisely in the economic growth of the new nation. According to Hamilton, such devices were absolutely necessary in underdeveloped frontier societies with vast tracts of uncultivated land and few manufactures, where the tendency was for capital to be diffused and currency depleted. The secretary wished to concentrate and mobilize American capital so that it would excite the industry and productivity of the American people; he especially wished to encourage production for export in order to rectify the chronic problem of an unfavorable balance of trade.[36] In his Reports on Public Credit (the second dealing with the Bank), Hamilton explained the importance of mobilizing capital in the young republic. His final major report, the Report on Manufactures, provided the capstone to his system in its suggestion of one important end toward which this capital should be employed.

In January 1790, Congress had instructed Hamilton to prepare a report on "the encouragement and promotion of such manufactures as will tend to render the United States independent of other nations for essential, particularly for military supplies."[37] What the secretary presented almost two years later, however, far transcended this modest request and explicitly tied his advocacy of manufactures to the evolving infrastructure of his "system." The Report on Manufactures was an ambitious theoretical defense of manufacturing, as well as a detailed prospectus for American industry. Most important, it confirmed the fundamental incompatibility, on both an ideological and a practical level, of the secretary's system of political economy and that of James Madison.

On the theoretical level, the report celebrated the benefits of a highly developed division of labor, or the "separation of occupations" in an advanced, commercialized society. Hamilton sought to shatter the romanticized image of the self-sufficient yeoman so popular in America by arguing that "the mere separation of the occupation of the cultivator,

---

36. For excellent discussions of Hamilton's economic purposes, see, among many: E.A.J. Johnson, *The Foundations of American Economic Freedom: Government and Enterprise in the Age of Washington* (Minneapolis, Minn., 1973), 121–151; Forrest McDonald, *The Presidency of George Washington* (Lawrence, Kans., 1974), 47–65; and John C. Miller, *Alexander Hamilton: Portrait in Paradox* (New York, 1959), chaps. 16, 18, and 19.

37. Miller, *Alexander Hamilton*, 282.

from that of the Artificer, has the effect of augmenting the *productive powers* of labour, and with them, the total mass of the produce or revenue of a Country."[38] If the cultivators of the land did their own manufacturing at home, as Madison and many other Americans wished, "the quantity of every species of industry would be less and the quality much inferior." Manufactures would be few and coarse, the land poorly cultivated, and industry "limited to the maintenance of each family in the simplest manner."[39] Thus, according to Hamilton, a predominantly agricultural nation with only household manufactures would be a stagnant, primitive society unable to achieve maximum efficiency or productivity in either its agriculture or its manufacturing. In a more complex society with an advanced division of labor and efficient public manufacturing, on the other hand, productivity could be much increased and diversified, and men would be more comfortable, refined, and civilized. As Adam Smith and many other eighteenth-century analysts had contended, and as Hamilton now agreed, a highly developed division of labor was the essence of social progress in its broadest sense. Unlike Smith, however, Hamilton did not seem to be concerned with the dehumanizing aspects of such progress.[40]

After making his case for the benefits of an advanced division of labor in America, the secretary proceeded to attack the idea that the United States might gain these advantages without resorting to its own public manufacturing, that it might, in other words, follow Adam Smith's (and James Madison's) plan and rely instead on free trade and an international division of labor that would permit the United States to continue its specialization in agriculture. "If the system of perfect liberty to industry and commerce were the prevailing system of nations," Hamilton conceded, "the arguments which dissuade a country in the predicament of the United States, from the zealous pursuits of manufactures would doubtless have great force," for "in such a state of things, each country would have the full benefit of its peculiar advantages to compensate for its deficiencies or disadvantages." But free trade was a chimera; the irrefutable fact of the matter was that "an opposite spirit" regulated "the general policy of Nations," with the inevitable consequence that "the

38. Syrett and Cooke, eds., *Hamilton Papers*, X, 251.

39. These quotations are taken from Hamilton's third draft of the report. Although this material was deleted from the final version, it illustrates well the secretary's celebration of an advanced division of labor. *Ibid.*, 80.

40. See above, chap. 1.

United States are to a certain extent in the situation of a country precluded from foreign Commerce."[41] America would always be able to get its necessary supplies from abroad; the problem, however, would continue to be the chronically fluctuating and inadequate foreign demand for its large agricultural surplus that resulted in a dangerously unfavorable balance of trade. Because a young and comparatively weak republic lacked the power to coerce the development of a Smithian international order, America had no choice but to reorient appropriately its domestic political economy. In view of the continually increasing surplus produce of American soil, and "weighing seriously the tendency of the system, which prevails among most of the commercial nations of Europe," Hamilton firmly concluded that "there appear strong reasons to regard the foreign demand for that surplus as too uncertain a reliance, and to desire a substitute for it, in an extensive domestic market."[42] To this degree, the Report on Manufactures was Hamilton's answer to Madison's defense of commercial discrimination.

Hamilton was convinced that America should move ahead into a more complex stage of social development, both because conditions favored this form of progress and because he regarded such change as inherently desirable. He cited traditional doubts about the potential for American manufactures only to dispel them. While Hamilton acknowledged that compared to Europe America had both a "scarcity of hands" and a "dearness of labor," he reminded his countrymen, as several observers had during the 1780s, that there were "large districts" already "pretty fully peopled" and therefore ripe for major manufacturing establishments. Labor surpluses in the form of idle women, children, and the poor could always be put to work in public factories, and recent advances in machinery promised a further solution to America's relative deficiency of labor.[43] Similarly, the problem of a "want of capital" had been largely overcome by the funding of the debt and the creation of a national bank; as always, Hamilton emphasized the potential for the public funds to operate as growth-inducing capital.[44] The inference to be drawn from

41. Syrett and Cooke, eds., *Hamilton Papers*, X, 262–263.

42. *Ibid.*, 259, 256–260. See also, 287–288.

43. *Ibid.*, 269–270. The American interest in machinery as a substitute for manual labor was very strong. See, for example, the Report of the Committee for Manufactures to the Board of Managers of the Pennsylvania Society, on the American Cotton Manufactory, in the *Pennsylvania Gazette* (Philadelphia), Nov. 12, 1788.

44. Syrett and Cooke, eds., *Hamilton Papers*, X, 275–283.

this train of logic was inescapable: all the United States lacked was the will and the necessary commitment to develop manufactures.

Not content with pleading his case for advancing to a higher stage of social development, Hamilton considered the requisite means to this end, and in so doing he gave additional evidence of his commitment to a vision of American growth modeled after the eighteenth-century English experience. It is curious that historians have generally portrayed Hamilton as the father of the American protective tariff, for the secretary went to some lengths in the Report on Manufactures to argue that "pecuniary bounties," more than tariffs on imports, would have a beneficial and direct impact on the development of a modern economy. He asserted that bounties had a distinct advantage over tariffs, in that bounties gave manufactures assistance in foreign markets as well as at home. This advantage was important to Hamilton, who was very concerned that American manufactures would have to compete with heavily subsidized European industries. He asserted, moreover, that bounties were appropriate only for public manufactures that were part of "a regular trade," and not for the household productions of private families; he added that with the exception of these crude household manufactures, bounties would ordinarily be indispensable to the introduction of any new branch of American industry.[45] This defense of bounties confirmed Hamilton's commitment to advanced, public manufactures, his lack of interest in household industry, and his desire to transplant the European system of direct government subsidy to America. His preference for bounties also betrayed his interest in developing American manufactures that would be suitable not only for domestic supply, as the instructions from Congress had specified, but also for exportation to foreign markets. As hostile readers of his report invariably pointed out, Hamilton's vision of a modern American republic bore a remarkable resemblance to the eighteenth-century English model that so many republicans despised.[46]

Indeed, Hamilton apparently never realized how offensive his Report on Manufactures would be to large numbers of Americans who were already suspicious of his economic programs. It should have been clear to the secretary that his blueprint for a modern America would terrify more traditional republicans. Tench Coxe, for example, was a particularly able advocate of native manufactures who shared Hamilton's sympathies

45. *Ibid.*, 300–301.
46. See above, chap. 2.

but who also sensed more shrewdly the need to placate traditional American fears and prejudices. Appropriately, he was much more solicitous of household, as opposed to strictly public manufactures, and he did not put the great stress on bounties that the secretary did.[47] Not surprisingly, other public defenders of the Hamiltonian program were self-consciously anxious to assuage republican anxieties. A writer in the *Gazette of the United States*, noting that manufactures would "afford a new source of employment for the poor, which will be constantly increasing," attempted to refute the insinuation that the establishment of manufactures "will tend to make menials of our citizens, while they are immured in the factories constructed for carrying on the works." "Let it be remembered," he argued, "that we are all under the protection of just and equal laws, that every man is free to chuse what occupation he pleases, and that our boundless western territories will forever afford a retreat from domestic imposition, as they now do from foreign tyranny."[48] Many Americans remained unconvinced, however, by efforts to reconcile republicanism and the Hamiltonian system. Ultimately, by early 1794, their opposition would come to a head in the revival of Madison's now familiar program of commercial discrimination.

[III]

As one historian has perceptively observed, "It is hard to imagine how, by deliberate attempt, Alexander Hamilton's economic program for the new nation could have been better calculated to stir the deepest fears in the Anglo-American heritage."[49] Since Hamilton set out to plant in America a British system of public finance that would promote the same kind of economic development that England had undergone since the

47. See Jacob E. Cooke, "Tench Coxe, Alexander Hamilton, and the Encouragement of American Manufactures," *WMQ*, 3d Ser., XXXII (1975), 377–380, and Leo Marx, *The Machine in the Garden: Technology and the Pastoral Ideal in America* (New York, 1964), 167–169. For a brief but adequate study of Coxe's thought and career, see Harold Hutcheson, *Tench Coxe: A Study in American Economic Development* (Baltimore, 1938). The definitive treatment of Coxe may be found in Jacob E. Cooke, *Tench Coxe and the Early Republic* (Chapel Hill, N.C., 1978).

48. *Gazette of the United States* (Philadelphia), Sept. 7, 1791.

49. Lance G. Banning, "The Quarrel with Federalism: A Study in the Origins and Character of Republican Thought" (Ph.D. diss., Washington University, 1971), 212.

Glorious Revolution, it is no wonder that scores of Americans saw his program as turning the revolution of 1776 upside down. Pecuniary bounties, manufactures for export, public factories—the Report on Manufactures seemed to describe a society ominously reminiscent of the English system that Franklin and the Revolutionaries had rejected.[50] Indeed, as Hamilton's "system" gradually took shape in the public mind, the character of the opposition to it changed dramatically. Early opposition to the secretary reflected tactical and strategic differences among political factions, competing interest groups, and geographic regions; eventually, however, this opposition assumed the more explosive form of ideological resistance. Many of Hamilton's opponents came to fear nothing less than a conspiracy to corrupt American society and smash the republican experiment by imitating British forms, manners, and institutions.[51]

This ideological resistance was triggered for Madison and many others by a wild scramble for the stock of the Bank of the United States on the part of speculators (some of whom were congressmen) in the summer of 1791 and by the ensuing financial panic of March 1792. Outraged republicans began hurling the epithet "Walpole" at Hamilton, for now they perceived in him the image of the notorious British minister who had regularized and consolidated the financial system allegedly responsible for the corruption of English government and society.[52] Madison and his followers were appalled by what they saw as a corrupted legislature—the supposedly republican Congress of the United States—manipulated by Hamilton from his vantage point in the Treasury and tied to a fiscal system that encouraged reckless speculation and immoral behavior in the society at large. To these republicans, Hamilton's delivery to Congress of the Report on Manufactures in December 1791 and his contemporaneous

50. See above, chaps. 2 and 4.

51. See especially Banning, *Jeffersonian Persuasion*, chaps. 5 and 6, and Banning, "Republican Ideology and the Triumph of the Constitution, 1789 to 1793," *WMQ*, 3d Ser., XXXI (1974), 167–188.

52. See Madison's general correspondence during this period; for example, Madison to Jefferson, Aug. 8, 1791, in Hunt, ed., *Writings of Madison*, VI, 58n–59n, and Madison to Henry Lee, Apr. 15, 1792, in *Letters and Other Writings of James Madison* (Philadelphia, 1865), I, 553–554. Madison also published during this general period an extended series of 17 essays (of which "Fashion" was one) that focused on threats to republicanism in America. See also, in particular, "Spirit of Governments," in Hunt, ed., *Writings of Madison*, VI, 93–95. See also McDonald, *Presidency of Washington*, 56–57, and Isaac Kramnick, *Bolingbroke and His Circle: The Politics of Nostalgia in the Age of Walpole* (Cambridge, Mass., 1968), chap. 2, for discussions of Walpole and his system.

assistance in the establishment of a grandiose corporative enterprise, the Society for Establishing Useful Manufactures, at Paterson, New Jersey, confirmed the existence of this insidious anti-republican conspiracy.[53]

To a great extent, the fears of Madison and his followers were constitutional, but in a broad, eighteenth-century sense. In his private correspondence, Madison's objections to the Report on Manufactures were focused on Hamilton's treatment of the "general welfare" clause of the Constitution. In urging pecuniary bounties as the best means of encouraging American manufactures, the secretary had asserted that Congress had virtually unlimited power to interpret that clause. "It is therefore of necessity left to the discretion of the National Legislature," Hamilton had declared, "to pronounce, upon the objects, which concern the general Welfare, and for which under that description, an appropriation of money is requisite and proper."[54] An alarmed Madison viewed this claim as "a new constitutional doctrine of vast consequences" that was utterly incompatible with limited republican government, for it purported to legitimate an unrestrained and "corrupted" legislature in its avaricious subversion of the public good. In Madison's eyes, the minority faction in control of the new federal government had arrogated to itself unlimited discretion in determining the scope of its operations.[55]

Viewed in this light, Hamilton's emphasis on "pecuniary bounties" provided indisputable evidence of his dark intentions. Instead of allowing manufactures to grow at a natural and proper pace, he would instead open the Treasury to subsidize "artificial" monopolies that would ruin

53. In a letter to Madison written shortly after the release of Hamilton's Report on Manufactures, Henry Lee of Virginia argued that the secretary envisioned the creation of a new species of human being who would not challenge the type of society Hamilton's policies were attempting to fashion. Indeed, Lee argued, those in power were "contriving ways and means to form a people as spurious as is their administration." The conspiracy, then, was ultimately directed toward corrupting the fundamental character of the American people. Lee to Madison, Jan. 8, 1792, James Madison Papers, Library of Congress (microfilm).

54. Syrett and Cooke, eds., *Hamilton Papers*, X, 303.

55. Madison to Edmund Pendleton, Jan. 21, 1792, Madison Papers. See also Madison to Henry Lee, Jan. 1, 1792, in Hunt, ed., *Writings of Madison*, VI, 81n. In his earlier opposition to Hamilton's Bank, Madison had prophetically warned that the drift of the secretary's doctrine of implied power would lead to a sanctioning of congressional power over "every object within the whole compass of political economy," including the right to "incorporate manufactures" and "give monopolies in every branch of domestic industry." *Annals of Congress*, 1st Cong., 3d sess., II, 1948–1949.

private, "natural" producers and foster dangerous, unrepublican disparities in wealth. These privileged groups would be beholden to the government for their sustenance, Madison feared, and this dependence would only enhance the secretary's corrupt influence. Who could doubt that corporate monopolies that corrupted the integrity of the political process and promoted inequality were anathema in a republic? In his ambitious prospectus for American industry, Hamilton threatened in one fell blow to subvert both the fundamental principles of republican government and the democratic social structure on which it depended.

Convinced that Hamilton was bent on consolidating the system of policies that had corrupted eighteenth-century England, Madison assumed that the secretary would now use the open-ended general welfare clause to fashion a distinctly unrepublican society where ministerial corruption, government-subsidized monopolies, and undemocratic inequality would hold sway. Madison dreaded the "Anglicization" of American society, particularly if it was unnecessarily induced by a corrupt, "Anglicized" system of government, and it seemed to him that Hamilton's system threatened to accelerate, rather than postpone, this regrettable process of social decay. Instead of using the new federal government to prevent America from following England's tragic path, as Madison wished to do through a program of commercial discrimination, the secretary was using the government to make America "old" and corrupt long before its time. This fundamental divergence in outlook arose in great part from Madison's and Hamilton's different ideological perspectives; what Hamilton applauded as positive growth and development, Madison shunned as corruption and decay.[56]

In November 1791, Madison began publishing a series of seventeen essays in Philip Freneau's *National Gazette*.[57] The first, "Population and Emigration," appeared just before the release of Hamilton's Report on Manufactures. Significantly, it was a defense of American westward expansion, which Hamilton and many of his supporters appeared anxious to restrain in the interest of concentrating and mobilizing capital. Centering his discussion on the problem of what could be done with "the surplus of human life," Madison praised the utility and general beneficence of emigration to virgin territory. Emigration from Europe to

56. See above, chap. 5.

57. Appearing between Nov. 1791 and Sept. 1792, the essays can be found in Hunt, ed., *Writings of Madison*, VI, 43*ff*.

America had benefited both continents; likewise, the movements that were "continually going forward" within the United States—from more compact to more sparse districts and from a less easy to an easier subsistence—should be welcomed rather than deterred. Such emigration had an especially salutary effect on private morality, Madison noted, for it discouraged the rampant vice prevalent in old, crowded settlements. In this way, Madison's initial essay reaffirmed the centrality of westward expansion to his system of political economy.[58]

All but one of the remaining essays appeared after the delivery to Congress of Hamilton's Report on Manufactures. Although the report was never explicitly mentioned in any of them, two essays obviously reflected its impact on Madison's thinking. In the "Republican Distribution of Citizens" essay of March 5, 1792, Madison discussed the relationship between the overall political and moral health of a society and the distribution of various occupations in it. After first noting that "the best distribution is that which would most favor *health, virtue, intelligence,* and *competency* in the *greatest number* of citizens," he asserted that the life of the husbandman was preeminently suited to individual comfort and happiness on all four counts. It avoided extremes both of want (poverty) and waste (luxury), evils that stemmed "from the distresses and vice of overgrown cities." For "those who work the materials furnished by the earth in its natural or cultivated state," Madison continued, it was most fortunate for the United States "that so much of the ordinary and most essential consumption, takes place in fabrics which can be prepared in every family, and which constitute indeed the natural ally of agriculture." Either Madison did not appreciate the potential advantages of a highly developed division of labor within America, as Hamilton did, or he believed that any such advantages would be more than compensated for by its liabilities. He expressed the strongest approbation for the private, household manufacturers whom the secretary had slighted in his report: "The class of citizens who provide at once their own food and their own raiment, may be viewed as the most truly independent and happy. They are more; they are the best basis of public liberty, and the strongest bulwark of public safety. It follows, that the greater the proportion of this class to the whole society, the more free, the more inde-

---

58. *Ibid.,* 48, 66, 43–66. For a similar defense of westward expansion in America, see Benjamin Rush, *Essays, Literary, Moral, and Philosophical,* 2d ed. (Philadelphia, 1806), 209–211, 223–224.

pendent, and the more happy must be the society itself." Madison's conclusion was not surprising: "In appreciating the regular [i.e., non-household] branches of manufacturing and mechanical industry, their tendency must be compared with the principles laid down, and their merits graduated accordingly. Whatever is least favorable to vigor of body, to the faculties of the mind, or to the virtues or the utilities of life, instead of being forced or fostered by public authority, ought to be seen with regret as long as occupations more friendly to human happiness, lie vacant."[59]

Madison's rather simplistic reaffirmation of traditional republican attitudes—celebration of the simple, virtuous, self-sufficient yeoman and suspicious distrust of commercialization and an advanced division of labor—was undoubtedly provoked by Hamilton's boldness in the Report on Manufactures. It is possible that Madison exaggerated and over-simplified his own views for partisan purposes; nonetheless, his essay is a revealing index of the extent to which Hamilton was defining and sharpening ideological divisions in American public debate, especially in the realm of political economy.

In his subsequent "Fashion" essay of March 22, 1792, Madison examined the liabilities of specific forms of non-household manufacturing enterprises. Citing his favorite example of the English buckle makers who were suddenly put out of work by "the mutability of fashion," he strongly cautioned Americans against developing luxury manufactures dependent on "the caprices of fancy." Workers in these industries could never enjoy a sure subsistence, because their livelihood was tied to the whimsical tastes of the fanciful rich. Such abject forms of dependence, characteristic of overrefined and enervated societies, were both repulsive and unrepublican. Moreover, Madison warned, if these luxuries were exported to foreign markets, they undermined national as well as individual independence, for in this case "the mutability of policy" in foreign governments compounded the uncertainty of demand.[60]

The content and timing of this essay must be understood in the broader context of Madison's fear that a Hamiltonian conspiracy might alter the basic institutions and character of American society. Several of his argu-

59. Hunt, ed., *Writings of Madison*, VI, 96–99.
60. *Ibid.*, 99–101. For a similar indictment of luxury manufactures, see James Anderson, *Observations on the Means of Exciting a Spirit of National Industry* (Dublin, 1779), I, 81–83.

ments in "Fashion" seem to have been drawn from a British tract, *Of Commerce and Luxury*, that had been reprinted in Philadelphia in 1791 at the request of "several enlightened patriots." These patriots, the tract announced, "set a proper value on the conveniencies and ornaments of civilized life; but detest that luxury which is the offspring of a frivolous taste, and the mother of profligacy, dishonesty, poverty—of numberless private and public vices and misfortunes."[61] Madison may well have been one of these "enlightened patriots," for the tract expressed many of his most basic concerns. It emphasized the distinction between an "oeconomical," natural, and beneficent trade on the one hand, and a licentious, debilitating "trade of luxury" on the other. No one could doubt that commerce was essential to civilized life, and that it would be foolish and impractical for modern men to attempt to turn back the clock by living in pure pastoral simplicity. Nevertheless, commerce had to be kept within "the bounds prescribed by nature," because an avaricious infatuation with speculation and the pursuit of easy wealth took men off the land, tempted them into frivolous and wasteful occupations, and produced a society geared to the enervating consumption of superfluities.[62] Indeed, if commerce was not kept within proper bounds, what resulted was precisely the inequality, servile dependency, and national weakness that Madison denounced in his "Fashion" essay and that he associated with Hamilton's system.

Madison did not object to plain and useful manufactures that prospered on their own, but from his perspective Hamilton was promoting something quite different: "artificial" forms of manufacturing that could not survive without government subsidy and special privilege. Because Madison was ideologically prone to interpret the secretary's system as part of a broader conspiracy to imitate British society, it is not surprising that he apparently feared a desire to bring to America the luxury manufactures, common to Europe, that he excoriated in "Fashion." After describing the sickening condition of England's buckle manufacturers, he appropriately invoked the traditional republican vision of America: "What a contrast is here to the independent situation and manly sentiments of American citizens, who live on their own soil, or whose labour is necessary to its cultivation, or who are occupied in supplying wants, which being founded in solid utility, in comfortable accommodation, or

61. *Of Commerce and Luxury* (Philadelphia, 1791), preface.
62. *Ibid.*, 2, 8, 11–12, 16.

in settled habits, produce a reciprocity of dependence, at once ensuring subsistence, and inspiring a dignified sense of social rights."[63]

By the close of the first session of the Second Congress in the spring of 1792, this ideological opposition to the emerging Hamiltonian system took on a bitter, at times hysterical, tone. Some of Hamilton's adversaries feared, in fact, that the Report on Manufactures would win legislative approval as quickly as had his previous reports.[64] The report left little doubt that the secretary was interested in the large-scale production of the advanced, "finer" manufactures, but whatever doubt existed was soon dispelled by his role in creating the Society for Establishing Useful Manufactures, a corporate enterprise chartered by the New Jersey legislature on November 22, 1791. Although the Society received its charter from a state legislature, its capital stock consisted largely of federal bonds (from the funded debt) and shares of the Bank of the United States. Furthermore, it was no secret that its promoters greatly desired additional assistance from the federal government. The Society had already received several impressive privileges and exemptions as part of its New Jersey charter, which alone were enough to provoke an outpouring of anti-monopoly outrage. To Hamilton as well as his enemies, the Society for Establishing Useful Manufactures was the Report on Manufactures put into practice.[65]

Hamilton's report had been unequivocal: the introduction of advanced manufactures in America would require extensive governmental encouragement, especially in view of the copious "bounties, premiums, and other artificial encouragements" that foreign governments extended to their manufacturers to give them a competitive edge.[66] John F. Amelung,

63. Hunt, ed., *Writings of Madison*, VI, 100.

64. George Logan noted, for example, that "experience justifies a belief, that the principles of this report will also be adopted, and will come forward under the sanction of the legislature in the form of a law." *Five Letters Addressed to the Yeomanry* (Philadelphia, 1792), Letter II.

65. Hamilton made an indirect reference to the Society for Establishing Useful Manufactures in the report when he announced that "measures are already in train for the prosecuting on a large scale, the making and printing of cotton goods." Syrett and Cooke, eds., *Hamilton Papers*, X, 328. The most thorough study of the Society and the ideological attacks on it is in Joseph Stancliffe Davis, *Essays in the Earlier History of American Corporations* (Cambridge, Mass., 1917), I, 349–522. See also Cooke, "Coxe, Hamilton, and American Manufactures," *WMQ*, 3d Ser., XXXII (1975), 380–392, and Cooke, *Tench Coxe*, chap. 9.

66. Davis, *History of American Corporations*, I, 363.

a German emigrant to America and an ambitious manufacturer, had earlier aired publicly this same point of view. In a passage guaranteed to make any straitlaced republican cringe, he had argued that "manufactures cannot subsist without particular necessary privileges." America must imitate Europe, where manufacturers customarily secured exemption from military service and taxation as well as loans from the public funds. As a further example, Amelung noted that in Europe, in the interest of assuring that the intricate "chain of business" would not be broken, factory laborers often could not be arrested or "taken to public services" without the consent of the owner, and, in the case of civil arrest, the owner was answerable for the worker.[67] Amelung's crude attempt to foster public support for manufactures was bound to misfire. To staunch republicans who would not tolerate special privilege, servile dependency, or the absence of equality before the law, his call for "necessary privileges" dramatically underlined the depravity of the European system of manufacturing.

Indeed, the New Jersey charter granted the Society many of the privileges Amelung described. Its employees were to be exempt from all taxes and from military duty except in emergencies. All "Lands, Tenements, Hereditaments, Goods and Chattels" belonging to the Society were also to be tax free for ten years. If that was not enough, the Society was also granted the right to raise money by lottery for its support and was given ample powers of eminent domain to aid construction of any necessary transportation facilities.[68] These privileges, the size of the enterprise (it was capitalized at one million dollars), and its close association with Hamilton and his circle of supporters elicited a vehement reaction, especially from small, "private" mechanics and manufacturers who feared they would be ruined by government-subsidized industries. How could the private manufacturer, who paid taxes and suffered losses without recourse to lotteries, hope to compete with the Society for Establishing Useful Manufactures? Like Madison, these opponents of the Society did not object to manufactures that were not forced or artificially supported by government, but in the Society they saw Hamilton's corrupt system of political economy extended into a new domain. "Under the

---

67. John Frederick Amelung, *Remarks on Manufactures* . . . (Frederick, Md., 1787), 7–8. For a discussion of Amelung's later lobbying efforts, see Johnson, *Foundations of American Economic Freedom*, 271, 275–277.

68. Davis, *History of American Corporations*, I, 383–387.

pretext of nurturing manufactures," wrote one critic, "a new field may be opened for favouritism, influence, and monopolies."[69] Now, it seemed, Hamilton's fawning favorites also included speculators who wanted to be the masters of American manufacturing houses modeled after those of the Old World.

Instead of viewing Hamilton's system as a forward-looking prospectus for economic growth, in short, these anguished republicans saw it as a blueprint for retrogression, as a falling away from the virtuous contours of the republican society that Franklin and the Revolutionaries had envisioned. For America to become like England was decay, not progress. The Society was, in effect, "planting a Birmingham and Manchester, amongst us," and this corporate monster was to be viewed more "as a production of the dark ages preceding the sixteenth century than of the present enlightened era."[70] Who could deny that the American republic was quickly slipping from freedom into slavery, thereby following the calamitous path of so many others that had gone before it? Such declension was especially tragic because it mocked the heartening portent of the French Revolution in Europe. The irony could hardly have been greater; at the very moment when the forces of reaction in Europe seemed to be tottering on the brink of collapse, they were gaining new life in America: "At a time when funding systems, excise laws, monopolies and exclusive privileges, have arrived at their last stage, and when the numerous evils flowing from them have come to a crisis, which seems to convulse Europe to its centre, and threatens to shake it to its foundations; instigated by a blind fatality altogether unaccountable, we seem to be treading in the very steps, and following the same paths, which has led the different nations of that quarter of the globe to their present alarming condition."[71] A crisis was at hand, with the fate of republicanism seeming to hang in the balance. By early 1794, opponents of the Hamiltonian system rallied behind Madison's final attempt to implement the cornerstone of his alternative system, a program of commercial discrimination.

69. *National Gazette* (Philadelphia), June 18, 1792. See also *ibid.*, Nov. 7, 1792; "Clitus," *General Advertiser* (Philadelphia), Nov. 24, 1791; "A Republican," *Dunlap's American Daily Advertiser* (Philadelphia), Feb. 4, 1792; Address of the president of the Germantown Society for Promoting Domestic Manufactures, *Gazette of the United States* (Philadelphia), Aug. 29, 1792; and Logan, *Five Letters*, esp. Letter III.

70. "A Mechanick," *Connecticut Courant* (Hartford), May 7, 1792, and "An Observer," *General Advertiser*, Jan. 7, 1792.

71. "Anti-Monopolist," *General Advertiser*, Jan. 23, 1792.

[IV]

The Report on Manufactures had done more than raise the specters of monopoly privilege and a federal government of unlimited power; it had directly challenged Madison's system of political economy by rejecting the theoretical basis for commercial discrimination. It followed from Hamilton's insistence that American access to foreign markets would continue to be severely limited by the immutable restrictions of European mercantilism that these markets would be increasingly insufficient for the absorption of the republic's agricultural surplus. This fact alone, he argued, pointed directly to the need for governmental assistance in the development of native manufactures and a more dependable home market. Such a program would foster a stronger, more balanced, sectionally interdependent economy: it would also gradually enhance American power to the point where a more mature United States might effectively contend for Madison's goal of commercial reciprocity.[72]

By denying the practicality of commercial coercion and concluding that America had no choice but to restructure its economy through the creation of publicly subsidized manufacturing enterprises, Hamilton put Madison in an increasingly precarious position; the secretary threatened to sustain the momentum of his earlier triumphs and consolidate a "system" that Madison thought antithetical to republicanism. The Virginian's counterattack came in January 1794, on the heels of Secretary of State Thomas Jefferson's Report on Commerce. Madison attempted to exploit a growing diplomatic crisis with Great Britain (occasioned by the wars of the French Revolution) by reviving his program of commercial discrimination, and the timing seemed perfect. There was universal outrage among Americans about renewed British violence against American vessels, and an already weak Britain appeared to be bogged down in an expensive military conflict that threatened once and for all, according to fervent republicans, to topple its precarious system of perpetual debt,

---

72. Miller, *Alexander Hamilton*, 292–295, 301. See also the conclusion of a speech written by Hamilton and delivered to Congress by William Loughton Smith in early 1794. *Annals of Congress*, 3d Cong., 1st sess., IV, 208. For typical statements of the home market argument by supporters of Hamilton, see, *Gazette of the United States* (Philadelphia), Jan. 18, 1792, and "Detector," *National Gazette* (Philadelphia), Sept. 8, 1792. The latter asked: "What would be the difference to the farmers, at this very moment, when their surplus productions are shut out of every port of Europe, by bad markets, if the country abounded in mechanics and manufacturers, to consume that surplus, and give in exchange the pro-

taxation, and war.[73] Madison's resolutions touched off a momentous congressional debate, in which Representative William Loughton Smith of South Carolina led the opposition to discrimination in a brilliant, day-long speech that Hamilton had assisted him in preparing. Echoing the message of the Report on Manufactures, Smith ridiculed "the impracticability and Quixotism of an attempt by violence, on the part of this young country, to break through the fetters which the universal policy of nations imposes on their intercourse with each other."[74]

As usual, Madison vigorously disputed this Hamiltonian argument, for he still believed that precisely because of its youth America would be strong enough to overcome this "universal policy." He was anxious, more than ever, to demonstrate that the young republic's "natural" economic power could shatter Old World mercantilist restrictions— restrictions that reinforced the Hamiltonian system not only by tying the American economy tightly to British credit and capital, but also by substantiating the secretary's claim that the United States was, by necessity, limited in its ability to extend its foreign commerce. In the realm of political economy, Madison's aim was not to stimulate American manufactures—at least not the type Hamilton wished to promote—but rather to undercut the crucial assumption behind Hamilton's prospectus for industrial development and to ensure the opening of adequate foreign markets for America's agricultural surplus. He hoped that the success of commercial discrimination would encourage further westward expansion and also preserve the virtuous character of America's farmers by assuring them a vent for their republican industry. In a broader sense, the policy's success would secure the institutional and moral base for a republican political economy by staving off, for as long as possible, America's advance into the more dangerous stage of social development described by Hamilton in the Report on Manufactures. Viewed in this context, commercial discrimination supported Madison's endeavor to preserve and expand across space the youthful, predominantly agricultural character of American society.[75] Just as Hamilton had done, in short, Madison

---

ductions of their labor, instead of the foreign articles which now render us tributary to foreign workmen?"

73. See, especially, Peterson, "Jefferson and Commercial Policy," *WMQ*, 3d Ser., XXII (1965), 584–610.

74. *Annals of Congress*, 3d Cong., 1st sess., IV, 196. For the whole debate see *ibid.*, 155*ff*. For a secondary account see, among many others, Varg, *Foreign Policies*, 99–101.

75. See above, chaps. 2, 3, and 5.

presented a coherent "system" in which his foreign policy objectives were integrally related to his approach to economic development and his vision of a future America.

The upshot of the 1794 crisis was a stunning defeat of the Madisonian system. Discrimination was never implemented, and the famous treaty that resulted from John Jay's mission to London consummated Hamilton's triumph, for that treaty explicitly bound the United States to a renunciation of discrimination for at least ten years. Madison and his Republican allies were horrified by this turn of events. Now the United States was tied even more closely to the nation that was attempting to smother the flames of republicanism on the European continent. The Jay Treaty marked, for these Republicans, a strengthening of the British "connection" that threatened ever more seriously to corrupt American government and society.[76] Indeed, America's "funding gentry," and not the American people, were served by this reconciliation with "the old, corrupt, and almost expiring government of Great Britain."[77] Referring to the Society for Establishing Useful Manufactures, one Republican cynically asked why the treaty was toasted "in the little circle of English manufacturers, on the banks of the Passayik."[78] Such a slavish submission to England marked an ominous decline of the republican spirit in America, offering a depressing contrast to the manly vigilance exhibited twenty years earlier: "Were our energies greater at the commencement of the late revolution, than they are now! Or have we become more corrupt? This is the rub, fellow citizens—the instrumentality of a *funding system*, aided by *British influence*, and directed by another Walpole, had not then enervated us. We were strangers to corruption, and principle incited us to the maintenance of our rights."[79] To these Republicans, the Jay Treaty was the fitting culmination of an American Walpole's plot to overturn the Revolution by fashioning a "corrupt, degenerate, and sinking" government and society similar to England's.[80]

But though the Hamiltonian system was victorious for the moment, its triumph was not without setbacks and ironies. By 1795 the Society for Establishing Useful Manufactures was defunct; its operations ceased

76. Banning, *Jeffersonian Persuasion*, chap. 8.

77. Caius, "Address to the President of the United States," July 21, 1795, printed in *The American Remembrancer* . . . (Philadelphia, 1795), 112, 106–114.

78. [Alexander James Dallas], *Features of Mr. Jay's Treaty* (Philadelphia, 1795), 25.

79. "Atticus," *American Remembrancer*, 68.

80. Lexington (Kentucky) Resolutions, *ibid.*, 270.

completely, and Paterson became a virtual "ghost town."[81] The colossal failure of this project thwarted Hamilton's desire to introduce this type of large-scale manufacturing rapidly into America. The reasons for the collapse of the Society were several, among them poor management and the absence of a skilled and disciplined labor force, but rapidly changing international conditions had much to do with the abortive effort to implement the Report on Manufactures. The European demand for American produce and raw materials, instead of diminishing as Hamilton had predicted, mushroomed to unprecedented heights after the outbreak of the wars of the French Revolution in early 1792. One historian has suggested that 1793 marked a turning point in the development of the American economy, for it "brought an end to the era that gave birth to the Constitution and the Federalist program," an era when inadequate foreign markets had cramped American exports and given rise both to conditions and ideas favoring the introduction of large-scale industry to America. This era ended when a change in international conditions made it most profitable for Americans to export produce, supply raw materials, and perform shipping services.[82]

Appropriately, the emphasis in the Federalist system gradually shifted from developing manufactures to reaping the profits of a burgeoning foreign commerce. Since Hamilton's program was geared to the accumulation and mobilization of capital, it required no major alterations to accomplish the transition. This capital, primarily in the form of government securities from the funded debt, could just as easily be channeled into commerce as industry.[83] Thus the short-lived but heated discussion about manufactures in the early 1790s had no major immediate policy repercussions; it did lay the basis, however, for a renewal of debate on this issue during the Jefferson and Madison presidencies.[84] In spite of domestic political chaos and a deepening, potentially dangerous involvement in European affairs, America entered the second half of the 1790s riding the wave of an unexampled and invigorating prosperity tied to the proliferation of its foreign commerce in a tumultuous era of international conflict.

81. Miller, *Alexander Hamilton*, 309–310, and Davis, *History of American Corporations*, I, 495–503.

82. Curtis P. Nettels, *The Emergence of a National Economy, 1775–1815* (New York, 1962), 125–126.

83. *Ibid.*

84. See chap. 9 of the present study.

CHAPTER SEVEN

"ONE GREAT COMMERCIAL REPUBLIC": COMMERCE, BANKRUPTCY, AND THE CRISIS OF THE NINETIES

Between the outbreak of the Anglo-French war in 1793 and the brief interlude of peace following the Treaty of Amiens in 1801, the expansion of American commerce fueled a vigorous, if precarious, prosperity. The dramatic growth of the re-export and carrying trades reflected America's advantages as a neutral in a world of belligerent maritime powers. Whereas the value of American domestic exports more than tripled during this period, earnings from the carrying trade nearly quadrupled, and the value of re-exports increased from approximately one million dollars in 1792 to almost fifty million in 1800.[1] This prosperity was precarious because it was spawned by exceptional circumstances and was enjoyed only at the expense of almost continual conflict with the major belligerents. Besides provoking a dangerous crisis in American politics and diplomacy, the commercial expansion of the 1790s sparked renewed debate over political economy. More seriously than ever, perhaps, Americans pondered the implications that commercialization and social progress held for the health of the republic.[2]

A concern with the nature and meaning of America's sudden pros-

1. Douglass C. North, *The Economic Growth of the United States, 1790–1860* (New York, 1961), 36–38, 221, 249.

2. See above, chaps. 1 and 2. Historians have generally ignored this dimension of the crisis of the 1790s, focusing their attention instead on the political and diplomatic developments of the decade. For an introduction to the politics and diplomacy of the late 1790s, see especially Stephen G. Kurtz, *The Presidency of John Adams* (Philadelphia, 1957), and Alexander DeConde, *The Quasi-War: The Politics and Diplomacy of the Undeclared War with France, 1797–1801* (New York, 1966).

perity arose as early as 1795 and 1796. Although many observers were quick to attribute their country's good fortune to the salutary influence of republican institutions, fears about the potentially corrupting effects of economic growth persisted. Americans were conscious of their society's apparent movement into a more complex stage of development, and they continued to take quite different views of the implications and significance of this process. By the late 1790s, an intensely partisan division within political economy surfaced in heated debates over issues such as the proposed naval protection of America's newfound carrying trade and the need for a national system of bankruptcy legislation. The bankruptcy debate was particularly revealing; it not only reflected the Federalist vision of America as an advanced commercial republic, but it also sharpened Republican anxiety about the rapid commercialization of American society. By the election of 1800, Jefferson and his supporters saw themselves engaged in a crusade to halt an unnecessary, deviously enforced "Anglicization" of American government and society. This process, they believed, would undermine the productivity and moral integrity of a republican citizenry, in part through the type of legal innovation represented in the bankruptcy act of that year.

[I]

Despite the intense political strife of the mid-1790s, Americans generally agreed that their country was experiencing an invigorating prosperity that reflected to a great extent the beneficence of their republican institutions. Few of them disputed, for example, the interdependence of republicanism and prosperity. The exceptional international conditions that underwrote America's economic growth did not, of course, go unrecognized. A Massachusetts minister predicted in 1795 that "the present plenty of money" and "the present extraordinary demand for all which we can supply foreign countries" would soon cease.[3] Nevertheless, many observers were confident that the basis for America's prosperity extended beyond a temporary profiting from Europe's distress, that the current boom portended, in short, a continued growth predicated on the solid rock of republican freedom. Americans stressed without hesitation and

3. Thomas Barnard, *A Sermon, Delivered on the Day of National Thanksgiving* . . . (Salem, Mass., 1795), 19.

with great pride the importance of their free institutions for molding an industrious and moral people capable of responding to the opportunities suddenly presented by European turmoil.

America's rapid growth to prosperity, contended Thomas Tudor Tucker, a South Carolina physician and congressman, had to be ascribed to its true cause, "the wholesome operation of our new political philosophy."[4] The Revolutionary separation from a corrupt and mercantilist Britain had laid the basis for a flourishing republican civilization. The key to this progress was the republican principle that every man was secure in his property, retaining a right to the fruits of his honest industry, a freedom that encouraged Americans to be industrious, productive, and hence virtuous.[5] The contrast with European countries still trapped in monarchy and mercantilism was striking. In countries with absolute governments, Americans arrogantly argued, the people were generally lazy, cowardly, turbulent, vicious, and poor; in republican societies they were active, brave, orderly, public-spirited, and prosperous. American success was a direct result of the absence of mercantilist restrictions on individual and national industry. In corrupt countries the people were lazy and dissolute because their property was extorted by a privileged, idle elite, but in America, even with Hamilton's system, the national wealth was never unjustly appropriated in massive sums as "revenue" as it was in the degenerate societies of the Old World. In a discourse delivered in Boston in early 1795, David Osgood proudly contrasted the glorious American experiment in popular government with the machinations of "arbitrary rulers, in every country, appropriating to themselves, under the name of revenues, the national wealth—revelling on the hard earnings of publick industry, and nourishing their luxury, pride, pomp and glory with the tears of general misery."[6] The vicious social inequality promoted by this

4. Thomas Tudor Tucker, *An Oration Delivered in St. Michael's Church* . . . (Charleston, S.C., 1795), 14.

5. See above, chap. 2.

6. David Osgood, *A Discourse Delivered February 19, 1795* . . . (Boston, 1795), 13–14. See also Samuel E. M'Corkle, *A Sermon, on the Comparative Happiness and Duty of the United States* (Halifax, N.C., 1795), 37; John Jones Spooner, *A Discourse . . . July 4th, 1794* (Petersburg, Va., 1795); Samuel Miller, *A Sermon, Delivered in the New Presbyterian Church* . . . (New York, 1795); William White, *A Sermon, on the Reciprocal Influence* . . . (Philadelphia, 1795); William Hunter, *An Oration, Delivered in the Baptist Meeting House* . . . (Newport, R.I., 1795); John Tyler, *The Blessings of Peace* (Norwich, Conn., 1795); and Joseph Barnes, *Treatise on the Justice, Policy, and Utility* . . . (Philadelphia, 1792). For

mercantilist system had been replaced in America by a more moderate, necessary, and just inequality that developed naturally from the exercise of each individual's equal right to reap the rewards of his labor. Such a republican order produced "a beautiful system of mutual dependencies" in the context of a burgeoning national prosperity.[7]

American ministers, orators, and statesmen, no matter what their partisan stance, stressed again and again this crucial interdependence of republicanism, public morality and industry, and national prosperity. Everyone could agree that the principle of security of property was the cornerstone of a republican political economy, since its protection encouraged the individual exertion and industry that promoted economic growth and civilized progress. These assumptions were vigorously expressed in 1792, for example, in Dr. John A. DeNormandie's analysis of the potential impact of the republican revolutions in Europe on the United States. DeNormandie, president of the Burlington County Society for Promoting Agriculture and Domestic Manufactures, suggested that American agriculture was overly dependent on "precarious foreign markets" that were bound to diminish as the spirit of liberty spread in Europe. "For as property in every country where liberty prevails, is secured to the cultivator and possessor," he noted, referring to recent developments in Europe, "they now have every stimulus that can excite them to industry, and increasing their agricultural productions." Countries with absolute governments often could not feed themselves, but this tragedy had nothing to do with natural inadequacies of soil or climate. France was a good example:

France, a country blest in the goodness of its soil, and a temperate climate, under the administration of its former tyrannical government, seldom was able to furnish its inhabitants with bread; but hereafter, we must expect grain will be raised, not only sufficient for their own consumption, but to supply foreign markets; as the deficiency did not arise from any sterility in the soil, or an unfavorable climate, but from exorbitant taxes, together with overbearing and greedy landlords, and a rapacious clergy, who amongst them, swept away the whole produce of the poor peasant's industry.

---

an earlier discussion of many of these same ideas during the ratification debates of 1787–1788, see the "Letters of Agrippa," in Paul Leicester Ford, ed., *Essays on the Constitution of the United States* . . . (Brooklyn, N.Y., 1892), esp. 54–55 and 109.

7. Tucker, *Oration*, 21.

Poland likewise was being "emancipated from its slavery, and from the same cause (that of enjoying the fruits of their own labor) the farmers will undoubtedly encrease the quantity formerly raised for exportation." Thus as republican principles spread to Europe, American farmers would face much stiffer competition in many of their customary markets, and DeNormandie concluded that it would be necessary to diversify the republic's economy away from its present emphasis on exporting an agricultural surplus.[8] Not all of DeNormandie's countrymen followed his reasoning to this particular conclusion; but his fundamental assumption that republican government, increased productivity, and economic prosperity were closely intertwined, both in the United States and in the foreign countries following its example, reflected at least a rudimentary national consensus in political economy.

Many Americans saw in the economic boom of the 1790s evidence of the republic's progress through the familiar stages of social development. "The present state of society in America," Samuel Whiting noted in 1796, "seems to be a fair medium between the rudeness of aboriginal simplicity, and the effeminacy and luxury which always mark the advanced stages of civil refinement." This intermediate stage was one "in which the virtues of hospitality, temperance, industry and oeconomy delight to dwell, and which, from its characteristic spirit of enterprise, exertion and vigour, is most favourable to the cultivation of the useful arts and sciences."[9] Voicing a traditional belief in the cyclical pattern of social growth and decay, Whiting characteristically preferred this middle stage to either undesirable extreme. "It has been said indeed," concurred Samuel West in 1795, "that as in nature there is a regular progress, increase, and decline, so nations have their helpless infancy, active youth, vigorous manhood and feeble old age, followed with inevitable dissolution."[10]

West and other commentators, however, went on to qualify this familiar analogy between national life and natural decline, exuding a brimming confidence in American progress. Although nature was governed by fixed laws "agreeable to which changes take place with inevitable necessity"—laws over which men could exercise no final control—the

8. DeNormandie's address is printed in the *Independent Gazetteer, and Agricultural Repository* (Philadelphia), Aug. 18, 1792.

9. Samuel Whiting, *An Oration . . . at Sheffield, July 4th, 1796* (Stockbridge, Mass., 1796), 9–10.

10. Samuel West, *A Sermon, Delivered upon the late National Thanksgiving* (Boston, 1795), 11.

fate of nations depended strictly on moral causes that were subject to regulation by men. The decay and "death" of a state were connected to its duration only by the pride, luxury, and immorality that advancing age brought with it; if these diseases could be stamped out, even an old, advanced nation might escape ruin.[11] Buoyed by the prosperity of the 1790s, some Americans occasionally flirted with just such a vision of virtually endless progress toward perfection. After citing the traditional metaphor of cyclical growth and decay, Thomas Barnard, a minister from Salem, Massachusetts, suggested that the United States might well be able to repeal the law of inevitable dissolution by becoming prosperous and powerful without becoming luxurious. "Let us convince the world, if possible," he exhorted his listeners, "that societies founded in wisdom, and trained up with discretion, may avoid the evils which have heretofore ruined the most celebrated nations which have existed."[12] America was making rapid progress; perhaps it might continue to develop and yet escape the corruption normally expected to accompany this social maturation.

Most Americans were also aware, however, that their present prosperity was grounded on the sudden expansion of foreign commerce, and this recognition evoked a hesitant skepticism about the country's future just as often as it elicited the dynamic confidence of optimists who talked of repealing the law of inevitable decay. This traditionally ambivalent view of commerce as a source of both civilization and corruption persisted throughout the 1790s.[13] Although defenders of commercial development continued to denigrate "those who think rudeness and ignorance essentially connected with virtue," and insisted that "encomiums too great cannot be lavished on Commerce," many of them also noted the dangers and evils of an expanding commerce.[14] Luxury, licentiousness,

11. *Ibid.*, 12.

12. Barnard, *Sermon*, 21–23. For an interesting discussion of the religious context of this optimism about America's social progress, see Ernest Lee Tuveson, *Redeemer Nation: The Idea of America's Millennial Role* (Chicago, 1968), chap. 4, esp. 109–110. See also John E. Crowley, "Classical and Other Traditions for the Understanding of Change in Post-Revolutionary America: The Idea of Decline," in John W. Eadie, ed., *Classical Traditions in Early America* (Ann Arbor, Mich., 1976), 213–253.

13. See above, chaps. 1 and 3.

14. Samuel Stanhope Smith, *The Divine Goodness to the United States . . .* , 2d ed. (Philadelphia, 1795), 21, and Jonathan Maxcy, *An Oration, Delivered before the Providence Association of Mechanics and Manufacturers* (Providence, R.I., 1795), 8–9.

and restless disorder too often accompanied commercial success unless precautions were taken to guard against the "arrogance of prosperity."[15] Many Americans feared that prosperity would loosen necessary social restraints and unleash a multitude of devastating vices. "Continued prosperity," Samuel Deane predicted in 1795, "is apt to bring political evils in its train; such as luxury and idleness, dissipation and extravagant expenses; which tend to, and end in, wretchedness and ruin."[16] Perhaps the strongest anxiety in this regard was that a booming prosperity would unleash a destructive spirit of speculation among the American people, a spirit that would upset the republican rhythm of economic life and promote social turbulence. This concern that a republican people might be tempted into ruin by "vain Speculations, imprudent and unfortunate Enterprises, and by very delusive Pursuits" intensified during the course of the 1790s, especially among opponents of the Federalist administrations who continued to accuse the national government of willfully and directly encouraging this calamity.[17]

Most Republicans, of course, traced the problem back to Hamilton's "system," which had first excited this spirit of destructive speculation. In 1792, James Sullivan argued in *The Path to Riches* that a distinction had to be made between an honorable spirit of commercial enterprise and the evils of avaricious speculation. Men naturally thirsted for wealth and

15. John Mitchell Mason, *Mercy Remembered in Wrath* (New York, 1795), 29. See also Phinehas Hedges, *An Oration, Delivered before the Republican Society* (Goshen, N.Y., 1795), esp. 11; Ezra Sampson, *A Discourse Delivered February 19, 1795 . . .* (Boston, 1795), esp. 12–20; and Thomas Thacher, *A Discourse, Delivered at the Third Parish in Dedham, 19th February, 1795* (Boston, 1795), 17.

16. Samuel Deane, *A Sermon Preached February 19th, 1795 . . .* (Portland, Mass., 1795), 19. To staunch New England Federalists, even the rioting and public disorder of the opponents of the Jay Treaty reflected the intoxicating licentiousness that could be induced by a rapid accumulation of wealth in a dynamically prosperous society. See, for example, David Osgood, *A Discourse Delivered on the Day of Annual Thanksgiving, November 19, 1795* (Boston, 1795), and Jonathan Strong, *A Sermon Delivered on the Day of the Annual Thanksgiving* (Boston, 1795).

17. Tyler, *Blessings of Peace*, 11. Although this fear was strongest among opponents of Federalism, some supporters of Hamilton and the Washington administrations shared it, in part because they saw the rewards of a speculative economy accruing to the wrong elements in society. See, for example, Henry Ware, *The Continuance of Peace* (Boston, 1795), 20–25. Ware insisted that it was necessary for government to hold up "as few objects of speculation as possible, which serve to discourage the exertions of patient industry, by enabling enterprising individuals, and often the least useful members of the community, to acquire large fortunes without industry, and without pursuing any regular business." *Ibid.*, 24–25.

comfort, and they had a right to acquire as much property as their honest industry would earn. All too often, however, men desired to gain without producing, by gambling, speculating, and manipulating. Such avarice was immoral, dishonorable, and socially dangerous. It encouraged men to expect rewards without the appropriate effort, excited a pernicious spirit of envy in the rest of the community, and, above all, tempted men away from useful, productive occupations like agriculture into idle and unproductive pursuits. Sullivan explained the attraction of these delusive pursuits by pointing to the weakness of human nature:

Mankind have a natural disinclination to labor and exertion. In a state of nature, hunger is a stimulous to the savage, or he would continue idle and inactive. In society, ambition, that natural, and avarice, that artificial passion, urge men to exertion; but nevertheless, labor is irksome, and all they who can devise some other method of gratifying their inclinations, and obeying the commands of their passions, will most certainly do it: hence it is, that we find every one, who can drive a bargain to advantage, forsaking the plough to do it.[18]

When permitted to flourish, this desire to profit without labor and industry, and especially the tendency to discourage steady industry in agriculture, ruined a society by corrupting its moral character and undermining its productive capacity. Most commentators, indeed, focused their attention on the neglect of agriculture occasioned by the feverish, unrepublican infatuation with speculation and quick profit that seemed to accompany the rapid commercialization of American society in the 1790s.

America's prosperity, Joseph Lathrop warned in 1795, must not be built on "an unbounded commerce." Although essential to industry and civilization, commerce became dangerous when carried to an extreme. "Commerce is, indeed, useful, and in some degree necessary to civilized and refined nations. This brings many conveniences, which cannot otherwise be obtained. It contributes to the increase of knowledge and the improvement of arts. It humanizes the manners, gives spirit to industry, and a spring to enterprize. But when it becomes the principal object, it is dangerous to a people. Carried to excess, it supplants more necessary occupations." Lathrop made it clear that agriculture was the most "necessary occupation." "That kind of wealth . . . is the most valuable,"

---

18. [James Sullivan], *The Path to Riches* (Boston, 1792), 43. See also, 5–6.

he observed, referring to the rewards of agricultural labor, because it "is immediately adapted to human use, affords necessary supplies for every member of society, prompts to general industry, yields the fewest temptations to vice, and is, in a competent degree, attainable by men of all conditions."[19] If America was to remain an orderly, just, and prosperous society, commerce would have to continue to subserve agriculture. As Samuel M'Corkle, a North Carolina minister, noted in 1795, some degree of commerce was necessary to maintain a spirited agriculture, but agriculture always had to remain the "principal object" of men's attention so it would "become the parent of commerce" and "hold her progeny in proper subjection." There was little doubt that when commerce exceeded its proper bounds, it ceased to nourish agriculture or wholesome industry and threatened instead to undermine and replace them with a ruinous spirit of speculative avarice.[20]

The fear that the commercialization of American society was spiraling out of control grew more pronounced by the late 1790s. As the French attacked America's mushrooming foreign trade, John Adams's administration advocated determined action, including rapid naval expansion, to ensure the protection of the country's burgeoning commerce. Opponents of the Federalists took vigorous exception to this proposal for a stronger navy, in large part because they opposed in principle certain aspects of the republic's recent commercial growth. Above all, these Republicans feared that America was developing a dangerously unbalanced political economy, one that was thoroughly at odds with the pattern of "natural" development. Directing their fire at the country's rapidly expanding carrying trade—the sector of American commerce that involved the transportation of goods neither produced nor consumed within the United States—they insisted that the protection of this commerce did not justify the expense and danger of a large navy. In early 1800 Jefferson, speaking of Federalist ambitions, lamented that "we are running navigation mad, and commerce mad, and navy mad, which is worst of all."[21] By the election of that year, he and his supporters had developed a coherent

19. Joseph Lathrop, *National Happiness, Illustrated in a Sermon* . . . (Springfield, Mass., 1795), 12–13.

20. M'Corkle, *Sermon*, 37, 35–37. See also, Pitt Clarke, *On the Rise and Signalized Lot* . . . (Boston, 1795), 24–26.

21. Jefferson to Joseph Priestley, Jan. 18, 1800, in Paul Leicester Ford, ed., *The Writings of Thomas Jefferson* (New York, 1892–1899), VII, 406.

public rationale for opposing the further extension and protection of certain forms of American commerce.

The Republican analysis closely paralleled Adam Smith's discussion in the *Wealth of Nations* of commerce and the "natural" order of economic development. Smith insisted that agriculture was the most advantageous and productive way for any society to employ its capital because, simply stated, in agriculture "nature labours along with men."[22] Ideally, he argued, no capital should be invested in commerce or manufacturing until a country's agriculture is fully developed. Smith also denoted several different types of commerce, again with a definite hierarchy of value and benefit. The carrying trade was the least productive and profitable, he contended, because it returned only freighting and shipping profits to the native country. Smith concluded that no country should force or allure more capital into this carrying trade than would naturally flow into it. When capital became superabundant in a fully mature, developed society, it should naturally disgorge itself into the carrying trade, but not before then. The gist of Smith's treatise was that in Europe this natural sequence of capital development had been entirely inverted by the pernicious interference of mercantilist ideas and policies, which was dramatically reflected in a misguided obsession with cultivating foreign commerce, especially the carrying trade. For a young, land-rich, and relatively undeveloped country like the United States to follow the same course would only be, from Smith's perspective, a tragic perversion of nature and good sense.[23]

During debates over the augmentation of the American navy in 1799, Albert Gallatin, the leading congressional opponent of the Federalist administration, argued that American commerce was already dangerously and unnaturally overextended. He contended that agriculture and commerce were naturally connected only when commerce directly encouraged agriculture; more than half of America's present foreign commerce, however, involved neither the exportation of native produce nor the importation of articles consumed in exchange for that produce. To this extent, America's carrying trade constituted "a sort of extraneous staple" that was hardly crucial to national prosperity. And since only the profits of a few merchants were at stake in this commerce, its protec-

22. Adam Smith, *An Inquiry into the Nature and Causes of the Wealth of Nations*, ed. Edwin Cannan (New York, 1937 [orig. publ. London, 1776]), 344–345.
23. *Ibid.*, 341–360.

tion did not justify the expense of a large navy.[24] Gallatin's practical argument typified Republican opposition to Federalist programs of the late 1790s. More formal statements, particularly in articles on "Political Arithmetic" by Thomas Cooper and Joseph Priestley, more fully developed the ideological context of this opposition to the carrying trade.[25]

Writing in 1799, Cooper remarked that America seemed determined to be a commercial country. In objection to this, he went on to argue that "until the home territory of a country be well cultivated and peopled," foreign commerce must be of secondary concern.[26] Cooper embraced Smith's argument that American capital could be more beneficially and productively invested in agriculture and in the "home trade" than in an overextended carrying trade. He urged, in this regard, that more emphasis be placed on increasing the productive, rather than the speculative and comparatively unproductive, employments in American society. According to Cooper, America suffered from a plethora of merchants rushing to engage in speculative ventures like the wartime carrying trade, and he further analyzed the impact of this trend on the republic's moral character and stability. By "the labours of agriculture," he asserted, "gains can be made but slowly, gradually and by the regular exertions of habitual, wholesome industry." The commercial speculator, on the other hand, "often gets rich by accident, by imprudent and unfair venturing, by sudden exertions. Wealth thus suddenly obtained, is, in many respects, detrimental to the community. It operates as a lottery; it tempts capital into trade beyond prudent bounds; it entices to unjustifiable boldness; it too often introduces ostentatious luxury, not warranted by the sober dictates of moderate and regular gains."[27]

A highly speculative economy, in short, upset the proper rhythm of economic life and disrupted the rational, equitable, and republican system of distributing rewards and benefits. The Jeffersonians were greatly concerned with the mode and tempo of acquiring wealth, and they argued that America's political economy was becoming dangerously unbalanced and unstable. By demanding protection for an overextended foreign

24. *Annals of Congress*, 5th Cong., 3d sess., IX, 2860–2861. See also Alexander Balinky, *Albert Gallatin: Fiscal Theories and Policies* (New Brunswick, N.J., 1958), 71–76.

25. See Dumas Malone, *The Public Life of Thomas Cooper, 1783–1839* (New Haven, Conn., 1926), 98.

26. Cooper's essay was reprinted in the *Emporium of Arts and Sciences*, N.S., No. 1 (June 1813), 164–179. See p. 165.

27. *Ibid.*, 173–174.

commerce, the Federalists threatened to exacerbate the unwholesome speculative spirit that fueled such precarious ventures as the premature expansion of America's carrying trade. Cooper concluded that although foreign commerce was always an important component in a republican economy, especially in its stimulation of agriculture, no governmental protection should be extended to highly speculative ventures or to the investment of capital beyond its natural and legitimate bounds. "If any profession is to be fostered," he concluded, "let it be the tiller of the earth: the fountain-head of all wealth, of all power, and all prosperity."[28]

Cooper's sentiments were echoed in the late 1790s by scores of Jeffersonians, including Joseph Priestley, who wrote in the *National Magazine* under the name of "A Back-Country Farmer." Priestley argued that the only part of America's commerce in serious danger from foreign attack was the carrying trade, whose importance hardly warranted the expense of a large navy. Since the carrying trade was conducted largely by agents of the British, an expanded navy would serve only to protect their speculative profits, not any crucial American commerce. Like Cooper and Gallatin, Priestley identified the core of America's commerce as the exportation of domestically produced "necessaries," a commerce that did not demand any extraordinary protection because its importance to foreigners ensured a fairly dependable and safe access to market. "What fashion is there," he asked, "in a bushel of wheat or a cask of flour?" Using James Madison's favorite example, Priestley contrasted American exports with "the plated candlesticks, or buckles, of Birmingham, and the velvets and muslins of Manchester," British superfluities that required "forced markets" because of their artificial, luxurious, and fashionable nature.[29] The implication was clear—only unnatural, adventitious economic ventures, whether they were luxury manufactures or a premature carrying trade, demanded the kind of extensive protection from government that the Federalists sought for American "commerce," a protection that could not be justified by republican standards. A truly republican political economy, the Jeffersonians contended, included neither an over-

28. *Ibid.*, 178–179. For a discussion of the persistence of a republican concern with the mode and tempo of acquiring wealth, see Marvin Meyers, *The Jacksonian Persuasion: Politics and Belief* (Stanford, Calif., 1957), esp. 18–24, and Fred Somkin, *Unquiet Eagle: Memory and Desire in the Idea of American Freedom, 1815–1860* (Ithaca, N.Y., 1967).

29. *National Magazine*, II, No. 5 (1800), 7–8. For the reference to Madison, see above, chap. 6. See also Abraham Bishop, *Connecticut Republicanism . . .* (New Haven, Conn., 1800), esp. 3.

extended commerce that was unrelated to the health and prosperity of the mass of republican producers nor a naval system that would, in defending such a commerce, threaten to embroil the United States in unnecessary, expensive, and potentially corrupting wars with the mercantilist powers of Europe.

[II]

A contemporaneous debate over the need for national bankruptcy legislation was intimately related to many of the concerns of the 1790s. It provided a focus for the clash between predominantly Federalist optimism about America's advance to a higher stage of social development and Jeffersonian fears about the republic becoming a corrupt and over-commercialized society. By 1800, bankruptcy had become an intensely partisan issue, and to a great extent the opposing viewpoints were shaped by different answers to some of the most fundamental questions in political economy that Americans had now pondered for three decades; in particular, those questions concerned which stage or stages of social development were most conducive to republicanism, and which stage actually corresponded to America's present condition. Americans had to decide if they had, or wanted to have, the kind of economy and society that required a more modern legal order, including the national bankruptcy system advocated by Federalists in the 1790s.[30]

When the dramatic economic growth of the 1790s generated an impetus for legal reform, bankruptcy logically became a central issue of debate. Several members of Congress and of the American mercantile community saw a need for the creation of a legal environment conducive to the prosperity of a flourishing commercial republic. In the words of James A. Bayard, the leading proponent of a national bankruptcy law,

---

30. See above, chap. 1. The bankruptcy debate of the 1790s has received very little attention from historians. For appropriate secondary discussions, see: Charles Warren, *Bankruptcy in United States History* (Cambridge, Mass., 1935), 3–22; Peter J. Coleman, *Debtors and Creditors in America: Insolvency, Imprisonment for Debt, and Bankruptcy, 1607–1900* (Madison, Wis., 1974), chap. 1 and 269–293; Morton Borden, *The Federalism of James A. Bayard* (New York, 1955), chap. 6; Kathryn Turner, "Federalist Policy and the Judiciary Act of 1801," *William and Mary Quarterly*, 3d Ser., XXII (1965), 3–32, esp. 10–11; and especially Charles R. Morgan, "The Legal Origins of the Bankruptcy Act of 1800" (M.A. thesis, University of Virginia, 1973).

the United States collectively formed "one great commercial Republic," and appropriate legal institutions had to be devised.[31] A bankruptcy law would support mercantile credit while facilitating the financial risk taking necessary in an advanced commercial society. A national law would ensure uniformity from state to state, which would further encourage merchants in their expansion of America's trade.

Bankruptcy in its modern form was a relatively new principle in English law. It applied only to merchants and traders, providing a procedure whereby those who had been devastated through accident, misfortune, and the like, rather than as a result of fraudulence, might settle with their creditors, discharge their debts, avoid being sent to prison, and thus have a chance for a fresh start. Modern bankruptcy, especially in its provision for the cancellation of all future obligations of the bankrupt, was a serious departure from traditional insolvency. The bankruptcy principle signified, above all, an acceptance of the instability and uncertainty of economic life that were inevitable in a modern world of commercial complexity. Falling into debt would no longer be considered as a punishable sign of moral turpitude, but rather as an unavoidable part of a business world in which merchants were forced to cope with the natural vicissitudes of trade. Proponents of an effective bankruptcy system in America contended that such legislation was necessary in an advanced commercial society, both to protect non-fraudulent debtors and creditors and to encourage the speculative extension of credit that fueled commercial growth.[32]

The Constitution granted Congress the power to legislate on bankruptcy, but although bills were introduced several times in the early 1790s, it did not become a serious issue until after 1797.[33] Bayard, a Federalist congressman from Delaware, became the leading and most articulate spokesman for the cause. He defended the need for a law modeled after the British bankruptcy statutes by asserting that America had reached a stage of social development comparable to England's. A bankruptcy law becomes necessary, he stated,

wherever a nation is in any considerable degree commercial. No commercial people can be well governed without it. Wherever there is an extensive com-

---

31. *Annals of Congress*, 7th Cong., 2d sess., XII, 549.
32. See especially, Morgan, "Legal Origins," chaps. 1 and 2.
33. Warren, *Bankruptcy*, 11–12.

merce, extensive credits must necessarily be given. Debts of great magnitude must be contracted; and the most honest and prudent man may, by accidents and misfortunes incident to commerce, be deprived of the means of making good his engagements. In a state of society, chiefly agricultural, a bankrupt system is not wanted, because credits of so great an extent are not given, nor are persons engaged in pursuits liable to so many unforeseen accidents.

The honest debtor in modern commercial society, Bayard stressed, must be given an opportunity "to begin the world anew" by reestablishing a "motive for industry or frugality."[34] Another congressional proponent of bankruptcy legislation, Harrison Gray Otis of Massachusetts, agreed that America's situation was "precisely similar" to England's in that "both we and they are a commercial people" with "large cities, populous villages, and a country more or less populous." Even though America's cities and villages were not quite as fully populated as England's, the important point was that "the same division of labor and of professions will be found in them."[35] Thus, according to Bayard and Otis, America had reached an advanced stage of society where a modern bankruptcy system was both appropriate and necessary.

Bayard and Otis were responding directly to Albert Gallatin, the leading congressional opponent of the Federalist bankruptcy bill, who presented several reasons for "the unfitness of this country for a bankrupt system." Listing the circumstances that had to exist before a country could justify the legal recognition of bankruptcy, Gallatin argued that in addition to being "in a considerable degree commercial," a country had to have a highly developed division of labor in which "the different professions and occupations" were thoroughly distinct. This condition was necessary because only full-time merchants and traders were meant to fall under the purview of the bankruptcy act. In this regard, Gallatin argued, the United States was in a very different situation from England:

In Great Britain, whence this system is borrowed, this distinction exists—the different trades and occupations of men being so well distinguished, that a merchant and a farmer are rarely combined in the same person; a merchant is a merchant, and nothing but a merchant; a manufacturer is only a manufacturer; a farmer is merely a farmer; but this is not the case in this country. Here, it is well known, that the different professions and traders are blended together in the

34. *Annals of Congress*, 5th Cong., 3d sess., IX, 2656–2657.
35. *Ibid.*, 2675.

same persons; the same man being frequently a farmer and a merchant, and perhaps a manufacturer.[36]

The absence of a highly developed division of labor reflected the new republic's relative youth. America's social development did not yet warrant a modern bankruptcy system; it was still, according to Gallatin, too agricultural, too undifferentiated, and too primitive.

Gallatin also worried that a premature national bankruptcy act would work against American farmers. Since the proposed bill included land as property liable to seizure, he feared that farmers might unjustly be considered "traders," declared bankrupts, and stripped of their land. Gallatin pointed to existing state insolvency laws (particularly in the South) that included the principle of *elegit*, which specifically exempted landed wealth from seizure for the payment of debts. These laws, which would conflict with the proposed national bankruptcy act, were necessary and just, according to Gallatin, because land, the value of which fluctuated greatly, was not easily converted into money.[37] Bayard, however, found this objection to the bankruptcy bill contemptible. This kind of state insolvency law was not the necessary and positive safeguard of justice Gallatin claimed it to be; it was a pernicious remnant of an archaic feudalism, an aristocratic vestige that must "give way to more liberal views of commerce." "Commerce, and a law like this," insisted Bayard, "cannot live and flourish on the same soil." Since America was rapidly becoming an advanced commercial society, the reactionary principle of *elegit* must be swept away (just as primogeniture had been earlier) by the legal reform embodied in the proposed bankruptcy act. In a fully commercialized society, Bayard contended, land could no longer be protected as a special form of wealth.[38]

Bayard and Gallatin clearly had different estimations of the present condition of American society as well as of the desirability of its moving into a more advanced stage of development. Other Republicans shared Gallatin's misgivings about America's readiness for a bankruptcy system. In late 1792, when Congress was considering an earlier version of the bankruptcy bill, Jefferson had expressed serious doubts about the young republic's need for this kind of law: "Is Commerce so much the basis of

36. *Ibid.*, 2649–2651.
37. *Ibid.*
38. *Ibid.*, 2660. See also Coleman, *Debtors and Creditors*, 291–292.

the existence of the U.S. as to call for a bankrupt law?" "On the contrary," he queried, "are we not almost [entirely] agricultural?"[39] On both political and legal grounds, opponents of bankruptcy feared that its centralizing tendencies were clearly designed to enhance the power and influence of the federal court system. Anthony New, a Republican representative from Virginia, complained that the act was "so constructed as to transfer to the Federal Courts a great portion of the jurisdiction now held by the State Courts."[40] Other Jeffersonians, like John Fowler of Kentucky, suspected that the law was "little more than a machine for extending the influence of the executive administration" that "certainly may be made an instrument to injure the incautious agriculturists."[41] Indeed, opponents of bankruptcy feared the new legislation was part of a larger social and economic scheme aimed at advancing the commercialization of American society to make it more like England, a process they regarded as a blatant repudiation of the republican revolution. Representative Thomas T. Davis explained his negative vote on the bill to his Kentucky constituents by observing that he believed it not only "replete with principles incompatible with a republican government," but also "a powerful political engine and the means of extending, with facility, British influence in the United States."[42] A national bankruptcy law was inappropriate, in sum, for the decentralized, predominantly agricultural republic that most Jeffersonians wanted America to remain.[43]

On an even broader moral level, opponents of bankruptcy feared that a Federalist bankruptcy system would only further incite an unhealthy spirit of reckless speculation among the American people, a spirit that would ultimately undermine the stable and rational moral order of an

39. Ford, ed., *Writings of Jefferson*, VI, 145.

40. Letter to Constituents, Apr. 8, 1800, in Noble E. Cunningham, Jr., ed., *Circular Letters of Congressmen to Their Constituents, 1789–1829* (Chapel Hill, N.C., 1978), I, 196.

41. Letter to Constituents, May 15, 1800, *ibid.*, 209.

42. Letter to Constituents, Mar. 29, 1800, *ibid.*, 184.

43. Coleman, *Debtors and Creditors*, 19, and Turner, "Federalist Policy," *WMQ*, 3d Ser., XXII (1965). See also James Willard Hurst, *Law and the Conditions of Freedom in the Nineteenth-Century United States* (Madison, Wis., 1956), and R. Kent Newmyer, *The Supreme Court under Marshall and Taney* (New York, 1968), esp. chaps. 2 and 3. Turner and Newmyer have particularly valuable discussions of the significance of enhancing the jurisdictional power and influence of the federal court system, an aspect of the bankruptcy debate not stressed in the present discussion.

agricultural republican economy. While supporters of a bankruptcy law generally viewed speculation as the necessary basis for economic growth, Republicans tended to consider it a dangerous activity to be discouraged, not promoted. Perhaps this fear of the social and moral repercussions of uncontrolled speculation was the strongest fear the Jeffersonians had, especially in the wake of a speculative fever in the early months of 1798 that resulted in a wave of defaults and insolvencies.[44] After Congress passed the bankruptcy act of 1800 by a slim margin (49–48 in the House of Representatives), Littleton W. Tazewell, a Virginia Republican, complained to Jefferson that the American law was copied directly from British statutes and that the intentions behind it were obvious. He was not surprised, however, by the passage of such legislation, since bankruptcy legislation was only the logical manifestation of a calculated Federalist design to model America's political economy after England's. "Protection to commerce and speculation and destruction to agriculture and industry," he lamented, "have long been the orders of the day."[45] Tazewell's point was clear: the national bankruptcy act was part of a determined effort to build an unrepublican political economy much like Britain's, which neglected agriculture, encouraged unproductive speculation, and subsidized such ventures as a swollen and dangerously overextended carrying trade.

Ultimately, the bankruptcy act of 1800 proved to be short-lived, since Congress repealed it in November 1803. Although dissatisfaction with the operation of the law among both Federalists and Republicans generated the movement for repeal, Republican opponents of bankruptcy continued to oppose the law on ideological as well as practical grounds. Congressman John Newton of Virginia, taking a somewhat different tack from Gallatin, criticized it as discriminatory, impolitic, and anti-republican. Since the law applied only to merchants and traders, it gave these groups an advantage that farmers and other citizens did not have, a

44. For Jefferson's account of this fever, see Jefferson to Madison, Jan. 3, 1798, in Ford, ed., *Writings of Jefferson*, VII, 188. William Gordon, a New Hampshire congressman, also referred to this situation in a speech on the bankruptcy bill in Jan. 1799, when he argued that it was not "owing to the natural operations of commerce, that a number of persons are now in jail; but, from a spirit of speculation which had raged to a great extent in this country." See *Annals of Congress*, 5th Cong., 3d sess., IX, 2667–2668.

45. Tazewell to Jefferson, Mar. 29, 1800, in Massachusetts Historical Society, *Collections*, 7th Ser., I (Boston, 1900), 71–73.

privilege that encouraged merchants to overextend themselves in dangerous and frivolous speculations.[46] However necessary bankruptcy legislation might be in England, whose prosperity depended almost wholly on trade, anti-commercial spokesmen insisted that "it became not a nation, the leading feature of whose character was agriculture, to tread in her footsteps." On the contrary, it was necessary "to avert rather than to hasten the period when such a system would be rendered necessary" in the United States.[47]

This last statement succinctly captured the essence of the Republican movement of the 1790s—a fervent desire to escape the national destiny that was foreshadowed and promoted by Federalist policies. The developments of the decade had created a sense of urgency among many Americans who saw a desperate need to seize control of the federal government from men who appeared bent on overturning the principles of a republican revolution. Following their convincing electoral victory in 1800, the Jeffersonians in power would indeed attempt to implement alternative policies that would postpone, for as long as possible, the tragic day when the American republic would assume a social character comparable to England's.

46. *Annals of Congress*, 7th Cong., 2d sess., XII, 555–562.
47. *Ibid.*, 8th Cong., 1st sess., XIII, 618.

CHAPTER EIGHT

THE JEFFERSONIANS

IN POWER: EXTENDING

THE SPHERE

Many years after his first election to the presidency, Thomas Jefferson commented that "the revolution of 1800" was "as real a revolution in the principles of our government as that of 1776 was in its form."[1] Jefferson was undoubtedly using the term "revolution" not in the modern sense of a radical creation of a new order, but in the traditional sense of a return to first principles, of a restoration of original values and ideals that had been overturned or repudiated. For him, the election of 1800 was a revolution because it marked a turning back to the true republican spirit of 1776.[2] Jefferson was excited by the prospect of the first implementation of the principles of America's republican revolution in the national government created by the Constitution of 1787, since in his eyes a minority faction consisting of an American Walpole and his corrupt minions had captured control of that government almost immediately after its establishment. From Jefferson's perspective, indeed, the Federalists had done more than threaten to corrupt American government by mimicking the English "court" model. Just as frightening was their apparent desire to mold the young republic's political economy along English lines, a desire reflected both in their call for the extensive development of government-subsidized manufacturing enterprises and in their attempt to stimulate a highly commercialized economy anchored to such premature and speculative ventures as an overextended carrying trade. Jefferson's fundamental goal in 1801 was to end this threatened

1. Jefferson to Spencer Roane, Sept. 6, 1819, Paul Leicester Ford, ed., *The Writings of Thomas Jefferson* (New York, 1892–1899), X, 140.
2. *Ibid*. See also Dumas Malone, *Jefferson the President: First Term, 1801–1805* (Boston, 1970), xv, 26–27.

"Anglicization" of both American government and society. In so doing he would restore the basis for the development of a truly republican political economy, one that would be patterned after Benjamin Franklin's vision of a predominantly agricultural empire that would expand across space, rather than develop through time.[3]

Within the Jeffersonian framework of assumptions and beliefs, three essential conditions were necessary to create and sustain such a republican political economy: a national government free from any taint of corruption, an unobstructed access to an ample supply of open land, and a relatively liberal international commercial order that would offer adequate foreign markets for America's flourishing agricultural surplus. The history of the 1790s had demonstrated all too well to the Jeffersonians the predominant danger to a republican political economy of corruption emanating from the federal government. They were especially troubled by the deleterious political, social, and moral repercussions of the Federalists' financial system, which they regarded as the primary vehicle of corruption both in the political system and in the country at large. Although Jefferson concluded rather soon after his election that his administration could not safely dismantle Hamilton's entire system with a few swift strokes, he was committed to doing everything possible to control that system's effects and gradually reduce its pernicious influence. Extinguishing the national debt as rapidly as possible, reducing government expenditures (especially on the military), and repealing the Federalist battery of direct and excise taxes became primary goals of the Jeffersonians in power, who sought by such means to purge the national government of Hamiltonian fiscalism in accordance with their cherished "country" principles.[4]

In itself, the electoral revolution of 1800 promised to remove the

3. See above, chaps. 2, 6, and 7.

4. See especially, Lance Banning, *The Jeffersonian Persuasion: Evolution of a Party Ideology* (Ithaca, N.Y., 1978), epilogue. For a discussion of the "moderate" nature of Jefferson's reform as president, see Richard E. Ellis, *The Jeffersonian Crisis: Courts and Politics in the Young Republic* (New York, 1971). My approach to Jeffersonian political economy should not be understood as an attempt to slight or de-emphasize the importance of antifiscalism in the Republican mind; the national debt, public credit, and banking were obviously fundamental concerns in the American understanding of political economy. My reason for not exploring this central dimension of the Jeffersonian mind in any great detail is simply that other scholars, including Banning, have already done so. My approach is meant to supplement, rather than challenge, their contributions.

primary threat to a republican political economy posed by the machinations of a corrupt administration. But the Jeffersonians also had to secure the other necessary guarantors of republicanism: landed and commercial expansion. Although the pressure of population growth on the supply of land in the United States had never been a problem of the same immediate magnitude as political corruption, the social and economic dislocations of the 1780s had prompted some concern with this matter.[5] Through the Louisiana Purchase of 1803, undoubtedly the greatest achievement of his presidency, Jefferson appeared to eliminate this problem for generations, if not for centuries, to come. But the third and thorniest problem, in the form of long-standing restrictions on American commerce, proved far more frustrating and intractable. Through an embargo and finally a war the Jeffersonians consistently tried but failed to remove this nagging impediment to the fulfillment of their republican vision.

The presidential administrations from 1801 to 1817 appear more consistent when viewed from this perspective—that is, as a sustained Jeffersonian attempt to secure the requisite conditions for a republican political economy. Securing such a political economy, as the Jeffersonians conceived of it, required more than merely capturing control of the government from a corrupt minority faction; it also required the elimination of specific dangers and the maintenance of certain conditions, and these concerns largely shaped the Jeffersonian approach to both domestic and foreign policy. There was never any question that positive, concrete measures would have to be taken to forestall the development of social conditions that were considered antithetical to republicanism. Hamilton and the Federalists had threatened to make American society old and corrupt long before its time. Now the Jeffersonians set out to reverse the direction of Federalist policy in order to maintain the country at a relatively youthful stage of development. Hoping to avoid the social evils both of barbarous simplicity and of overrefined, decadent maturity, the Jeffersonians proposed to escape the burden of an economically sophisticated society without sacrificing a necessary degree of republican civilization. Their aspiration to evade social corruption and the ravages of time was a fragile and demanding dream, and the quest to fulfill it was not without its ironies.

5. See above, chap. 4.

On the one hand, the Republican party attracted political support from scores of Americans whose outlook can properly be termed entrepreneurial. Opposition to the Federalist system was never limited to agrarian-minded ideologues who unequivocally opposed a dynamic commercial economy. Many Jeffersonians were anxious to participate in the creation of an expansive economy and to reap its many rewards. Frustrated by the failure of Federalist policies to serve their immediate needs, ambitious men-on-the-make, engaged in a variety of economic pursuits, enlisted under the banner of Jeffersonianism in a crusade to secure the advantages and opportunities they desired.[6] Perhaps some of them saw no contradiction between their personal material ambitions and the traditional vision of a simple, bucolic republic articulated by the leader of their party. Assessing the economic psychology of many of these enterprising Jeffersonians, one scholar has suggested the complex paradox "of capitalists of all occupations denying the spirit of their occupations," adding that "it appears that many Republicans wanted what the Federalists were offering, but they wanted it faster, and they did not want to admit that they wanted it at all."[7] Such a characterization cannot be applied, however, to Jefferson and Madison, and in their case we observe a more poignant irony. As their experience as policymakers soon demonstrated, the Jeffersonian endeavor to secure a peaceful, predominantly agricultural republic demanded a tenaciously expansive foreign policy—a foreign policy that ultimately endangered both the peace and the agricultural character of the young republic.

6. Explaining how and why different groups in American society supported each of the two political parties is, of course, an exceedingly complex problem. Many relevant variables, from ethnicity and religion to social connections, affected partisan allegiance. An excellent discussion of some general trends can be found in David Hackett Fischer, *The Revolution of American Conservatism: The Federalist Party in the Era of Jeffersonian Democracy* (New York, 1965), 201–226. For evidence of the entrepreneurial wing of the Republican party, see, for example, Roland M. Baumann, "John Swanwick: Spokesman for 'Merchant-Republicanism' in Philadelphia, 1790–1798," *Pennsylvania Magazine of History and Biography*, XCVII (1973), 131–182. For an interesting discussion of the argument that Albert Gallatin was the quintessential "petty capitalist" who became an appropriate spokesman for the entrepreneurial wing of the Jeffersonian party, see Edwin G. Burrows, "Albert Gallatin and the Political Economy of Republicanism, 1761–1800" (Ph.D. diss., Columbia University, 1974).

7. John Zvesper, *Political Philosophy and Rhetoric: A Study of the Origins of American Party Politics* (Cambridge, 1977), 131.

[I]

In developing his analysis of Britain's mercantilist political economy during the 1760s and 1770s, Benjamin Franklin had recognized that corruption could result from both natural and artificial causes. A high population density brought about by the biological pressure of population growth on a limited supply of land was one route to social decay. But as Franklin and many other eighteenth-century writers so often noted, decay also resulted from a corrupt political system that deviously induced extreme social inequality, depopulation of the countryside, urban squalor, luxury manufacturing, and the like. Both routes to corruption had devastating consequences; the difference was that while one was natural and seemingly inevitable, the other was not. During the 1780s James Madison had pondered this distinction, most notably in his correspondence with Jefferson, and had reached the rather pessimistic conclusion that even in the absence of a corrupt political system "a certain degree of misery seems inseparable from a high degree of populousness."[8] Ultimately, he suggested, republican America would offer no exception to this rule. Although Jefferson agreed that the United States would remain virtuous only "as long as there shall be vacant lands in any part of America" and people were not "piled upon one another in large cities, as in Europe," he was confident that such a crisis would not arise "for many centuries."[9] If social decay was to afflict the young republic, Jefferson believed the threat stemmed more from artificial than from natural causes, from a corrupt political system rather than from the inevitable pressure of population growth on the American supply of land. Nevertheless, Jefferson was not totally unconcerned with the problem of land, especially in the realm of theory and speculation. His confidence about the American future betrayed his assumption that America's western (and perhaps northern and southern) boundaries would be regularly extended, always bringing in a fresh supply of virgin land.[10] Should that assumption be challenged, especially by a formidable foreign power,

8. Madison to Jefferson, June 19, 1786, in Julian P. Boyd *et al.*, eds., *The Papers of Thomas Jefferson* (Princeton, N.J., 1950–), IX, 659–660. See also above, chap. 5.

9. Jefferson to Madison, Dec. 20, 1787, Boyd *et al.*, eds., *Jefferson Papers*, XII, 442.

10. As Merrill Peterson has noted, when Jefferson referred to the United States in his first inaugural address as "a chosen country, with room enough for our descendants to the thousandth and thousandth generation," he surely did not mean the United States as it was

however, a theoretical problem might indeed become a more immediate and practical one.

It is interesting, in this regard, to observe Jefferson's reactions to the writings of Thomas R. Malthus, the British parson and political economist who popularized the theory of population pressure on subsistence, especially since Jefferson gave Malthus's writings particularly close attention near the end of his first presidential administration. Malthus had first presented his views on population in an anonymous pamphlet published in 1798, and his basic thesis was straightforward. Reacting against the optimistic forecasts of social improvement that were common in the late eighteenth century in the writings of William Godwin, the marquis de Condorcet, and others, Malthus argued that given the biological facts of population and subsistence, such visions of perfectibility for the mass of mankind were chimerical. Instead, the widespread vice, misery, and poverty that so appalled these "speculative philosophers" were the inevitable lot of humanity. The problem, simply stated, was that "the power of population is indefinitely greater than the power in the earth to produce subsistence for man."[11] The irrepressible passion between the sexes, when unchecked, resulted in a geometrical rate of population growth, whereas the supply of food and available means of nourishment could increase only arithmetically at best. This "perpetual tendency in the race of man to increase beyond the means of subsistence," Malthus explained, "is one of the general laws of animated nature, which we can have no reason to expect will change."[12]

Malthus suggested, in short, that all societies were destined to proceed rapidly through the familiar stages of social development toward a state of overpopulation, corruption, and old age. Old age might be postponed, especially in a society with an abundance of land, but not forever. In discussing population growth in America, Malthus emphasized the point that there was no final escape from the predicament he described, for not even a vast reservoir of fertile land could repeal the natural laws of population and subsistence. "Perpetual youth" for a nation was impossible; anyone who expected the United States to remain a land with relatively little poverty and misery forever, he commented, "might as

---

then bounded by the 31st parallel, the Great Lakes, and the Mississippi River. See Merrill D. Peterson, *Thomas Jefferson and the New Nation: A Biography* (New York, 1970), 746.

11. [Thomas Robert Malthus], *An Essay on the Principle of Population . . .* (London, 1798), 13.

12. *Ibid.*, 346.

reasonably expect to prevent a wife or mistress from growing old by never exposing her to the sun and air."[13] "It is, undoubtedly, a most disheartening reflection," he grimly concluded, "that the great obstacle in the way to any extraordinary improvement in society, is of a nature that we can never hope to overcome."[14]

Malthus's arguments should have been especially discouraging to Americans, since he contended that the necessary social basis for republicanism was precariously ephemeral. Extreme inequality, widespread poverty, extensive landless dependency—indeed, everything Americans considered antithetical to republicanism—were, according to Malthus, biologically inevitable. American readers could take solace only in the English parson's concession that there were "many modes of treatment in the political, as well as animal body, that contribute to accelerate or retard the approaches of age." Like Adam Smith and the French physiocrats, Malthus was a determined foe of "the mercantile system" of political economy, and like them he emphasized the need to achieve maximum agricultural productivity. Pointing to Europe, he admitted that "by encouraging the industry of the towns more than the industry of the country," mercantilist governments had "brought on a premature old age," and, indeed, that "a different policy in this respect, would infuse fresh life and vigour into every state."[15] Thus the best approach to ameliorating the misery of the poverty-stricken masses in Europe would be to remove all unnatural restraints on agricultural production, including all of the mercantilist strictures that Adam Smith and others had rightly condemned for encouraging commerce and manufacturing at the expense of agriculture. Like Franklin, in short, Malthus saw an artificially contrived as well as a natural basis for the misery of densely populated societies. Although the English cleric consistently emphasized the biologically inevitable basis for this social crisis, he never neglected the exacerbating influence of a mercantilist political system, and this subsidiary dimension of his commentary on population was bound to catch the attention, and even approval, of careful American readers.

In 1803 Malthus published a revised and greatly expanded version of his tract that softened "some of the harshest conclusions of the first

13. *Ibid.*, 343, 344.

14. *Ibid.*, 346.

15. *Ibid.*, 343, 344. For a succinct analysis of Malthus's opposition to "the mercantile system," see Bernard Semmel, "Malthus: 'Physiocracy' and the Commercial System," *Economic History Review*, 2d Ser., XVII (1964–1965), 522–535.

essay."[16] He retreated substantially from the bald and uncompromising pessimism that was always to remain associated with his name, admitting that there were "preventive" checks to population growth (particularly "moral restraint" in sexual relations) that he had not sufficiently considered.[17] By further tempering his belief in the natural and inevitable basis for social misery, Malthus brought his views more in line with those of the few Americans who had read his work. To the extent that American commentators paid any attention to Malthus in the early years of the nineteenth century, they were generally unsympathetic to his best-known theory, that of the inexorable biological basis for social decay and corruption. Instead, they stressed the idea that poverty and social misery were primarily attributable to pernicious mercantilist institutions, even suggesting that "Malthusianism" was a vicious rationalization purporting to free the privileged classes of responsibility for the social crisis they directly promoted.[18] To sensitive American readers, therefore, Malthus's revised version of his essay was much more satisfactory, since it de-emphasized the most objectionable aspect of his population theory.

President Thomas Jefferson was one such reader. By early 1804 he was perusing a borrowed copy of "the new work of Malthus on population," and he pronounced it "one of the ablest I have ever seen."[19] Writing to the French economist Jean Baptiste Say, he described it as "a work of sound logic, in which some of the opinions of Adam Smith, as well as of the economists [i.e., the physiocrats], are ably examined."[20] "A review of Malthus's anonymous tract [i.e., the initial 1798 version]," Jefferson noted, "had given me great prejudices against his principles, but he has greatly mended their appearance in his last work." "He has certainly furnished some sound correction of former errors, and given excellent

16. T. R. Malthus, *An Essay on the Principle of Population . . .* , 2d ed. (London, 1803), vii.

17. *Ibid.*, chap. 2. The physiocratic, or at least pro-agrarian, cast of this second edition was also quite pronounced. Malthus's anti-mercantilist argument was developed fully in Book III, chaps. 7–9, 420–451.

18. See George Johnson Cady, "The Early American Reaction to the Theory of Malthus," *Journal of Political Economy*, XXXIX (1931), 601–632, and Joseph J. Spengler, "Population Doctrines in the United States. I. Anti-Malthusianism. II. Malthusianism," *ibid.*, XLI (1933), 433–467, 639–672.

19. Jefferson to Joseph Priestley, Jan. 29, 1804, Andrew A. Lipscomb and Albert Ellery Bergh, eds., *The Writings of Thomas Jefferson* (Washington, D.C., 1903–1904), X, 447–448.

20. Jefferson to Say, Feb. 1, 1804, *ibid.*, XI, 1.

views of some questions in political economy."[21] Along with his friend and political ally Thomas Cooper, however, Jefferson continued to chide Malthus for failing to recognize the value of emigration as a remedy for the population problem. Jefferson's reaction to Malthus's first essay, as Cooper recalled it, had been to suggest that "a well regulated System of gradual colonization might prove an effectual remedy, without adding to the inevitable mass of human misery."[22] Now, in early 1804, Jefferson reiterated this belief. Even in the revised edition of his essay Malthus had insisted that contrary to general expectations, emigration to new territory was "a very weak palliative," at best only "a partial and temporary expedient."[23] Jefferson vigorously dissented from this belief, agreeing with Cooper that Malthus was "particularly defective in developing the resources of emigration." "Were half the money employed under the poor laws in England, laid out in colonizing their able bodied poor," the president noted, "both the emigrants and those who remained would be the happier."[24]

Jefferson's reaction to the revised edition of Malthus was indicative of his general state of mind toward the end of his first presidential administration. Ironically, what Jefferson found least useful and convincing in Malthus was the population theory that the parson was best known for; the president's general praise for the essay appears to have been prompted by its restatement of laissez-faire, anti-mercantilist doctrine.[25] Jefferson particularly chastised Malthus for failing to recognize the ir-

21. Jefferson to Thomas Cooper, Feb. 24, 1804, Jefferson Papers, Library of Congress (microfilm). Jefferson was responding to a letter from Cooper, who noted that although he had perused Malthus "with deep interest and melancholy conviction of the general truth of his Theory," he could not help thinking that "he carried it much too far." Cooper to Jefferson, Feb. 16, 1804, *ibid.*

22. *Ibid.*

23. Malthus, *Essay on Population*, 2d ed., 394–395.

24. Jefferson to Cooper, Feb. 24, 1804, Jefferson Papers.

25. Malthus stressed, for example, the primary importance of agriculture and the necessary role of an agricultural surplus in supporting the "sterile" occupations of commerce and manufacturing. He also berated "all corporations, patents, and exclusive privileges of every kind, which abound so much in the mercantile system"; and he lamented England's switch from an "agricultural system" to a "commercial system" of political economy, a process that he claimed had taken place during the second half of the 18th century. Malthus, *Essay on Population*, 2d ed., 436–437, 439, 443. According to Malthus, England had developed a dangerously unhealthy economic system, putting a premium on exporting manufactures while importing raw produce. He argued that it was far better, as well as natural, for a country to adopt the reverse pattern of exporting produce and importing

relevance of his population theory to the American experience. "From the singular circumstance of the immense extent of rich and uncultivated lands in this country, furnishing an increase of food in the same ratio with that of population," Jefferson noted, "the greater part of his book is inapplicable to us, but as a matter of speculation."[26] Population pressure on subsistence would never be an immediate problem in America because "the resource of emigration" to virgin territory was always available. Discussing Malthus's theory with the French economist Say, Jefferson expanded this observation into a more general statement. "The differences of circumstance between this and the old countries of Europe," he wrote, "furnish differences of fact whereon to reason, in questions of political economy, and will consequently produce sometimes a difference of result." Echoing Franklin's observations of fifty years earlier, Jefferson continued: "There, for instance, the quantity of food is fixed, or increasing in a slow and only arithmetical ratio, and the proportion is limited by the same ratio. Supernumerary births consequently add only to your mortality. Here the immense extent of uncultivated and fertile lands enables every one who will labor, to marry young, and to raise a family of any size. Our food, then, may increase geometrically with our laborers, and our births, however multiplied, become effective."[27] Jefferson went on to argue, in this regard, that America provided a further exception to the European rule of balanced economies and national self-sufficiency:

Again, there the best distribution of labor is supposed to be that which places the manufacturing hands along side the agricultural; so that the one part shall feed both, and the other part furnish both with clothes and other comforts. Would that be best here? Egoism and first appearances say yes. Or would it be better that all our laborers should be employed in agriculture? In this case a double or treble portion of fertile lands would be brought into culture; a double or treble creation of food be produced, and its surplus go to nourish the now perishing births of Europe, who in return would manufacture and send us in exchange our clothes and other comforts. Morality listens to this, and so invariably do the laws of nature create our duties and interests, that when they seem to be at variance, we ought to suspect some fallacy in our reasonings. In solving this question, too,

---

manufactures (*ibid.*, 449), and one can easily imagine Jefferson nodding vigorously in assent as he read.

26. Jefferson to Cooper, Feb. 24, 1804, Jefferson Papers.

27. Jefferson to Say, Feb. 1, 1804, Lipscomb and Bergh, eds., *Writings of Jefferson*, XI, 2–3.

we should allow its just weight to the moral and physical preference of the agricultural, over the manufacturing, man.[28]

This statement was a striking reaffirmation of Jefferson's fundamental beliefs on the subject of political economy, a statement that differed very little from his well-known observations in the *Notes on Virginia* of twenty years earlier.[29] Jefferson's encounter with Malthus thus served, in the end, to reconfirm his basic vision of a predominantly agricultural America that would continue to export its bountiful surpluses of food abroad. Such a republic, he believed, would best serve not only its own citizens, by permitting them to pursue a virtuous way of life, but also the European victims of a Malthusian fate, by providing them with the subsistence they desperately needed. It seems clear, above all, that Jefferson's brimming confidence during this period—expressed both in his response to Malthus and in his restatement of agrarian beliefs—must be viewed in the context of the Louisiana Purchase. With the Federalists properly and, Republicans hoped, permanently displaced from power in the national government, there was no need to worry about the dangers to a republican political economy from political corruption. With Louisiana safely added to the Union, there was also no need to worry about the danger of foreign powers choking off the American supply of land. The acquisition of Louisiana probably removed any Malthusian doubts Jefferson might have had about the long-range viability of republicanism in America.[30] Indeed, the Louisiana question touched on so many aspects of the Jeffersonian vision of a republican political economy that it deserves much closer investigation.

28. *Ibid.*

29. See Thomas Jefferson, *Notes on the State of Virginia*, ed. William Peden (Chapel Hill, N.C., 1955), 164–165, and above, chap. 1.

30. Even in Nov. 1803, while discussing the problem of the distribution of occupations in populous countries, Jefferson could still express the fear that there was "too strong a current from the country to the towns" in America, including "instances beginning to appear" of the urban misery that characterized Europe. "Although we have in the old countries of Europe the lesson of their experience to warn us," he noted, "yet I am not satisfied we shall have the firmness and wisdom to profit by it." He spoke here, however, of great cities that were "the sinks of voluntary misery," which attracted both those who desired "to live by their heads rather than their hands" and those "who have any turn for dissipation." He was not referring, in short, to the Malthusian problem of a biologically induced and involuntary misery. Jefferson to David Williams, Nov. 14, 1803, Lipscomb and Bergh, eds., *Writings of Jefferson*, X, 430–431.

[I I]

The Mississippi crisis of 1801–1803, which culminated in the Louisiana Purchase, affected crucial and long-standing American concerns. Since the 1780s most Americans had regarded free navigation of the Mississippi River and the right of deposit at New Orleans as essential to the national interest. Without the access to market that these conditions permitted, westward expansion would be stalled, because settlers in the trans-Appalachian regions necessarily depended on the Mississippi and its tributaries to sustain them as active and prosperous republican farmers.[31] The Pinckney Treaty of 1795 temporarily resolved this nagging problem, since the Spanish agreed in the treaty to grant the United States free navigation of the Mississippi with a three-year right of deposit at New Orleans. This treaty, along with the Jay Treaty of the same year, cleared the way for a burst of western settlement. By 1801 the Mississippi River provided the primary access to market for the produce of more than half a million Americans living in the trans-Appalachian West, especially in Kentucky and Tennessee. When Spain made a secret agreement in 1800 to transfer possession of Louisiana back to France, however, the old problem took on a new and more ominous dimension. As Jefferson and most Americans immediately recognized, Napoleonic ambitions in the Mississippi valley posed a far more serious threat to the westward course of American empire than Spain ever had.[32]

To add insult to injury, before formally transferring Louisiana to Napoleon, the Spanish intendant at New Orleans revoked the American right of deposit in violation of the Pinckney Treaty. Many Americans, including eastern Federalists as well as westerners, responded with outraged belligerence and threats of war. Jefferson shrewdly contained this war fever and proceeded cautiously, employing a strategy that ultimately contributed to the convergence of circumstances that made the Louisiana Purchase possible. The Purchase solved once and for all the Mississippi problem that had festered for twenty years—the United States gained

---

31. See above, chap. 5.

32. See especially Arthur Preston Whitaker, *The Mississippi Question, 1795–1803: A Study in Trade, Politics, and Diplomacy* (New York, 1934). Other useful secondary discussions include: Paul A. Varg, *Foreign Policies of the Founding Fathers* (East Lansing, Mich., 1963), chap. 8; Peterson, *Jefferson and the New Nation*, 745–754; and Malone, *Jefferson the President: First Term*, chaps. 14 and 15.

formal control of the river, both its eastern and western banks, and of New Orleans.[33]

In the minds of many Americans, the question of the Mississippi River involved much more than a narrow concern with the prosperity or profits of western farmers. What they saw to be at stake in the Mississippi crisis of 1801–1803 was the very character of western society itself. This concern with social character, especially with the interdependence of economic life and the moral integrity of the individual personality, was part of a fundamentally republican world view. To Americans committed to the construction of a republican political economy, it was imperative that public policy be directed toward the creation of social conditions that would permit and even foster the maintenance of a virtuous people.[34] The crisis in the Mississippi valley was commonly conceived of and discussed in these terms. What the Louisiana Purchase made possible, according to many commentators, was the existence of a republican civilization in the American West.

Most important, control of the Mississippi permitted westerners to engage in a secure and dynamically expanding foreign commerce and, as always, Americans saw the significance of commerce in very broad social and moral terms. It was repeatedly asserted that an active commerce that provided a secure and dependable access to foreign markets was absolutely necessary to establish and maintain the republican character of western society. A primary concern here was the familiar emphasis on "industry" as the cornerstone of the republican personality. Obstructions to foreign commerce, it was argued, always "palsied" the labor of American farmers and discouraged their industry by destroying incentives to production. Eventually, such obstructions led to indolence, lethargy, dissipation, and barbarous decadence—characteristics hardly befitting a republican people. In a pamphlet celebrating the Louisiana Purchase, Allen Bowie Magruder, a Kentucky lawyer who later removed to Louisiana, pithily stated this common argument in the following terms:

There are innumerable circumstances that combine to render it absolutely necessary, that the Western Republics should enjoy an active commerce. Without it,

33. Peterson, *Jefferson and the New Nation*, 755–768, and Malone, *Jefferson the President: First Term*, chap. 16.

34. See above, chaps. 3, 4, and 5.

even the natural luxuriance of the soil, would produce the worst impression upon the morals of the people. Without commerce to yield a market to the products of agriculture, that agriculture would languish, and the mass of society be thrown into a state of listless indolence and dissipation. The human mind must be active; and provided it is not excited by the more useful and inoffensive passions, it will yield to the dominion of the more dangerous and ferocious kind. The immense fertility of the soil, where human life is supported without that constant labor which requires an assiduous employment of time, would produce the same effect upon morals that acquired luxury does.[35]

Foreign commerce, in short, was the necessary solvent of idleness and the depravity idleness bred, especially in a fecund region like the Mississippi valley where the struggle for mere subsistence appeared to require very little exertion or moral discipline.

Americans commonly argued that the alternative to this active foreign commerce and the republican civilization it underwrote was a lethargic subsistence agriculture at an undesirably primitive stage of social development. Following the Spanish removal of the American right of deposit at New Orleans in October 1802, several senators graphically portrayed the anticipated consequences of a disruption of American commerce on the Mississippi in these terms. American settlers in the West had "explored and settled a wilderness," in the process planting "polished societies" where "but a few years since was heard only the savage yell"; now that their industry was threatened with obstruction, their very status as a civilized people "enjoying peace, happiness, industry, and commerce" was seriously endangered.[36] Referring to American farmers in the West, a writer in the *Kentucky Gazette* similarly argued that without the "market for their surplus produce" that had been assured by the Louisiana Purchase, they would have "degenerated into savages, because they had no incentive to industry."[37]

By rectifying the chronic problem of an uncertain, rapidly fluctuating demand for western agricultural surpluses, the Purchase thus served an important social and moral purpose. "No ruinous fluctuations in com-

35. Allan Bowie Magruder, *Political, Commercial, and Moral Reflections on the Late Cession of Louisiana to the United States* (Lexington, Ky., 1803), 50.

36. See especially, speeches by Samuel White of Delaware and William Cocke of Tennessee, *Annals of Congress*, 7th Cong., 2d sess., XII, 113, 140. See also speeches by James Ross of Pennsylvania and DeWitt Clinton of New York, *ibid.*, 84–85, 131.

37. "Phocion," *Kentucky Gazette and General Advertiser* (Lexington), Oct. 4, 1803.

merce need now be apprehended," noted another western commentator, for "agriculture may depend upon those steady markets which trade shall open to industry." There could be no doubt that a "want of markets for the produce of the soil" always had disastrous consequences, for "it saps the foundations of our prosperity; subverts the end of society, and literally tends to keep us in that rude, uncultivated state, which has excited the derision and contempt of other communities." "As long as this is the state of our country," the same observer queried in familiar fashion, "what encouragement is there for the mind to throw off its native ferocity?"[38] By permanently securing control of the Mississippi River and the promise of boundless foreign markets beyond, the Louisiana Purchase did more than pave the way for economic prosperity. By providing the incentive to industry that shaped a republican people, it laid the necessary basis for the westward expansion of republican civilization itself.

[III]

Federalists as well as Jeffersonians applauded certain aspects of the Louisiana Purchase. Indeed, with few exceptions, even opponents of the Jefferson administration recognized the importance and significance of resolving the crisis in the Mississippi region. Virtually no one could deny the need to gain control of the river and of New Orleans. Federalists criticized Jefferson on only two points; first, for failing to respond vigorously enough to the crisis when it first arose (many of them advocated immediate military action), and second, for acquiring in the process of resolving that crisis "a vast wilderness world which will . . . prove worse than useless to us."[39] Purchasing New Orleans and guaranteeing American navigation of the Mississippi were commendable achievements, even if, as Alexander Hamilton claimed, they were "solely owing to a fortuitous concurrence of unforseen and unexpected circumstance, and not to any wise or vigorous measures on the part of the American govern-

38. "Reflections on Political Economy, and the Prospect Before Us, Addressed to the Citizens of the Western Country," *Ky. Gazette*, Sept. 6, 1803, and Sept. 27, 1803. This series of essays, which also appeared in the *Scioto Gazette* (Chillicothe, Ohio) was signed by "Aristides."

39. Everett Somerville Brown, ed., *William Plumer's Memorandum of Proceedings in the United States Senate, 1803–1807* (New York, 1923), 13, 6–13.

ment."[40] But Federalists viewed the purchase of an "unbounded region west of the Mississippi" as unnecessary, frivolous, and dangerous. The United States already had more than enough land, much of it as yet unsettled. If this new territory was opened to immediate emigration, "it must not only be attended with all the injuries of a too widely dispersed population, but by adding to the great weight of the western part of our territory, must hasten the dismemberment of a large portion of our country, or a dissolution of the Government."[41] Advancing the Antifederalist argument of 1788, ironically, the Federalists claimed that republican government could not function effectively over such a large area; hence, American interest should extend no further west than the Mississippi River. "Now, by adding an unmeasured world beyond that river," lamented Fisher Ames, "we rush like a comet into infinite space."[42]

Many Jeffersonians, including the president himself, agreed that the new territory should not be settled immediately.[43] For the moment, Jefferson wanted to settle only Indians on the western bank of the river, thus making the acquisition "the means of filling up the eastern side, instead of drawing off its population." Later, however, when "we shall be full on this side," new states would be laid off on the western bank, with American settlement "advancing compactly as we multiply."[44] Indeed, unlike Ames and the Federalists, most Jeffersonians enthusiastically welcomed the acquisition of this "infinite space," even if it were to be of no immediate use. In addition to resolving the Mississippi crisis, the Louisiana Purchase was important to the Jeffersonians precisely because

40. See Douglass Adair, "Hamilton on the Louisiana Purchase: A Newly Identified Editorial from the *New-York Evening Post*," *William and Mary Quarterly*, 3d Ser., XII (1955), 274, 268–281.

41. *Ibid.*, 276. See also the hostile reaction to the Purchase reprinted from the *New England Palladium* (Boston) in the *Alexandria Advertiser and Commercial Intelligencer* (Va.), Aug. 9, 1803.

42. Fisher Ames to Christopher Gore, Oct. 3, 1803, in Seth Ames, ed., *Works of Fisher Ames* (Boston, 1854), I, 323–324. See also the speech of Congressman Gaylord Griswold of New York, *Annals of Congress*, 8th Cong., 1st sess., XIII, 433. This Federalist opposition was prompted to a great extent, of course, by partisan fears that the Purchase would ensure the continued dominance of an agricultural Republican majority in American politics.

43. See, for example, St. George Tucker's *Reflections on the Cession of Louisiana to the United States* (Washington, D.C., 1803), esp. 3, 19–20.

44. Jefferson to Breckinridge, Aug. 12, 1803, *State Papers and Correspondence Bearing upon the Purchase of the Territory of Louisiana* (Washington, D.C., 1903), 235.

it promised to preserve the fundamentally agricultural, and hence republican, character of American society for centuries to come. In simplest terms, the Purchase guaranteed that the American empire would be able to continue to expand across space, rather than be forced to develop through time.

Jeffersonian supporters of the Louisiana Purchase never hesitated, of course, to point out the advantages it offered to American merchants and to easterners in general. Commerce was always an important part of the republican vision of an empire across space, and the Jeffersonians were anxious to convince easterners that they could play a significant role in the development of that empire. Above all, Republicans argued that the elimination of a threatening foreign presence in the Mississippi valley opened the way for enterprising merchants of the eastern states to move in and take undisputed control of the region's lucrative trade. American "merchants of capital and character" could now settle at New Orleans and provide western farmers with the secure commercial connections they needed. Republicans customarily emphasized this need for "a strict union of the interests of the cultivator and exporter"; such an alliance would overcome the debilitating fluctuations in America's Mississippi commerce that had prevailed when "merchants in the eastern states had not regularly formed connections there, and the arrival of vessels was uncertain."[45] One commentator even suggested that the Purchase would be a boon to eastern merchants because trade with the new territory might replace the undependable, heavily restricted West Indies trade. Louisiana plantations would be able to produce everything the West Indies did, he argued, and they might also provide a market for products that Americans were often forbidden to carry to the West Indies. In this way, eastern merchants might eventually discover in Louisiana an invaluable and secure network of commerce that would compensate for the chronic irregularities and deficiencies of the West Indies trade.[46]

But this emphasis on the commercial aspects of the Louisiana Purchase rarely led to the articulation of a predominantly commercial vision of empire. One writer in the *Charleston Courier*, effusive in his praise of the

45. "Phocion," *Ky. Gazette* (Lexington), Oct. 4, 1803, and "Aristides," *ibid.*, Sept. 6, 1803, Sept. 20, 1803, and Oct. 18, 1803. See also Chapman Johnson, *Oration on the late Treaty with France* . . . (Staunton, Va., [1804]), esp. 11.

46. "Considerations in favor of our seaport towns, and of the Eastern and Northern States, arising out of the purchase of Louisiana," *Philadelphia Aurora*, July 21, 1803. This essay was signed by "Columbus."

Purchase, did anticipate an American empire modeled on the English tradition. Predicting that the United States would one day be a commercial emporium second to none in human history, he exulted that "America will in time be what its founder Great Britain once was—or rather another Britain, but on a scale of unbounded extent."[47] Most commentators did not share this emphasis, however, and would have been very uncomfortable with it. If the Louisiana Purchase portended anything to most Republicans about America's future social development, it was the development of a landed and timelessly youthful empire that would be quite unlike England's.

No one doubted that the Purchase would influence the course of American economic and social development. "What are the consequences then which we may expect?" asked a writer in the *Kentucky Gazette*.

> Only that our labour will continue in the old direction. But are we certain that any other would be more profitable, more advantageous, or more fortunate to our character and morals? The great body of the people at present obtain foreign manufactures in exchange for their produce at less expence and trouble than they could, were they to manufacture themselves. And unless they should be determined to abandon the pure air of the country for the shop of the artizan, to leave their farms for the sinks of vice (towns and cities) they must not think of manufacturing for themselves.[48]

As usual, such a statement did not mean that Americans should abjure all domestic manufactures, but only that they should not resort to manufacturing on a large scale or on an extensive and permanent basis. To some extent Americans would always have to manufacture for themselves, but the Louisiana Purchase would presumably reduce the need for such activity to a minimum.[49] By guaranteeing the commerce of the Mississippi River and by providing a reservoir of open land, the Purchase seemed to guarantee the viability of a political economy based on the exportation of burgeoning agricultural surpluses. In the process, it extended "the empire

47. *Charleston Courier* (S.C.), Dec. 2, 1803.

48. "Phocion," *Ky. Gazette*, Oct. 11, 1803. For a limited but quite useful discussion of Louisiana's influence on American perceptions of economic and social development, see Isabelle Claxton Deen, "Public Response to the Louisiana Purchase: A Survey of American Press and Pamphlets, 1801–1804" (M.A. thesis, University of Virginia, 1972), esp. 34–44.

49. See, for example, "Aristides," *Ky. Gazette*, Sept. 13, 1803.

of republicanism, by giving corresponding influence to the agricultural class, who in all ages have been peculiarly devoted to liberty."[50]

If the American republic was in a race against time, as many Republicans believed, the Louisiana Purchase indeed offered a boost to the republican cause. "The history of the world," noted Abraham Bishop, a prominent Connecticut Republican, "teaches that nations, like men, must decay. Ours will not forever escape the fate of others. Wealth, luxury, vice, aristocracies will attack us in our decline: these are evils of society, never to be courted, but to be put to as distant a day as possible."[51] Viewed in this light, the acquisition of Louisiana was of crucial importance to all Americans, not just to southerners and westerners, for it pushed far into the future that dreaded day when America would become a densely populated society characterized by inequality, luxury, and dependence. "We see in Louisiana an assurance of long life to our cause," Bishop exulted. "The Atlantic states, as they advance to that condition of society, where wealth and luxury tend to vice and aristocracies, will yield to that country accessions of enterprizing men. The spirit of faction, which tends to concentrate, will be destroyed by this diffusion."[52] Expansion across space was the only effective antidote to population growth, development through time, and the corruption that accompanied them. "What territory can be too large," David Ramsay asked rhetorically in 1804, "for a people, who multiply with such unequalled rapidity?"[53] "By enlarging the empire of liberty," noted President Jefferson in 1805, "we multiply its auxiliaries, and provide new sources of renovation, should its principles, at any time, degenerate, in those portions of our country which gave them birth."[54]

50. *Ibid.*, Sept. 6, 1803.

51. Abraham Bishop, *Oration, in honor of the Election of President Jefferson, and the Peaceable Acquisition of Louisiana . . .* (Hartford, Conn., 1804), 4.

52. *Ibid.*, 6.

53. David Ramsay, *An Oration, on the Cession of Louisiana, to the United States . . .* (Charleston, S.C., 1804), 16.

54. Jefferson to the president and legislative council, the speaker and house of representatives of the territory of Indiana, Dec. 28, 1805, Jefferson Papers, Library of Congress, as cited in Adrienne Koch, *The Great Collaboration* (New York, 1950), 244–245. See also Jefferson's message to Congress, Oct. 17, 1803, *State Papers and Correspondence Bearing upon the Purchase of the Territory of Louisiana*, 251–253.

[IV]

Jefferson's notion of a continuously expanding "empire of liberty" in the Western Hemisphere was a bold intellectual stroke, because it flew in the face of the traditional republican association of expansion and empire with luxury, corruption, and especially despotism. The familiar bugbear of the Roman Empire and its decline through imperial expansion was the most common source of this association.[55] According to Jefferson and most American republicans, expansion would preserve, rather than undermine, the republican character of America. In addition to forestalling development through time and diffusing the spirit of faction, expansion was crucial to American security in its broadest sense. Removing the French from Louisiana also removed the need for a dangerous military establishment in the face of a contiguous foreign threat. It greatly reduced, too, the likelihood of American involvement in a ruinous war that would impose on the young republic the vicious Old World system of national debts, armies, navies, taxation, and the like. For a plethora of reasons, in short, peaceful expansion was sustaining the Jeffersonian republic.[56]

But if the Louisiana Purchase removed some serious obstacles to the realization of Jefferson's republican empire, it also exposed some of the tensions and contradictions within that vision. Since the proper functioning of the empire required both westward and commercial expansion, an assertive, even aggressive, foreign policy would often be necessary to secure the republic. The Jeffersonians frequently boasted of the isolation and independence of the United States; curiously, this claim obscured the fact that American republicanism demanded both an open international commercial order and the absence of any competing presence on the North American continent. The United States could isolate itself from foreign affairs and the potential for conflict only if it was willing to resign its tenacious commitment to westward expansion and free trade. To do this, however, would be to abandon the two most important pillars of the Jeffersonian vision of a republican political economy. Indeed, given

55. The best discussion of this matter is in Gerald Stourzh, *Alexander Hamilton and the Idea of Republican Government* (Stanford, Calif., 1970), chaps. 4 and 5.

56. *Ibid.*, esp. 189–201. See also Julian P. Boyd, "Thomas Jefferson's 'Empire of Liberty,'" *Virginia Quarterly Review*, XXIV (1948), 538–554. For a contemporary statement of the broad Jeffersonian definition of security, see Magruder, *Reflections on the Cession of Louisiana*, 42–43.

the commitment to that vision, the national independence and isolated self-sufficiency boasted of by the Jeffersonians were illusory.

This tension or contradiction was reflected both in Jeffersonian tracts on political economy and in the course of public policy itself. In a lengthy pamphlet celebrating the Louisiana Purchase, Allan Bowie Magruder touched on the key elements of the Jeffersonian republican vision. The Purchase enhanced American security and lessened the danger of a corrupting war; it bolstered the influence of the agricultural class, always the best repository of republican virtue; and it laid the basis for a flourishing commerce in the West that would cultivate an active, industrious, and republican people. Magruder also stressed the familiar theme of the importance of the complete protection to property offered by American institutions, an advantage that would underwrite the development of a prosperous, republican civilization in the Mississippi valley.[57]

Magruder also insisted, however, on denigrating commerce and merchants (who were "venal" and "avaricious"), emphasizing the "peculiarly agricultural" character of America, and boasting of America's complete lack of dependence on commerce. "Neither the elements of her happiness," the gratification of her wants, or the preservation of her independence," he argued, "rest upon the fate of commerce."[58] But as the rest of Magruder's pamphlet so vividly illustrated, this assertion was true only in a very narrow and limited sense. To be sure, Americans could always feed themselves and provide their own basic "necessaries," and to this extent they were independent of foreign commerce and the outside world. But if America was to be more than an extremely rude and simple society based on subsistence agriculture and household manufactures, more than a crude society that was hardly the foundation for any realistic conception of republicanism, it required rapidly expanding export markets to absorb the surplus that its active, industrious, republican farmers would inevitably produce. As Magruder himself, in fact, explicitly recognized, this had been the lesson of America's experience in the Mississippi valley—"there are innumerable circumstances that combine to render it absolutely necessary, that the Western Republics should enjoy an active commerce."[59] There was more and more talk of the prospect of a highly developed domestic commerce that might replace America's need for

57. Magruder, *Reflections on the Cession of Louisiana*, esp. 42–43, 50–51, 75–78, 103.
58. *Ibid.*, 81.
59. *Ibid.*, 50. See also above, chap. 3.

foreign trade, but most commentators, including Magruder, seemed to recognize that domestic trade could never be an adequate substitute for foreign commerce, at least not in the immediate future. As long as this situation persisted, foreign commerce would remain an indispensable factor in the republican equation.

In this regard, Magruder was particularly interested in American acquisition of the Floridas. He insisted that Americans must enjoy all the advantages of "the Gulph trade." Referring to the Tombigbee, Alabama, and Perdido rivers (as well as to the important port of Mobile), he argued that complete control of "the rivers which run parallel with the Mississippi, a considerable distance up the interior parts of the country" was absolutely necessary. "Much remains yet to be done," Magruder asserted, "to establish the rights of ingress and egress to our rivers upon a secure foundation; and to give to our Western commerce, the highest possible degree of prosperity." Magruder's interest even extended to Cuba, which he felt must come under American control, ideally through purchase. Cuba was "the key to the commerce of almost one half of the empire; and should not be submitted to the caprice, or the jealousy of any foreign nation whatever."[60] For Magruder, the Louisiana Purchase was only the beginning; the United States had much more to do in the Southwest if it was to promote its basic security as a republic.

Both President Jefferson and Secretary of State Madison shared Magruder's interest in the rivers and ports of Florida and, to a lesser extent, in Cuba. Indeed, Jefferson's interest after 1803 in acquiring the Floridas bordered on an obsession.[61] The precise boundaries of the Louisiana Purchase were ambiguous, and the administration advanced the rather dubious claim against the Spanish that West Florida, an area between the Mississippi and Perdido rivers, had been part of America's purchase from Napoleon. Jefferson and Madison cared much less about the small amount of land in question than they did about the rivers and ports at stake. On all these rivers, Madison had noted prior to the purchase of Louisiana, "the country within the boundary of the United States . . . is fertile." "Settlements on it are beginning; and the people have al-

60. Magruder, *Reflections on the Cession of Louisiana*, 104–107.

61. Relevant secondary discussions of Jefferson and the Florida question include: Peterson, *Jefferson and the New Nation*, 768–770, 808–810, 816–817, 825–826; Varg, *Foreign Policies*, 157–167; and Malone, *Jefferson the President: First Term*, 303–309. See also Isaac Joslin Cox, *The West Florida Controversy, 1798–1813* (Baltimore, 1918).

ready called on the Government to procure the proper outlets to foreign markets. . . . In fact, our free communication with the sea through those channels is so natural, so reasonable, and so essential, that, eventually, it must take place: and in prudence, therefore, ought to be amicably and effectually adjusted without delay."[62] When the administration failed to budge the Spanish on the Florida question, Jefferson became increasingly frustrated and irritated, and during the summer and fall of 1805 he even considered effecting an alliance with Spain's enemy, England. Although the administration soon became distracted by more pressing foreign policy problems, this Republican interest in the Floridas (and to a lesser degree in Cuba) did not disappear.[63] The Florida question became even more complicated during Madison's presidency, and it was not resolved until the Adams-Onis Treaty of 1819, by which the United States finally acquired the territory so coveted by Jefferson.

The Florida problem reflected a central tension in the Jeffersonian conception of a republican political economy. The establishment and security of a relatively simple, peaceful, predominantly agricultural republic paradoxically required a dynamically expansive foreign policy that promised to involve the republic in serious and potentially dangerous disputes with other nations. The Jeffersonian interest in obtaining the Floridas stemmed from a concern for the republic's security in both an immediate and a long-range sense. New Orleans had to be protected, and there was always the danger that Spain might cede the Floridas to a more formidable and threatening power like England. But above all the commercial angle was paramount. It was imperative that the United States control these rivers and ports, as well as the Mississippi and New Orleans, because they provided the necessary avenue to foreign markets for American farmers in the West. The Jeffersonian vision of an expanding republican civilization demanded this unimpeded access to foreign

---

62. Madison to Livingston and Monroe, Mar. 2, 1803, *State Papers and Correspondence Bearing upon the Purchase of the Territory of Louisiana*, 127. See also *ibid.*, 84–88, and Walter LaFeber, "Foreign Policies of a New Nation: Franklin, Madison, and 'The Dream of a New Land to Fulfill with People in Self-Control,' 1750–1804," in William Appleman Williams, ed., *From Colony to Empire: Essays in the History of American Foreign Relations* (New York, 1972), 35–37.

63. Varg, *Foreign Policies*, 161. For expressions of Jefferson's continuing interest in the Floridas and Cuba, see Jefferson to Madison, Aug. 16, 1807, Lipscomb and Bergh, eds., *Writings of Jefferson*, XI, 327, and Jefferson to Madison, Apr. 27, 1809, *ibid.*, XII, 276–277.

markets—for economic, social, and moral reasons—and to this extent the republic was something less than the fully autonomous and self-sufficient entity the Jeffersonians usually portrayed it to be. If the necessary guarantors of the Republican vision included an interventionist foreign policy, territorial aggression, Indian removal or management, and even war, might not the means of achieving an escape from time subvert their fundamental purpose? Ultimately, as the events of Jefferson's second administration and Madison's presidency demonstrated, the struggle to secure the Jeffersonian republic culminated in the need to wage a second war for American independence.

CHAPTER NINE

THE JEFFERSONIANS

IN POWER:

EMBARGO AND WAR

Shortly after Thomas Jefferson's election to the presidency in early 1801, George Logan, a close friend and political ally, wrote to congratulate the Virginian and to suggest "two objects" of "national importance" that demanded the immediate attention of the new Republican administration. First, prompt action should be taken to promote American manufactures. "As long as we are dependent on Great Britain for our cloathing and other necessaries," Logan warned, "we must be influenced by her baneful politics." Second, the United States should cooperate with the smaller states of Europe to ensure "that the Sea, as the great highway of all Nations, should be perfectly free."[1] Although Jefferson did not respond directly to Logan's advice regarding manufactures, he concurred "in a sense of the necessity of restoring freedom to the ocean." The president rejected only his friend's suggestion that the United States pursue this goal by joining the European league of "armed neutrality." Instead, the young republic should, if necessary, make independent use of what Jefferson referred to as "the means of peaceable coercion." "Our commerce is so valuable to them [the nations of Europe]," the president reassured Logan, "that they will be glad to purchase it when the only price we ask is to do us justice."[2]

Because a brief interlude of peace in Europe and the Louisiana crisis focused American attention elsewhere, neither of Logan's "two objects" received much attention during Jefferson's first administration. His letter and Jefferson's response did anticipate, however, the issues and con-

1. Logan to Jefferson, Feb. 27, 1801, Thomas Jefferson Papers, Library of Congress (microfilm).

2. Jefferson to Logan, Mar. 21, 1801, Paul Leicester Ford, ed., *The Writings of Thomas Jefferson* (New York, 1892–1899), VIII, 23.

cerns that dominated Jefferson's second administration as well as the presidency of his successor, James Madison. The Jeffersonians soon discovered that the Louisiana Purchase alone could not ensure the basis for a republican political economy in America. The Purchase provided an abundant reservoir of open land for the future, and it afforded western farmers a safe route to the ocean; but it could not guarantee Americans the unrestricted access to foreign markets they needed. When the renewal and intensification of the European war brought this matter to a head after 1805, the Jeffersonians responded to massive restrictions on American trade with an experiment in commercial coercion on an unprecedented scale—the great embargo that lasted from December 1807 to March 1809. Conceived of as an alternative to the decadent European system of war, this ambitious venture failed to achieve its primary goal of liberating the republic's commerce, and eventually the Jeffersonians had to accept war as the dangerous but necessary means of furthering the Revolutionary vision of free trade.

In addition to culminating in a declaration of war against England in 1812, the failure of "peaceable coercion" prompted a renewed concern with the place of manufactures in the American economy. The embargo's tendency to encourage native manufactures was universally recognized, and some Americans—Federalists and Republicans alike—regarded the advancement of manufacturing as one of the primary purposes of commercial coercion. But the prolonged duration of the embargo, which few Jeffersonians had anticipated, greatly compounded any intended effect on the economy. As the Jeffersonians struggled to come to grips with the repercussions of their commercial policy, they debated the meaning that contemporary developments held for the future of a republican political economy. Their effort to accommodate encroaching economic realities was usually guided by a remarkably faithful attention to the latent implications of the original Revolutionary vision. For Jefferson and many Republicans, indeed, an active commitment to manufactures during and after the embargo did not represent a significant departure from their traditional conception of a republican political economy; they continued to think principally in terms of those very simple small-scale manufactures ("necessaries") that were appropriate to a predominantly agricultural stage of social development.[3] To this degree, the Jeffersonians'

3. See above, chaps. 4 and 6.

attention to manufactures in this period actually supported, rather than supplanted, their vision of a relatively young agricultural republic.

[I]

Jacob Crowninshield, a Republican merchant from Massachusetts, first informed President Jefferson in September 1805 of a new British justifi- cation for the seizure of American ships. Writing from Salem, Crownin- shield reported that the British had tightened their stand against America's participation in the neutral trade between France and Spain and their colonies by invoking a strict interpretation of the so-called "Rule of 1756." The *Essex* decision indicated that the subterfuge of the "broken voyage" would no longer be tolerated. If American merchants were to engage in a re-export trade of colonial produce, henceforth they would have to prove conclusively that their initial importation of enemy pro- duce into the United States had been in good faith, without prior inten- tion to re-export, rather than part of a devious attempt to disguise what the British regarded as illegal commerce. This new ruling clearly was designed to stifle America's mushrooming re-export trade, which had expanded rapidly after the renewal of war in Europe in 1803. Crownin- shield reported to Jefferson that the merchants in his region were "all very uneasy on this subject, as it strikes deeply at our export trade in foreign articles and will ultimately injure the whole commerce of the Country."[4]

Crowninshield's fears were shared by merchants from all over the United States, who began in early 1806 to flood Congress with memorials and petitions. New York City merchants stressed that British attacks on the re-export trade rendered the future of all commercial operations uncertain. The United States could not afford to concede the immediate principle, they argued, because such a concession would only encourage

4. Crowninshield to Jefferson, Sept. 11, 1805, Jefferson Papers. For more detailed discus- sions of the American re-export trade, the *Essex* decision, and the events of this period, see Dumas Malone, *Jefferson the President: Second Term, 1805–1809* (Boston, 1974), 59–61; Bradford Perkins, *Prologue to War: England and the United States, 1805–1812* (Berkeley, Calif., 1961), 77–84; Paul A. Varg, *Foreign Policies of the Founding Fathers* (East Lansing, Mich., 1963), 175–186; and Herbert Whittaker Briggs, *The Doctrine of Continuous Voyage* (Baltimore, 1926).

further British infringements on American commerce.[5] A common argument among Americans was that the *Essex* decision was only the entering wedge in an insidious British plot to clip the wings of their new commercial rivals in America. "We have reason to believe," asserted Congressman Barnabus Bidwell of Massachusetts, "that Great Britain is acting upon a systematic calculation, and with a design to engross the commerce of the world."[6] Thus, although the *Essex* principle directly affected only one branch of American commerce, immediate and firm resistance was necessary, for "if we acquiesce in their capturing a part," as Crowninshield put it, "Great Britain will extend her captures still further, and make a sweep of our whole trade."[7]

As Congress began debating possible responses to the *Essex* decision in early 1806, many Republicans, led by the indomitable John Randolph of Virginia, vigorously denied the need for any retaliation by the national government. Their argument was hinged on a familiar and very limited conception of the American "carrying trade" affected by the *Essex* doctrine. Nothing of real national significance, these Republicans contended, was actually at stake. What was in dispute was not "the fair, the honest, and the useful trade that is engaged in carrying our own productions to foreign markets, and bringing back their productions in exchange"; the British attacked only "that carrying trade which covers enemy's property, and carries the coffee, the sugar, and other West India products, to the mother country." "This mushroom, this fungus of war," as Randolph referred to the trade in question, was the product of exceptional circumstances and therefore destined to evaporate "as soon as the nations of Europe are at peace."[8] It was a trade, moreover, "totally unconnected with agriculture, and enjoyed by a few merchants only."[9] Since only the personal profits of these few merchants would be protected if the American government took retaliatory action, the potential costs and risks of such a policy were hardly justified by the threat.

According to Randolph and his supporters, in short, the young republic must not be trapped into protecting an unnatural and temporary

---

5. *Memorial of the Merchants of the City of New York* (New York, 1806). See also *The Memorial of the Merchants and Traders of the City of Baltimore* (Baltimore, 1806).

6. *Annals of Congress*, 9th Cong., 1st sess., XV, 654.

7. *Ibid.*, 554. See also a speech by Nathan Williams of New York, *ibid.*, 578.

8. *Ibid.*, 557.

9. *Ibid.*, 673. The quotation is from a speech by Congressman Joseph Nicholson of Maryland.

commerce at the expense of its more permanent and important interests. Such a practice was common to the decadent mercantilist governments of Europe, which all too often were dragged into corrupting wars as a result. "I, for one," declared Randolph, "will not mortgage my property and my liberty, to carry on this trade." Referring to the Republican attitude toward this "carrying trade" during the crisis of 1798–1799, he asserted that "the nation said so seven years ago—I said so then, and I say so now."[10]

Outside of Congress, other commentators agreed with Randolph that "no nation has ever denied or interrupted our necessary commerce, that is carrying out our own produce, or carrying in for home consumption, and beside that, we ought nationally to have nothing to do."[11] Drawing extensively on Adam Smith's *Wealth of Nations* for support, the pamphleteer Clement C. Moore vigorously argued that the only foreign commerce "truly advantageous" to a young country like the United States was that "which serves to promote the internal industry of the people, by affording a free vent for their surplus produce, and by bringing back, in return for it, foreign articles which could neither be so well nor so cheaply made at home." The wartime carrying trade, however, served no such purpose. Its "rapid and exorbitant" profits only fed the luxury of a mercantile elite, drained capital away from agriculture and the "natural commerce" allied to it, and threatened to disrupt the beneficial course of social development that Smith and good American republicans advocated. Moore admitted that when America's agricultural surplus became too great to find an advantageous market abroad, surplus capital would then have to be transferred to domestic manufacturing. Similarly, when the American population became "so great as to render it difficult for many to find employment, and to procure a competent subsistence at home" in either agriculture or manufacturing, these "supernumerary hands" might then properly have recourse to the carrying trade. The important point for Moore was that "the possibility of this superabundant population in our country is so remote as to bear the appearance of a chimera."[12] Given this fact, the federal government should ignore the

10. *Ibid.*, 557. See also a later Randolph speech, *ibid.*, 876. For other statements of this position by different congressmen, see *ibid.*, 623–628 (Peter Early), 643–650 (David R. Williams), 660–666 (Christopher Clark), and 686–698 (Nathaniel Macon). For a discussion of the Republican view of the carrying trade during the late 1790s, see above, chap. 7.

11. *Philadelphia Aurora*, Jan. 15, 1807. See also the previous issue of Jan. 14, 1807.

12. [Clement Clarke Moore], *An Inquiry into the Effects of Our Foreign Carrying Trade*

present clamor of merchants for protection of the lucrative but unnecessary commerce affected by the *Essex* decision.

This familiar Jeffersonian argument was now vigorously challenged, however, by a spate of Republican congressmen who took a very different approach to the "carrying trade" in question. Led by Crowninshield, they insisted that a matter of crucial and widespread significance was indeed at stake. As "an essential link in the chain of our commerce," America's re-export trade could not be sacrificed without serious consequences for the economy as a whole, because this trade was intimately "connected with the sales of our native exports, and indeed grows out of them."[13] American merchants exchanged domestic agricultural surpluses in the East and West Indies for tropical staples that had to be resold in Europe. If this circuitous trade was in any way obstructed, therefore, American farmers would eventually suffer the loss of valuable markets for their surpluses. As congressional critics of Randolph suggested, "what is called with us the carrying trade, and the direct trade, cannot be easily separated," and by necessity the American farmer had as much interest in that carrying trade as did the merchant.[14]

Crowninshield and his supporters argued, moreover, that a prosperous re-export trade was the vital and necessary means of offsetting America's chronically unfavorable balance of trade with England. They noted that the United States regularly purchased at least twelve million dollars more in imports from England than it sold her in exports and that this deficit could be overcome only through profits from the re-export trade.[15] The merchants of New York made this argument by stressing "the necessity of a circuitous trade, to enable us to realize the great value of exports in our native productions, by which alone we acquire the power to liquidate the balance against us, in our commerce with Great Britain."[16]

Viewed in this light, the *Essex* decision threatened not just one minor,

---

upon the Agriculture, Population, and Morals of the Country ... (New York, 1806), 11–12, 17, 13.

13. *Annals of Congress*, 9th Cong., 1st sess., XV, 656. The quotation is from a speech by Barnabus Bidwell.

14. *Ibid.*, 619. The quotation is from a speech by William Findley. See also *ibid.*, 634 (Ebenezer Elmer), 726–727 (John Jackson), 753–754 (Crowninshield), 795–796 (Willis Alston), and 865–872 (Thomas Newton).

15. *Ibid.*, 619 (Findley), 628–630 (William McCreery), 634 (Elmer), and 711–712 (George W. Campbell).

16. *Memorial of the Merchants of New York*, 24.

perhaps superfluous, segment of American commerce but the basic integrity of a highly interdependent American economy as well. If one link in the chain was broken, the economy would falter seriously, perhaps necessitating some fundamental structural changes. Conceding the *Essex* principle to the British, the New York merchants suggested, might "require us to divert much of our capital and industry to new employments."[17] Above all, the problem of America's large deficit in its trade with England reflected the primitive state of domestic manufactures. The United States always had to export its agricultural surpluses in order to pay for its heavy importation of necessary manufactures. If a serious disruption of the re-export trade made this balancing impossible, some commentators implied, the United States might be compelled to manufacture much more for itself. In this sense, a prosperous re-export trade even underwrote the viability of America's predominantly agricultural economy.[18]

President Jefferson's and Secretary of State Madison's response to this debate was to agree emphatically with Crowninshield that the re-export trade had to be defended. Jefferson noted in a message to Congress that the *Essex* doctrine challenged American rights "too evident and too important to be surrendered."[19] Thomas Cooper, who supported Randolph on this issue, was sharply rebuked by the president for suggesting that the endangered commerce did not warrant protection from the government. Jefferson never explicitly endorsed the arguments of Crowninshield and other Republicans in Congress about the broader importance of the re-export trade to American agriculture and to the economy as a whole; he simply insisted to Cooper that the government was obligated to protect the violated rights of American citizens engaged in that commerce.[20] But it seems reasonable to assume that Jefferson and Madison were influenced by the Crowninshield argument, especially since the Salem merchant often advised the administration on commercial matters.[21] By 1806,

17. *Ibid.*, 25.

18. See especially, *ibid.*, 19, 25, and the speech by Thomas Newton, *Annals of Congress*, 9th Cong., 1st sess., XV, 865–867.

19. Jefferson to Congress, Jan. 17, 1806, in James D. Richardson, comp., *A Compilation of the Messages and Papers of the Presidents, 1789–1908* (New York, 1908), I, 383. Madison apparently wanted to implement a permanent retaliatory system of commercial discrimination at this time. See Henry Adams, *History of the United States during the Administrations of Jefferson and Madison* (New York, 1891), III, 148–149.

20. Jefferson to Cooper, Feb. 18, 1806, and Cooper to Jefferson, Mar. 16, 1806, Jefferson Papers.

21. Later, in the fall of 1806, for example, Crowninshield provided Madison (at the

as the contrast with Randolph, Cooper, and other Republicans clearly indicates, Jefferson and Madison apparently believed that America's "carrying trade" was much more important than most Republicans had generally conceded during the late 1790s.

By late 1807, when the British began to escalate their campaign against American commerce by placing restrictions on the republic's direct trade with Europe, this debate over the importance of the re-export trade became less pressing. Predictions that the *Essex* decision portended further attacks on the republic's commerce proved correct. In November 1807 new British orders-in-council prohibited any neutral trade with Continental ports that were in enemy control except under British license. All American trade with the Continent, in other words, would now have to pass first through England. These orders represented more than retaliation against Napoleon's comparable Berlin Decrees; they were a further, thinly disguised attempt to protect British commerce against American competition. Most important, they dramatically changed the nature of the dispute between the United States and the European belligerents. Much more was now at stake than Randolph's "fungus of war," the debatable carrying trade. America's right to export its native produce directly to foreign markets—the cornerstone of its economy—was under siege.[22]

The British orders of November 1807 were the last in a series of provocations that prompted Jefferson's decision for a major experiment in "peaceable coercion." The embargo approved by Congress in December 1807, which prohibited American vessels from sailing to foreign ports and foreign vessels from taking on any cargo in the United States, ultimately lasted fourteen months. Although the theory behind this embargo was part of a tradition that went back to the non-importation movements before the Revolution, its extended length made it a novel experiment of unparalleled magnitude. The rationale for the embargo can probably best be deduced from earlier Jeffersonian statements, especially Jefferson's Report on Commerce in 1793 and Madison's defense of commercial

---

secretary's request) with a detailed report on American commerce as it affected Anglo-American relations, and Madison subsequently submitted a draft of the proposed Monroe-Pinkney Treaty to Crowninshield for his evaluation. See John H. Reinoehl, ed., "Some Remarks on the American Trade: Jacob Crowninshield to James Madison, 1806," *William and Mary Quarterly*, 3d Ser., XVI (1959), 83–118.

22. See, among many others, Varg, *Foreign Policies*, 193–194.

discrimination during the early 1790s.[23] Neither Jefferson nor Madison made any coherent or systematic statement of principle on the theory of the embargo throughout its duration, but a series of three articles published in the *National Intelligencer* shortly after the embargo began probably came from the pen of Madison.[24] These three articles are the best immediate clue to the rationale and objectives of the embargo.

The first article, which appeared December 23, 1807, unequivocally admitted the embargo's coercive purpose. Although the author made every effort to demonstrate that the embargo would be neutral and impartial, he could not fully disguise the fact that Great Britain, with its control of the seas and its alleged aim of monopolizing world trade, was the principal target. All the belligerents would suffer from the absence of American trade, to be sure; but Britain would feel it almost everywhere, "in her manufactures, in the loss of naval stores, and above all in the supplies essential to her colonies."[25] This familiar argument had been developed at such length in earlier debates on Jeffersonian commercial policy that it needed little elaboration. Foreigners, especially the British, would suffer much more than Americans in any test of commercial strength, since Americans would temporarily be deprived only of markets for their agricultural surplus, while foreigners would "feel the want of necessaries." The young republic could always feed itself, but the corrupt, mercantilist societies of the Old World and their colonies could not. They were directly dependent on the United States for subsistence, especially in wartime. Without American produce and without American customers to sustain their manufacturers, the familiar argument ran, these countries might literally starve. The European powers would thus have no choice but to grant America commercial justice.[26]

The *Intelligencer* articles suggested, moreover, that the embargo would serve an additional purpose—by necessitating a rejection of foreign luxuries, encouraging frugality, and promoting a renewed commitment to domestic industry it would rejuvenate America's political economy.

23. See above, chap. 6.

24. Malone, *Jefferson the President: Second Term,* 487–490. Malone suggests, in this regard, that Madison's faith in the embargo as a coercive weapon may have been greater than the president's. Irving Brant, Madison's biographer, believes that the secretary's authorship of the *Intelligencer* articles is unmistakable. See *James Madison: Secretary of State, 1800–1809* (Indianapolis, Ind., 1953), 402–403.

25. *National Intelligencer and Washington Advertiser* (D.C.), Dec. 23, 1807.

26. *Ibid.,* Dec. 28, 1807. See also *ibid.,* Dec. 25, 1807.

The embargo would "extend those household manufactures, which are particularly adapted to the present stage of our society," and would even favor "the introduction of particular branches of others, highly important in their nature." In this way, the American commitment to "peaceable coercion" would conclusively demonstrate to foreigners that the young republic was not abjectly dependent on foreign commerce and the finer manufactures it provided. The virtue of America would be aroused and its "national character" vindicated. "With other injured nations," the third article concluded, "there may be no choice, but between disgraceful submission or war." America was uniquely fortunate in that "a benignant providence" had given it a "happy resource for avoiding both," a resource that would also reaffirm the youthful vigor of its social character.[27]

This emphasis on frugality and domestic industry, which formed a crucial dimension of the Jeffersonian conception and public defense of the embargo, created a great deal of misunderstanding among hostile Federalists. Many of Jefferson's opponents were quick to accuse him of being fundamentally anti-commercial, since they viewed his embargo as indisputable evidence of a deep-seated hostility to the expansion of foreign commerce. They specifically charged that the Virginian favored a "passive commerce" for the United States, whereby any minimal economic contact with the outside world would be conducted solely by foreign merchants and shippers. According to Federalists, Republicans advocated a system of "passive commerce" because it was inexpensive and did not require the naval protection that an "active commerce" in American ships demanded. Convinced that Jefferson was bent on destroying native (particularly New England) merchants and shippers, enraged Federalists defended an independent American navigation system as the necessary guarantor of republicanism, echoing Noah Webster's declaration in 1800 that "public virtue depends greatly on steady attention to business, and business at home depends on a constant market for surplus produce, which must inevitably fail if we cease to be our own carriers."[28] Who could deny, the Federalists demanded during the embargo, either "the value of active commerce, that great promoter of

---

27. *Ibid.*, Dec. 28, 1807. See also *Reasons in Justification of the Embargo . . .* (Salem, N.Y., 1808), and Christopher Manwaring, *Individual and National Dependance . . .* (Hartford, Conn., 1808).

28. [Noah Webster], *A Rod for a Fool's Back* (New Haven, Conn., 1800), 4.

national wealth, industry, and morality" or "the futility and absurdity of a national system of passive commerce?"[29]

Driven by this fear that the real purpose of the embargo was the annihilation, rather than the liberation, of America's foreign commerce, scores of Federalists responded to the crisis of 1808 with a passionately ideological defense of commerce that drew on the rich, eighteenth-century heritage of pro-commercial writings. Americans were reminded that commerce was the source of industry, enterprise, civilization, and social progress, not to mention personal liberty itself; "her victories are over ferocious passions, savage manners, deep rooted prejudices, blind superstition and delusive theories."[30] In his alleged endeavor to destroy America's foreign commerce, Jefferson threatened to erase this salutary influence and promote a devastating reversion to savagery. Many Federalists insisted that Jefferson advocated a "Chinese" approach to political economy and that his policies were therefore directed toward the creation of an isolated, barbarous, and crudely self-sufficient America. If Jefferson had his way, they charged, Americans would be shut off from all foreign commerce; they would then "enjoy an eternal rusticity and live, forever, thus apathized and vulgar, under the shelter of a selfish, satisfied indifference."[31] The favorite Federalist analogy to Jefferson's ideal society was the ancient republic òf Sparta where, they did not fail to remind American republicans, slave labor had been the basis of a primitive, despotic, pre-commercial social order. To Federalists who never doubted the existence of a Jeffersonian conspiracy to impose the decadent Virginia way of life on the rest of the country, Noah Webster's injunction that "no nation, but *barbarians* and *slaves*, have ever been without commerce" seemed ominously apposite during the trying days of the embargo.[32] One Federalist observer, insisting that he bore no un-

29. *Remarks on the Embargo Law . . . by Civis* (New York, 1808), 13.

30. James Richardson, *An Oration, Describing the Influence of Commerce, on the Prosperity, Character and Genius of Nations* (Boston, 1808), 6. See also [Daniel Webster], *Considerations on the Embargo Laws . . .* (Boston, 1808).

31. *An Inquiry into the Present State of the Foreign Relations of the Union . . .* (Philadelphia, 1806), 19. See also *A Free Enquiry into the Causes . . . by a Citizen of Vermont* (Windsor, Vt., 1808).

32. [N. Webster], *Rod for a Fool's Back*, 5. See Richardson, *Oration*, 9–12, 18–20, and John Lowell, *The New-England Patriot: Being a Candid Comparison of the principles and conduct of the Washington and Jefferson administrations* (Boston, 1810), 100–101. See also Linda K. Kerber, *Federalists in Dissent: Imagery and Ideology in Jeffersonian America* (Ithaca, N.Y., 1970), chap. 2.

reasoning animosity toward Jefferson, offered a characteristically cynical but relatively charitable analysis of the president's motives and abilities:

I think him possessed of talents, of useful information, but they are not of that kind which qualify him for the government of an empire so extensive, so important, and so enterprizing, as that of the United States. In a republic like that of Lacedemon, if there is such in existence, insulated from all kinds of commerce with the world, unacquainted with the luxuries of any clime but its own, and having no temptation to industry or enterprise, I think he might be extremely useful in dealing out some useful precepts of philosophy or temperance, or measuring out with a ladle some dishes of the Spartan soup to a large family.[33]

Other Federalists, equally critical of Jefferson, took a somewhat different tack from those who accused him of attempting to mold a precommercial Spartan social order. They agreed that Jefferson was an enemy to foreign commerce who intended "a change in our habits, manners, and occupations," but they also accused him of desiring to force the development of advanced, large-scale manufactures in America. Rather than pushing America back in time toward a state of barbarous simplicity, in other words, he was deliberately pushing it ahead into a state of overrefined and corrupt social decadence. Under the Jeffersonian system, charged one Connecticut Federalist, America's proper status as a simple society—"bottomed on agriculture, connected with commerce"— would be exchanged "for the dissipated and effeminate manners and habits, which extensive establishments of manufactures, never fail to bring in their train."[34] A Boston writer added that "manufactures generally create large cities, and accumulate great numbers of individuals, who obtain a bare subsistence." He did not categorically oppose the establishment of manufactures in America, objecting only to the alleged Jeffersonian attempt to achieve this end by annihilating foreign commerce. "Would the existence of our present form of government," he asked, "be compatible with such a populace as exists in Lyons, Manchester, or Birmingham?"[35]

These Federalist charges, uniformly based on the assumption that the

---

33. *Remarks . . . by Civis*, 33–34. See also [John Park], *An Address to the Citizens of Massachusetts . . .* (Boston, 1808), and Thomas Thacher, *The Principles and Maxims on which the Security and Happiness of a Republic depend . . .* (Boston, 1811), esp. 12–13.

34. *Connecticut Courant* (Hartford), Apr. 6, 1808.

35. *Monthly anthology, and Boston Review*, VI (1809), 50.

Jeffersonians were purposely destroying the republic's commerce, remained common well into Madison's presidency and took on an even greater intensity during the War of 1812.[36] Madison himself was astounded by these accusations, labeling as "incomprehensible" the suggestion that he and Jefferson intended any "systematic exclusion of commerce." The "avowed object" of Jeffersonian policy, Madison contended, had always been "to liberate our commerce from foreign restrictions." "Temporary abridgements or suspensions of it," he insisted, always had "for their object its permanent freedom."[37] During the difficult days of the embargo, Republican writers emphasized their commitment to commerce as a pillar of republicanism in an effort to fend off Federalist criticism. Some painted a horrible picture of the consequences of an American failure to resist foreign aggression on the seas; if all of the belligerents' orders and decrees were successfully enforced, the republic would lose as much as half of its vital export trade.[38] Federalists easily retorted that as long as the embargo was in effect, all the trade was lost anyway. Defenders of the embargo were thus prompted to express both their confidence in the embargo's efficacy and their enthusiasm for the new world of free trade it would unquestionably produce. Once the oppressive edicts of the warring powers were lifted, "the embargo would no longer exist, and commerce would again enliven every town and village in the nation, every sail would be unfurled to the wind, and the merchant and the mariner, the farmer, the mechanic, and the labourer would all have full employment, and receive an adequate reward for their labour."[39] No one denied that the embargo was causing serious and extensive hardship; but ought not a virtuous people be able to endure temporary privations for the long-term well-being of the republic?[40] "We feel a confidence," announced a New Hampshire Republican in support

---

36. See, for example, George Grennell, *An Oration, Pronounced at Northampton on the anniversary of American independence, 1811* (Northampton, Mass., 1811); Justus E. Bollman, "A Cursory Inquiry into the Embargo Policy of the American Government," *American Review of History and Politics . . .* , III (April 1812), 306–332; and "Conspiracy Against Commerce," *Conn. Courant,* Jan. 11, 1814. See also Lowell, *New-England Patriot.*

37. Madison to David Humphreys, Mar. 23, 1813, James Madison Papers, Library of Congress (microfilm).

38. *Reasons in Justification of the Embargo,* 36–38.

39. *A Political Essay addressed to the people of Maryland, By a Farmer of Caecil County* (Baltimore, 1808), 38.

40. Selleck Osborn, *An Oration, Commemorative of American Independence . . .* (New Bedford, Mass., 1810).

of the embargo, "that we shall again navigate the ocean, free from insult, capture, or robbery, from any nation under heaven."[41]

Many defenders of the embargo made it clear that they supported an "active commerce" in American ships as much as any Federalist, but that peaceable coercion was the only means of achieving that end. Charles Jared Ingersoll, a Philadelphia lawyer who broke with his Federalist background by endorsing Jefferson's embargo, stressed his continuing commitment to an independent system of navigation. "Without an export trade in our own ships," he argued in defense of Republican policy, "the foreign demand would be very precarious, because it would be regulated, not by the interests of this country, but of that which monopolized the exportation." He asserted that the purpose of the embargo was not to drastically reorient the republic's economy toward manufacturing by de-emphasizing commerce, but rather to ensure the prosperity of an economy based squarely on agriculture and commerce. In this regard, Ingersoll reported that while he did not regret the appearance of manufacturing establishments in the neighborhood of Philadelphia during the embargo, he was acutely conscious of "the immorality, diseases, deformity, the slavish and mutinous tempers, the debauchery and miseries which are said to be the inmates of great factories." Citing the horrible British system that was supported by high taxes, pauper laborers, and wealthy masters of manufacturing houses, he rejoiced that the United States had not yet reached "this gradation of society" and decried any attempt to force this system on the republic prematurely. The key to American growth was the exportation of an agricultural surplus, and Ingersoll foresaw no problem with an inadequacy of foreign demand. Once the principle of free trade was established through the influence of the embargo, new markets for American farmers and merchants would open all over the globe. And in such a world, Ingersoll was confident, the United States' prosperity as an agricultural republic would be nothing short of staggering.[42]

While there can be no doubt that the Jeffersonians expected their commercial policies to encourage some degree of domestic manufacturing, this indirect result was not their primary goal, nor did most of them ever

41. Joseph Bartlett, *An Oration, Delivered at the Request of the Republican Citizens . . .* (Portsmouth, N.H., 1809), 11.

42. Charles Jared Ingersoll, *A View of the Rights and Wrongs, power and policy, of the United States of America . . .* (Philadelphia, 1808), 12, 13–14, 18, 19–28. See also [John Phelps], *The Present State of Our Country . . .* [n.p., 1808].

intend to alter the predominantly agricultural character of American society. The basic purpose of commercial coercion was to liberate American commerce from devastating foreign restrictions in order to underwrite and secure the prosperity of an agricultural republic. The unexpected duration and ultimate failure of "peaceable coercion" gave added reason for a Republican interest in the promotion of manufactures, but it never resulted in the serious redefinition of America's political economy that many Federalists imagined. In this connection, to understand fully and accurately the Jeffersonian approach to manufactures in this period, it is first necessary to examine the renewal of debate on manufactures that began just prior to the embargo.

[II]

Public debate on American manufacturing, which had been extensive during the 1780s and early 1790s, began to revive during Jefferson's first administration and climaxed in a congressional committee report of early 1804. Many different Americans embraced the cause of domestic manufactures, but they varied greatly in the nature and degree of their commitment. George Logan, for example, was light years apart from Alexander Hamilton in his political economy; yet he had always shared with Hamilton an interest in developing manufactures. The important point is that Logan and Hamilton meant something entirely different by "manufactures."

Logan is an excellent example of the zealous advocate of American manufactures who never wavered in his commitment to a relatively simple, overwhelmingly agricultural society. He consistently emphasized the importance of reducing an excessive importation of debilitating foreign luxuries by substituting domestic manufactures conducive to "those plain and simple manners, and that frugal mode of living, which are absolutely necessary in the infant state of our Country, and best suited to our Republican form of Government."[43] Logan's desire was never to make America "in the common acceptance of the Word, a Manufacturing Country," like England; he neither contemplated "any Manufactured

43. George Logan, *A Letter to the Citizens of Pennsylvania* . . . , 2d ed. (Philadelphia, 1800), 8. For a useful discussion of Logan's life and career, see Frederick B. Tolles, *George Logan of Philadelphia* (New York, 1953).

Article for an export Trade" nor wanted any American counterparts to those pathetic and exploited British workers who had been reduced by their employers through subsistence wages "to a mere animal existence." For Logan, in short, American manufacturing was not to be part of the mercantilist system that characterized European industry: "We want not that unfeeling plan of Manufacturing Policy, which has debilitated the Bodies, and debased the Minds, of so large a Class of People as the Manufacturers of Europe," he wrote. "Nor are we ambitious to see a Manufacturing Capitalist, as in the great Manufacturing Towns of Europe, enjoy his Luxuries, or fill his Coffers, by paring down the Hard-earned Wages of the laborious Artists he employs."[44] American manufacturers were to be independent citizens, either household producers or virtuous artisans, instead of the dependent "slaves" found in the large public manufactories of Europe.

Logan's approach to manufactures was quite similar to the position stated in an important congressional committee report of January 1804, which was a response to a deluge of petitions seeking public support for domestic manufactures. The report rejected the petitioners' plea for extensive governmental assistance by arguing that American manufactures were already making the right kind of progress without such aid. "Our works in wood, copper, hemp, leather, and iron," the committee noted, "are already excellent and extensive," and if America was not making similar progress "in the manufacture of the finer articles of cotton, silk, wool, and the metals," this deficiency should be viewed as a blessing, not as a problem to be overcome. "We may felicitate ourselves that, by reason of the ease of gaining a subsistence and the high price of wages," the report asserted, "our fellow-citizens born to happier destinies are not doomed to the wretchedness of a strict discipline in such manufactories." America could produce simple, coarse manufactures, in other words, but for the finer goods that required factories or large public establishments, the republic should happily rely on Europe. Indeed, the best political economy for America was one based on coarse manufactures and the exportation of agricultural surpluses that could be exchanged for these finer manufactures: "In a country devoted to agriculture, the cluster of arts and trades which minister to its wants spring up, of course, and almost from necessity. The plainer, coarser, and more useful fabrics in wool, leather, iron, flax, cotton, and stone, are manufactured with tol-

44. Logan, *Letter to Citizens*, 7, 19.

erable skill; while the more fine, costly, and high wrought articles of those several kinds can be procured more conveniently from foreign parts." Given the basic needs of an agricultural American economy, the committee warned in conclusion, any misguided attempt to force domestic manufactures by barring the importation of foreign manufactures would have dangerous consequences if it provoked retaliation against American exports. Eventually, "by the adoption of such a measure, we should have no market abroad for our produce, and industry [i.e., the character trait] would lose one of its chief incentives at home."[45]

This congressional report reaffirmed the traditional American commitment to small-scale manufactures that developed naturally at a predominantly agricultural stage of social development. Other Americans, however, were becoming increasingly impatient with this point of view. Especially in the more densely populated areas of New England, there was more and more talk of the need to go beyond these simpler manufactures. In Connecticut, for example, the fear of losing too many people to less heavily populated states through emigration supported a commitment to fostering manufactures "on an increasing scale."[46] Similarly, in eastern urban areas like New York, the chronic problem of idle, poverty-stricken city dwellers generated schemes for public workshops that could promote a fuller and more efficient employment of the republic's human resources.[47]

Perhaps the most coherent and incisive critique of the position expressed in the congressional committee report came in a direct reply to it published anonymously by Tench Coxe. The tone of Coxe's rhetoric was almost abusive. Congress, he charged, was only repeating outmoded and silly prejudices that were part of a colonial attitude instilled in Americans by their former mother country. Citing the passage in the report that spoke of America not being doomed to produce the finer manufactures,

45. The report may be found in the *Annals of Congress*, 8th Cong., 1st sess., XIII, 946–949.

46. *Conn. Courant*, May 14, 1806. See also the *American Mercury* (Hartford, Conn.), May 26, 1803, and May 28, 1807. David Humphreys made a serious effort to demonstrate that large-scale manufactures could thrive in America without ruining the health and morals of a laboring force. For a history of his Humphreysville, Connecticut, enterprise, see Frank Landon Humphreys, *Life and Times of David Humphreys* (New York, 1917). See also Richard J. Purcell, *Connecticut in Transition, 1775–1818* (Washington, D.C., 1918).

47. *New-York Evening Post*, Feb. 24, 1803. See also Raymond A. Mohl, "Poverty, Politics, and the Mechanics of New York City, 1803," *Labor History*, XII (1971), 38–51.

he ridiculed the insinuation "that wretchedness is inseparably connected with the arts necessary to polished society." Coxe contended that America could have its factories and more advanced manufactures without necessarily abandoning large numbers of its citizens to the miserable "wretchedness of a strict discipline," and he added that it was imperative that America move on to this "new and more exalted stage of industry, and consequent refinement." He insisted, moreover, that the development of the "complex manufactures" that would move America to this "more exalted state of civil society" necessitated congressional intervention. After outlining the familiar sequence of social development through the intermediate stage of agriculture with its cluster of necessary arts (the present stage of American social development celebrated in the congressional report), Coxe argued that "no step farther can be made . . . in the finer arts, which minister to the comforts of polished society, but by the direction of the legislature." "What enlightened princes have formerly done to excite their subjects to a more advanced state of society," he concluded, "must, in these confederated republics, be expected only from the wisdom of an enlightened Congress."[48]

Coxe's pamphlet was accompanied by a memorial to Congress from "The Society of Artists and Manufacturers of Philadelphia." This memorial reiterated Coxe's major arguments and suggested further that America was suffering from all the evils of "luxury" without enjoying any of its benefits. Instead of importing foreign luxuries, as it currently did, the United States should manufacture its own, for then it could enjoy all the benefits and advantages of luxury that had been described by numerous "political writers." Luxury, the memorial reminded Congress, "makes the rich contribute to the ingenious poor; calls forth talents, and circulates the wealth of a nation."[49] The striking contrast between this endorsement of luxury and advanced manufactures, Mandevillian in tone as well as content, and Logan's traditional approach dramatizes the serious differences in outlook among the various groups of early nineteenth-century Americans who advocated increased manufacturing.

Tench Coxe was a Jeffersonian, and undoubtedly there were others in the Republican fold who shared his enthusiasm for advanced manufac-

---

48. [Tench Coxe], *An Essay on the Manufacturing Interest* . . . (Philadelphia, 1804), 7, 15, 21, 25, 26.
49. *Ibid.*, appendix, v.

tures. But when Jefferson himself began discussing the impact of his embargo on the development of American manufactures, he placed himself much closer to the position of Logan and the congressional report. His primary interest was always in coarse, household manufactures. A major advantage of the embargo, he contended, was that it encouraged Americans to produce coarse manufactures ("in our families") in greater abundance than before, which lessened the need to import foreign goods of the same nature. Speaking of Virginia in early 1809, Jefferson noted that he could "affirm with confidence that were free intercourse opened again to-morrow, she would never again import one-half of the coarse goods which she has done down to the date of the edicts."[50] Here, in Virginia, he wrote to John Adams several years later, "we do little in the fine way, but in coarse and middling goods a great deal." "Every family in the country is a manufactory within itself, and is very generally able to make within itself all the stouter and middling stuffs for its own clothing and household use. We consider a sheep for every person in the family as sufficient to clothe it, in addition to the cotton, hemp and flax which we raise ourselves." "The economy and thriftiness resulting from our household manufactures," Jefferson concluded, "are such that they will never again be laid aside; and nothing more salutary for us has ever happened than the British obstructions to our demands for their manufactures. Restore free intercourse when they will, their commerce with us will have totally changed its form, and the articles we shall in future want from them will not exceed their own consumption of our produce."[51]

The embargo, Jefferson thus contended, had finally forced Americans to realize their full potential in *household* manufacturing, a momentous achievement that had always been implicit in the Revolutionary impulse. The important point for Jefferson was that this breakthrough eliminated the basis for the chronically unfavorable balance of trade with England that had traditionally crippled the republic. It is interesting, in this regard, that during the embargo Jefferson began to denounce viciously

50. Jefferson to David Humphreys, Jan. 20, 1809, Andrew A. Lipscomb and Albert Ellery Bergh, eds., *The Writings of Thomas Jefferson* (Washington, D.C., 1903–1904), XII, 235.

51. Jefferson to John Adams, Jan. 21, 1812, *ibid.*, XIII, 122–123. See also Jefferson to Du Pont de Nemours, June 28, 1809, Dumas Malone, ed., *Correspondence between Thomas Jefferson and Pierre Samuel Du Pont de Nemours, 1798–1817* (Boston, 1930), 124–125.

America's overextended carrying trade.[52] The embargo had been necessary, in part, to defend that trade, which provided a means of overcoming the unfavorable balance with England. In the future, however, since a more self-sufficient America would no longer face the problem of this unfavorable balance, such a vast carrying trade would be unnecessary. The American economy could thus be more balanced and less prone to foreign danger, and this change, for Jefferson, was the most permanent and valuable consequence of the embargo and the conditions that had provoked it. "An equilibrium of agriculture, manufactures, and commerce," he noted in April 1809, "is certainly become essential to our independence." He then laid down the following guidelines: "Manufactures, sufficient for our own consumption, of what we raise the raw material (and no more). Commerce sufficient to carry the surplus produce of agriculture, beyond our own consumption, to a market for exchanging it for articles we cannot raise (and no more). These are the true limits of manufactures and commerce. To go beyond them is to increase our dependence on foreign nations, and our liability to war."[53] As a result of the embargo, in short, Americans had substituted household manufactures for a dangerously overextended carrying trade.

Although Jefferson always stressed the importance of coarse, household manufactures, he was well aware that his embargo had also encouraged some of the finer, more advanced, large-scale manufactures, especially in northern cities. He was not convinced, however, that their development was extensive, nor did he think they would be permanent. By 1811, Jefferson's friend and correspondent, Du Pont de Nemours, feared that the United States was beginning to manufacture too much, and he emphasized the potentially dangerous effects of decreased trade and greater self-sufficiency on America's system of taxation. Du Pont suggested that if adequate revenue could not be procured in the future through import duties, the reimposition of odious direct and excise taxes, which the Jeffersonians were determined to avoid, might be neces-

52. See Jefferson to Colonel Larkin Smith, Apr. 15, 1809, Lipscomb and Bergh, eds., *Writings of Jefferson*, XII, 272. See also Merrill D. Peterson, *Thomas Jefferson and the New Nation: A Biography* (New York, 1970), 911, and Burton Spivak, *Jefferson's English Crisis: Commerce, Embargo, and the Republican Revolution* (Charlottesville, Va., 1979), esp. chap. 7.

53. Jefferson to Gov. James Jay, Apr. 7, 1809, Lipscomb and Bergh, eds., *Writings of Jefferson*, XII, 271.

sary.[54] Jefferson's response to this fear reflected his precise attitudes and expectations about America's future development.

It is true we are going greatly into manufactures; but the mass of them are household manufactures of the coarse articles worn by the laborers and farmers of the family. These I verily believe we shall succeed in making to the whole extent of our necessities. But the attempts at fine goods will probably be abortive. They are undertaken by company establishments, and chiefly in the towns; will have little success, and short continuance in a country where the charms of agriculture attract every being who can engage in it. Our revenue will be less than it would be were we to continue to import instead of manufacturing our coarse goods. But the increase of population and production will keep pace with that of manufactures, and maintain the quantum of exports at the present level at least: and the imports must be equivalent to them, and consequently the revenue on them be undiminished.[55]

Once commerce was reopened, in sum, a predominantly agricultural America would continue to import in sufficient quantities for revenue purposes the finer manufactures that it was not suited or, from the Jeffersonian perspective, not doomed to produce.[56] Jefferson was particularly pleased that the tax on these imports would fall exclusively on "the rich," or on those who consumed such luxuries, with the result that "the poor man in this country who uses nothing but what is made within his own farm or family, or within the U.S." might not have to be taxed at all. When Jefferson gazed into the future and anticipated the extinction of the national debt, he foresaw a surplus of revenue accruing from this taxation of imported luxuries, a surplus that might be put to advantageous use in the support of a wide variety of internal improvements. His vision of such a political economy in a debt-free America even took on a utopian cast.

Our revenues once liberated by the discharge of the public debt, and its surplus applied to canals, roads, schools, etc., and the farmer will see his government supported, his children educated, and the face of his country made a paradise by the contributions of the rich alone, without his being called on to spare a cent

54. Du Pont to Jefferson, July 23, 1808, and Sept. 14, 1810, Malone, ed., *Correspondence between Jefferson and Du Pont de Nemours*, 109, 127–129.

55. Jefferson to Du Pont, Apr. 15, 1811, *ibid.*, 132.

56. See also Jefferson to James Maury, June 16, 1815, Lipscomb and Bergh, eds.,

from his earnings. The path we are now pursuing leads directly to this end, which we cannot fail to attain unless our administration should fall into unwise hands.[57]

Despite Jefferson's emphasis on traditional household industry, it is important to recognize that he never abandoned his long-standing interest in adapting new advances in machinery to American manufacturing. As early as 1793, when Jefferson had first encountered news of Eli Whitney's cotton gin, he had anticipated the potential success of such inventions "for family use."[58] By 1812, he boasted to correspondents that American manufactures were "very nearly on a footing with those of England," which, he claimed, had "not a single improvement which we do not possess, and many of them better adapted by ourselves to our ordinary use." "We have reduced the large and expensive machinery for most things," Jefferson asserted, "to the compass of a private family, and every family of any size is now getting machines on a small scale for their household purposes."[59] Apparently Jefferson had visions of literally domesticating the industrial revolution. In America, technological advance would be assimilated to the traditional framework of small-scale industry, as Jefferson saw no necessary connection between the new machinery and more advanced, large-scale forms of production. By the end of the War of 1812, the ex-president noted that "carding machines in every neighborhood, spinning machines in large families and wheels in the small, are too radically established ever to be relinquished."[60]

Writings of Jefferson, XIV, 318–319, and Jefferson to Mr. Lithson, Jan. 4, 1805, *ibid.*, XI, 55–56.

57. Jefferson to Du Pont, Apr. 15, 1811, Malone, ed., *Correspondence between Jefferson and Du Pont de Nemours*, 133–134. Jefferson's interest in these future "internal improvements" is emphasized in Richard Ellis, "The Political Economy of Thomas Jefferson," Lally Weymouth, ed., *Thomas Jefferson: The Man, His World, His Influence* (London, 1973), 81–95. See also Joseph H. Harrison, Jr., "The Internal Improvements Issue in the Politics of the Union, 1783–1825" (Ph.D. diss., University of Virginia, 1954), chap. 4.

58. Jefferson to Eli Whitney, Nov. 16, 1793, Ford, ed., *Writings of Jefferson*, VI, 448.

59. Jefferson to General Thaddeus Koscuisko, June 28, 1812, Lipscomb and Bergh, eds., *Writings of Jefferson*, XIII, 170. Tench Coxe, in *A Statement of the Arts and Manufactures of the United States of America for the year 1810 . . .* (Philadelphia, 1814), also discussed the successful application of labor-saving machinery to household manufacturing. See also Samuel Rezneck, "The Rise and Early Development of Industrial Consciousness in the United States, 1760–1830," *Journal of Economic and Business History*, IV (1931–1932), 784–811, esp. 799.

60. Jefferson to James Maury, June 16, 1815, Lipscomb and Bergh, eds., *Writings of Jefferson*, XIV, 318.

Jefferson's emphasis on the small-scale production of simple, coarse manufactures was characteristic of many Republicans. President Madison's public references to America's budding manufactures stressed "household fabrics" and "useful manufactures." He did not fail to note the rise of "professional occupations" in addition to family industry, but he always emphasized the need to promote basic manufactures that would be central "to our defense and our primary wants."[61] In a Report on Manufactures presented to Congress in April 1810, Secretary of the Treasury Albert Gallatin made a clear distinction between "family manufacture" and "establishments, on an extensive scale." Although Gallatin acknowledged with pleasure that both forms were making rapid progress in the United States, he was particularly impressed by the recent extraordinary increase in household manufactures. He estimated, in this regard, that almost two-thirds of the clothing and linen of rural Americans was now "the product of family manufactures."[62] In some instances, the public incorporation of relatively large-scale manufacturing enterprises after the embargo served as a means of extending this household industry, rather than supplanting it. The 1811 General Incorporation Statute in New York, for example, was designed to encourage the construction of textile mills that would produce thread for household weaving. Thus even when public manufacturing was directly promoted, Americans still remained committed to the extension of small-scale, household industry.[63]

Henry Clay summarized a rough Jeffersonian consensus in 1810 when he observed that "in inculcating the advantages of domestic manufactures, it never entered the head, I presume, of any one to change the habits of the nation from an agricultural to a manufacturing society."[64] What Clay meant was that America would manufacture its own "necessaries," especially its coarse clothing, but nothing more. Above all, the republic would not manufacture extensively for export, as England did, for then the whole decadent system of large urban manufactories and

61. Madison's first (Nov. 29, 1809), second (Dec. 5, 1810), and third (Nov. 5, 1811) annual messages, Richardson, ed., *Messages and Papers of the Presidents*, I, 461–462, 469–470, and 480.

62. Gallatin's report is printed in *Annals of Congress*, 11th Cong., 2d sess., XXI, appendix, 2223–2239. See especially 2227, 2230.

63. See Ronald E. Seavoy, "Laws to Encourage Manufacturing: New York Policy and the 1811 General Incorporation Statute," *Business History Review*, XLVI (1972), 85–95.

64. *Annals of Congress*, 11th Cong., 2d sess., XX, 627, 626–630.

poverty-stricken landless laborers that Benjamin Franklin had first condemned in the 1760s and 1770s might be transferred to the United States.[65] Clay seemed less tightly riveted than many other Jeffersonians to household industry, but his emphasis on integrating specific kinds of manufactures—simple, coarse "necessaries"—into a basically agrarian, republican mold represented well the predominant Jeffersonian outlook of the immediate post-embargo period.[66]

Nevertheless, several Federalist congressmen felt compelled during Madison's first admini ration to argue strenuously against the excessive development of An.rican manufactures, a threatening prospect that they continued to attribute to the impact of Jeffersonian policy. They reminded their Republican listeners that America's happiness depended on its always remaining a predominantly agricultural society and that this condition required the republic's extensive participation in foreign commerce.[67] Such warnings were to most Jeffersonians, however, quite unnecessary. Most of them had never committed themselves to any manufactures beyond the simple household or small workshop scale, and they never envisioned a completely isolated America that did not require a considerable foreign commerce. As Jefferson acknowledged in his correspondence with Du Pont de Nemours, the United States would always have to export a large part of its agricultural surplus—no domestic market could ever absorb all of it—and it would always be necessary, therefore, to import some foreign manufactures in return. The Jeffersonians now hoped to limit these importations to the finer manufactures that an old, crowded, and corrupt Europe was peculiarly suited to produce. In this way, a more independent United States, producing all of its own coarse manufactures, might finally escape the trap of an unfavorable balance of trade with England, and, above all, never be dependent on foreign commerce for the basic necessaries of life.

Although the embargo had succeeded to this extent in furthering the

65. See above, chap. 2.

66. See also, for example, *Annals of Congress*, 11th Cong., 1st sess., XX, 185–186; *ibid.*, 11th Cong., 2d sess., XXI, 1845, 1894, 1899–1900; *ibid.*, 11th Cong., 3d sess., XXII, 760. For an interesting discussion of the place manufactures came to hold in the outlook of some groups of Jeffersonian theorists, see Richard J. Twomey, "Jacobins and Jeffersonians: Anglo-American Radicalism in the United States, 1790–1820" (Ph.D. diss., Northern Illinois University, 1974), chap. 5.

67. *Annals of Congress*, 11th Cong., 1st sess., XX, 1166–1167 (David Sheffey), and *ibid.*, 11th Cong., 2d sess., XXI, 1904–1906 (Philip Barton Key).

Jeffersonian vision, its disappointing failure to coerce the removal of foreign restrictions on the republic's commerce left much to be done. Indeed, the continuing American need to export its agricultural surplus to foreign markets remained a matter of the most fundamental concern to the Jeffersonians, as their ultimate decision to declare war on England in June 1812 indicated.

[I I I]

The Republicans' decision for war reflected their consistent commitment to the Revolutionary ideal of free trade, and to most of them free trade meant the unrestricted flow of exports to foreign markets. By 1812 President Madison and the Jeffersonians faced a choice of two basic alternatives. Either they could accept the failure of peaceable coercion to remove restrictions on American commerce and submit to the British orders-in-council, or they could attempt, through military means, a forcible assertion of America's right to an independent and unrestricted access to foreign markets. The first alternative was a humiliating prospect to most Republicans, and it was particularly unacceptable because it also implied that it might be necessary to reorient significantly America's political economy.

As western Republicans like Felix Grundy of Tennessee argued, the bone of contention between England and the United States had become "the right of exporting the productions of our own soil and industry to foreign markets."[68] A New England Republican reminded his listeners that back in 1806 many Americans had cried out for the government to defend the carrying trade; "but what is our precarious interest and disputed right in the carrying trade," he now asked, "compared with the extensive, necessary and direct commerce between us and continental Europe?"[69] As long as Great Britain closed off direct trade with the Continent, restricted the West Indian market, and dominated American

68. *Ibid.*, 12th Cong., 1st sess., XXIII, 424. See also Henry Clay's comments, *ibid.*, 600. For President Madison's views, see especially Madison to Jefferson, May 25, 1810, and Madison to the House of Representatives of the State of South Carolina, Jan. 8, 1812, in Gaillard Hunt, ed., *The Writings of James Madison* (New York, 1900–1910), VIII, 102, 174–175.

69. [Nathaniel Ruggles], *An Address to the Citizens of Norfolk County . . .* (Dedham, Mass., 1812), 15.

commerce in general, adequate markets and prices for the produce of American farmers would, according to most Republicans, be impossible. Restricted markets inevitably meant glutted markets, which in turn meant falling prices, idle American farmers, and a debilitating social malaise. To this extent, indeed, the basic integrity of America's republican political economy was at stake.[70]

Most Jeffersonians were unwilling to accept this seriously circumscribed foreign commerce and the alternative political economy it implied. If America were forced to become a "world within itself" on any kind of permanent basis, either its agricultural surplus would be seriously diminished for want of adequate markets, which raised the problem of how to sustain active, industrious, and prosperous republican farmers in an isolated and undeveloped America, or a vast domestic market would have to be created to absorb this large surplus, which implied the need to develop the large-scale, urban manufacturing most Jeffersonians could not accept. Both versions of this alternative political economy were incompatible with the traditional Jeffersonian conception of a republican political economy, and both were implicitly rejected in the decision for war in 1812.

It is interesting to note, in this regard, that in April 1812 Jefferson was reminded through personal experience of just how dependent American farmers were on foreign markets to sustain them. A sixty-day general embargo, generally recognized as the necessary prelude to a declaration of war, caught Virginia farmers, including Jefferson, with a large part of their spring harvest unmarketed. The ex-president noted to several correspondents, including President Madison, that a vent for this surplus was so absolutely necessary that even trade with "our enemies" would be desirable. Assuming the inevitability of war, Jefferson suggested that it might prove necessary to sanction a limited trade with the enemy, by license, in order to clear American surpluses and keep the republic's farmers contented. Madison rejected Jefferson's scheme of a license trade, but he agreed that somehow American surpluses would have to find their way to foreign markets.[71] Thus by June 1812, when the declaration of

---

70. For useful secondary discussions, see especially George Rogers Taylor, "Agrarian Discontent in the Mississippi Valley Preceding the War of 1812," *Journal of Political Economy*, XXXIX (1931), 471–505; Marshall Smelser, *The Democratic Republic, 1801– 1815* (New York, 1968), chap. 10; and Roger H. Brown, *The Republic in Peril: 1812* (New York, 1964).

71. Jefferson to Patrick Gibson, Apr. 12, 1812, and Jefferson to Madison, Apr. 17,

war finally came, the Jeffersonians appeared to acknowledge that, in the end, the American economy was just as dependent on Europe as the European economies were on America. The War of 1812 was more than a second war for American independence. To the Jeffersonian Republicans, it was a war to vindicate the promise of a republican political economy.

1812, Jefferson Papers. See also Irving Brant, *James Madison: The President, 1809–1812* (Indianapolis, Ind., 1956), 447–448.

CHAPTER TEN

THE REPUBLIC SECURED?

The Jeffersonians' decision for war in June 1812 initiated a critical period of readjustment in their endeavor to secure a republican system of political economy. The original conception of such a system, articulated by Benjamin Franklin in the 1760s and 1770s, had presumed the existence of conditions that were not uniformly realized. The hope for a steady westward expansion across the continent, with its promise of virtually unlimited free land, remained viable for the immediate future. But the dream of a liberal revolution in international commerce that would assure American producers the foreign markets they needed had been consistently frustrated. Certainly the second war for American independence did not, in itself, resolve this problem. Although the end of the Napoleonic conflict in Europe automatically brought with it the removal of many of the most burdensome restrictions on American commerce, others remained. For example, the United States would remain locked in peaceful combat with England over the critical West Indies trade for at least a decade to come.[1] As Thomas Jefferson remarked in 1816, Americans had come to experience what they had not believed possible thirty years earlier, "that there exist both profligacy and power enough to exclude us from the field of interchange with other nations."[2] The Jeffersonians could no longer anticipate with sufficient certainty secure and adequate markets abroad, a circumstance that eventually prompted them to make adjustments in their traditional republican outlook.

The "republican revolution" in political economy was based on the assumption that America would remain at a "middle stage" of social development. This synthetic vision represented an effort to adapt the

1. For a brief discussion of the West Indies controversy during the Monroe and Adams administrations, see George Dangerfield, *The Awakening of American Nationalism, 1815–1828* (New York, 1965), 148–151, 154–155, 158–159, 211, 258–260, and 264–265. For the reference to Franklin and the republican revolution, see above, chap. 2.

2. Jefferson to Benjamin Austin, Jan. 9, 1816, Andrew A. Lipscomb and Albert Ellery Bergh, eds., *The Writings of Thomas Jefferson* (Washington, D.C., 1903–1904), XIV, 391.

moral and social imperatives of classical republicanism to modern commercial society. According to this hybrid republican vision, American society was to grow prosperous and civilized without succumbing to luxury. As a people, Americans were to be active, diligent, and industrious, but not avaricious. Their republic was thus to be a more advanced, commercialized society than many of the primitive, even barbarous, republics of the past, but it was to stop far short of a perilous descent into Mandevillian decadence. Above all, this republican America was to be characterized by an unprecedented degree of social equality, whereby even the poorest man would at least be secure, economically competent, and independent. Indeed, the United States was to be a revolutionary society precisely because it would not have the permanent classes of privileged rich and dependent poor that Americans associated with the "old" societies of mercantilist Europe. Such was the republican dream, a utopia anchored to westward expansion and free trade.[3]

Despite persistent fears about the corrupting influence of foreign trade, commerce had always played an integral role in the republican vision. As a necessary solvent of idleness and degeneracy, commerce was the vital stimulus to industry that would establish Americans as a virtuous people. Virtuous republicans had to be industrious; in a bountiful America, productive farmers had to rely on foreign markets to absorb the prodigious fruits of their republican labor and thereby support sustained industry in agriculture beyond the labor necessary for mere subsistence. To this degree, America depended on foreign commerce to maintain its moral character. Should sufficient markets abroad not be available, the republic appeared to face the prospect either of declining into a state of uncivilized indolence or of being compelled to pursue incentives to industry and exertion other than those provided by agriculture and the export trade. This latter strategy had always suggested the uninviting alternative of cultivating advanced manufactures and the other accouterments of a "luxury" economy that were customarily thought necessary to provide employment for the idle members of a populous society.[4]

From this perspective, America's republican challenge remained that of keeping its people industriously employed in virtue-sustaining occu-

---

3. *Ibid.*, chaps. 1, 2, and 3. For a typical restatement of the "middle stage" concept as it related to commerce, see William C. Jarvis, *The Republican, or A Series of Essays on the Principles and Policy of Free States* (Pittsfield, Mass., 1820), 202.

4. See above, chaps. 3 and 4.

pations. To some extent, as James Madison had suggested as early as the 1780s, America's dilemma in political economy paradoxically arose from its tremendous productive capacity—from its ability to produce a massive surplus beyond subsistence, and not from the Malthusian specter of nature's inability to provide adequate sustenance for an expanding population. Indeed, the republic's ability to yield an easy subsistence, which reflected its great natural wealth, might ironically become a curse if republican incentives to industry and exertion, capable of keeping the American people virtuously employed, were not secured.[5]

Viewed in this light, the Jeffersonians' commitment to war in 1812 marked the culmination of their struggle to vindicate the Revolutionary goal of free trade with its promise of abundant markets abroad that might stabilize a virtuous republic. This commitment was made, however, in the midst of growing doubts and anxieties about the capacity of foreign markets to sustain a republican political economy in America. These doubts became more intense during and immediately after the war, when Americans examined and debated at some length the meaning of their post-Revolutionary experience. Emerging from this debate was a noticeable reorientation of Republican political economy toward a more definite emphasis on the development of domestic manufactures and an extensive home market for American produce. Implicitly acknowledging the logic of Alexander Hamilton's argument of the early 1790s, even many Jeffersonians now admitted the need to integrate large-scale manufactures (beyond the simple household or small workshop scale) into their conception of a republican political economy. This concession did not represent a sudden capitulation to the Hamiltonian vision, but the cumulative force of experience nudged many Jeffersonians into accommodating much of what they had traditionally feared and rejected. Their original vision was never consciously abandoned; it was subtly adapted to the exigencies of a world that could not be molded to the shape of their Revolutionary dreams.

Indeed, these adjustments in the Republican outlook were generally made within the traditional framework of perception and debate. Most Jeffersonians continued, in other words, to interpret the interdependent realm of polity, economy, and society in the light of the same fears and concerns that had informed Franklin's outlook on the eve of the Revolution. Certainly Jefferson and Madison remained committed to the goal of

5. *Ibid.*, chap. 5.

securing a youthful and predominantly agricultural republic, one that would escape to the greatest possible extent the adverse effects of social development through time. But as these two elder statesmen in retirement contemplated the fate of America's republican revolution, they came to differ significantly in their identification of the most serious obstacle to its fulfillment. Continuing to evade a confrontation with the most devastating threat to his vision, the institution of black slavery, Jefferson became preoccupied with the specter of political corruption in the form of a revived Hamiltonianism. Madison's attention was focused more on the implications of the sensitive relationship between demographic expansion, foreign markets, and American social character. Neither of these concerns was new; each emerged from a well-known republican context. And although neither Jefferson nor Madison ever succumbed completely to pessimism and despair, both men remained troubled by an unhappy, apparently unshakable truth: the republican social order that they had labored so long to secure was necessarily ephemeral.

[I]

Perhaps the most important wartime debate in political economy concerned the relative importance of foreign and domestic commerce. This debate had been brewing for some time. The subject had become a pressing one in England by the early years of the nineteenth century, and it took on enhanced relevance in America after the embargo.[6] In both England and America, critics of foreign commerce condemned the traditional emphasis on an extensive overseas trade and argued instead the comparative merits of a highly developed internal trade. Defenders of foreign commerce always responded vigorously to such attacks. Participants in the American debate rarely took the extreme position of arguing that America should forgo either foreign or domestic commerce; the dispute was over which form of trade was more valuable, more productive, and therefore worthy of greater encouragement and support.

Commentators on both sides of the American controversy were tremendously concerned with the familiar problem of generating sufficient incentives to industry among a republican people. Especially after 1805,

6. For a statement from the English debate, see James Mill, *Commerce Defended . . .* (London, 1808). In this tract Mill reviews the range of arguments on both sides.

an enhanced interest arose in providing stimulants for industry in what was often seen to be an underdeveloped, even stagnating, America. Joel Barlow, for example, argued in precisely those terms the value of cultivating the "fine arts" in America: "In proportion as they multiply our wants, they stimulate our industry, they diversify the objects of our ambition, they furnish new motives for a constant activity of mind and body, highly favorable to the health of both."[7] In the wake of the embargo, indeed, more and more Americans expressed the fear that America was stagnating, that the republic was wasting its abundant resources by failing to generate adequate sources of industry. It was not correct to say, argued Robert Hare in 1810, that "we produce already as much as we can," since "the prodigious amount of our exports during periods of extraordinary foreign demand, sufficiently proves that in ordinary times, we have not full employment for our means of production."[8] "We should omit no exertions," agreed Laommi Baldwin in the conclusion to his *Thoughts on the Study of Political Economy* in 1809, "to call into useful activity the latent energies of the country."[9]

The subsequent wartime debate over the relative merits of foreign and domestic commerce was usually focused on this matter of calling into "useful activity" the dormant energies of the young republic. Defenders of foreign commerce pointed to its primary importance, especially in a predominantly agricultural economy, as a source of industry, prosperity, and civilized refinement. They argued that foreign trade was more valuable than domestic commerce in this capacity, because foreign trade excited a greater degree of native industry by extending the lure of new, different, and exotic products.[10] "A nation, when trying to withdraw from the great society of nations, and to suffice to herself," noted one vindicator of foreign commerce, "assumes a situation, probably not the most favourable for the attainment of either civilization or pros-

7. Joel Barlow, *Prospectus of a National Institution, to be Established in the United States* (Washington, D.C., 1806), reprinted in William K. Bottorff and Arthur L. Ford, eds., *The Works of Joel Barlow* (Gainesville, Fla., 1970), I, 496.

8. Robert Hare, *A Brief View of the Policy and Resources of the United States . . .* (Philadelphia, 1810), 89.

9. Laommi Baldwin, *Thoughts on the Study of Political Economy . . .* (Cambridge, Mass., 1809), 72.

10. Charles Ganilh, "An Introduction to the Study of Political Economy," *American Review of History and Politics . . .* , IV (October 1812), 345, 306–353.

perity."[11] The important point was that foreign commerce always put a greater amount of national industry into motion than domestic commerce, thereby rescuing many men from idleness, barbarism, and even starvation. A highly developed international division of labor, taking the greatest possible advantage of a natural diversity among both men and nations, was thus the best means of promoting the amelioration of the human condition in all countries. As one observer put it in 1813, "The utmost division of labour, . . . unabated activity, unremitted exertions to extend improvements, enlarged ideas, and their great result—a steady progress of civilization—are only compatible with those prudential considerations that ultimately guide the conduct of individuals, in a country enjoying an extensive foreign trade."[12]

Such defenders of foreign commerce usually recognized, however, that they had to deal more convincingly with the common rejoinder that domestic trade could perform many of the same functions just as well, especially in a vast empire like China (or potentially in the United States) that appeared to have the capacity to form "a world in itself."[13] According to supporters of foreign commerce, there was one final, irrefutable argument in their favor: foreign trade was essential to the prosperity of the laborers and producers of every society because the domestic market for their industry was necessarily limited. Supply eventually exceeded domestic demand; as production increased to the point of glutting the home market, prices sank to their lowest rates, and the ensuing struggle for employment ultimately relegated more and more laborers to poverty and even starvation. Since "foreign consumption, on the contrary, has no limits," and since "the merchants—the agents between domestic producers, and foreign consumers, are constantly on the watch to extend its sphere," the conclusion was obvious: "Foreign commerce is the surest, and perhaps the only means, of maintaining the staple commodities of a nation, at prices which will insure to the mass of the people the enjoyment of substantial comforts, and allow them to be rational beings, and men, instead of mere drudges, and beasts of burthen."[14] From this per-

---

11. Dr. E. Bollman, in the *Emporium of Arts and Sciences*, N.S., II (December 1813), 121.

12. *Ibid.*, 135.

13. *Ibid.*, 136.

14. *Ibid.*, 159–161.

spective, foreign commerce and the markets it provided were the only solution to the problems of surplus production, a glutted home market, and social decay.

This argument was one that James Madison and American republicans of his ilk generally appreciated, for they had consistently stressed the importance of foreign markets to the health and security of the republic. Yet more and more of them were gradually coming to question this emphasis, in large part because its rationale no longer jibed with reality. Foreign markets for America's surplus had hardly proved to have "no limits," and many Americans began to wonder if the potential of the republic's domestic market had yet been tapped. In this regard, one commentator argued that a home market was dangerously limited only in overpopulated and badly governed countries like England, where a mercantilist emphasis on the exportation of manufactures created a depressed, exploited, and poverty-stricken labor force that had little purchasing power. In republican America this situation would not obtain, and perhaps, therefore, strictures against domestic commerce on this count might not be relevant.[15]

Defenders of domestic commerce and the home market became increasingly vocal during the war. These critics of foreign commerce stressed the precarious nature of overseas trade and its inability to provide a constant, secure demand for domestic industry. American agriculture needed a more dependable home market, and that home market had to be systematically cultivated. For this reason, a more compact population that would permit manufacturing on a substantial scale was desirable, since there would be greater industry and exertion among the American people if they were brought closer together and encouraged to engage in a civilizing commerce among themselves. As the domestic division of labor increased, a greater refinement of manners and the cultivation of Barlow's "fine arts" would naturally result. Above all, once the potential for this home market was realized, there would no longer be a need to rely so heavily on foreign markets to absorb America's agricultural surplus and thereby sustain the industry and moral integrity of its citizens.[16] A more compact, closely integrated republic would not require, in short, an elusive world of free trade to support it.

15. *Ibid.*, 159. The commentator was Thomas Cooper, the editor of the *Emporium of Arts and Sciences*, reacting to Bollman's defense of foreign commerce.

16. See, for example, *ibid.*, N.S., I (June 1813), 1–14; "On Density of Population," *Port*

Critics of foreign commerce often emphasized this final point. They claimed that the burden of idleness and unemployment in the American republic had become serious enough to warrant significant alterations in its political economy. In the West, argued one observer, the chronic problem of idleness emanated from the simultaneous presence of a vast productive potential and the "want of a market" for that potential surplus. "In these regions upon which nature has smiled," he noted, "there is a redundance of physical force," along with "a want of employment, a want of that stimulus to action, which nothing would so effectually create as a well directed factory." This commentator even complained that the embargo had been temporary, for it was time, he argued, to abandon the chimera of free trade and boundless markets abroad and build instead a dynamic, self-sufficient economy "independent of foreign commerce."[17]

Few Republicans went quite so far. But during and immediately after the war many of them did put a greater emphasis on both domestic manufactures and the creation of a more dependable home market. A common explanation, among the many given for this shift, was the inadequacy of foreign markets for bringing into operation the full productive labor of the country.[18] Isaac Briggs, a Republican surveyor from Maryland, advanced this argument for manufactures on several occasions. Briggs always presented himself as a zealous advocate and friend of American agriculture. "Agriculture must, in the nature of things," he noted in 1816, "be governed by the market for its surplus production," and it was therefore necessary for Americans to "enquire into the possibilities of the present and future markets" accessible to them. Briggs estimated that in all probability the annual demand for America's surplus

---

folio, 4th Ser., VI (August 1815), 164–175; and "Letter on Domestic Manufactures," *American Review of History and Politics*, IV (October 1812), 367–375. For relevant secondary studies, see: Kenneth Wyer Rowe, *Mathew Carey: A Study in American Economic Development*, Johns Hopkins University Studies in Historical and Political Science, LI (Baltimore, 1933); Richard Gabriel Stone, *Hezekiah Niles as an Economist* (Baltimore, 1933); Charles Patrick Neill, *Daniel Raymond: An Early Chapter in the History of Economic Theory in the United States*, Johns Hopkins University Studies in Historical and Political Science, XV (Baltimore, 1897); and Dumas Malone, *The Public Life of Thomas Cooper, 1783–1839* (New Haven, Conn., 1926).

17. "Letter on Domestic Manufactures," *American Review of History and Politics*, IV (October 1812), 370, 372. See also "Political Economy," *Emporium of Arts and Sciences*, N.S., III (June 1814), 172–173.

18. See also "Political Economy–No. I," *Niles' weekly register*, June 7, 1817, 225–227.

produce would never exceed forty-two million dollars, a figure he took from the commercial statistics for 1803. The American capacity to produce a surplus, however, was constantly expanding. By 1817, Briggs estimated, this potential would reach eighty-four million dollars, or twice the normal foreign demand. The consequences were clear: "Either a vast amount of surplus produce would lie dead upon our hands; or, by attempting to force a sale, we should reduce the price; in either case, the necessary stimulus being withdrawn, industry would languish."[19] Eventually, the moral integrity of the American republic would be undermined by this faltering economy, "for as markets fail, the demand for labor will diminish; many will become idle for want of employment; our streets and highways will be infested with mendicants and robbers; our prisons will be filled and crimes will increase." In such a situation, America would develop its own substantial class of wandering poor, and the republican revolution would be overturned. Briggs worried that the return of peace and stability to Europe, by seriously diminishing foreign demand for the American surplus, would make this prospective crisis even more acute. The immediate construction of a more balanced economy with a dependable home market was therefore imperative.[20]

There were other reasons for an enhanced Republican attention to manufactures. Jefferson, Madison, and James Monroe, among others, stressed the importance of manufactures to America's independence and military security.[21] The pre-war crisis as well as the war itself had demonstrated the danger of relying on a precarious foreign commerce "for articles necessary for the public defense or connected with the primary wants of individuals."[22] Americans must learn to manufacture all such "necessaries," it was argued, if the United States was ever to be a truly independent republic. The embargo and the war had provided a welcome

19. Isaac Briggs addressing the chairman of the Committee of Commerce and Manufactures, Jan. 25, 1816, *ibid.*, Feb. 3, 1816, 390, 389–392.

20. Isaac Briggs's address to the Oneida Society for the Promotion of American Manufactures, *ibid.*, Nov. 29, 1817, 213, 212–214. See also *ibid.*, May 10, 1817, 166–167.

21. See, for example, Jefferson to Austin, Jan. 9, 1816, Lipscomb and Bergh, eds., *Writings of Jefferson*, XIV, 387–393; Madison's fifth (Dec. 7, 1813), seventh (Dec. 5, 1815), and eighth (Dec. 3, 1816) annual messages, in James D. Richardson, ed., *A Compilation of the Messages and Papers of the Presidents, 1789–1908* (New York, 1908), I, 524–525, 552, 559; and Monroe's first inaugural address (Mar. 4, 1817) and first annual message (Dec. 2, 1817), *ibid.*, 577–578, 587.

22. Madison's seventh annual message, Richardson, ed., *Messages and Papers of the Presidents*, I, 552.

boost in the right direction. Now the federal government must offer post-war protection for those useful manufactures that had grown up. The result of this logic was the moderately protective tariff passed by Congress in 1816. To a great extent, Republican support for this tariff stemmed from a concern for the republic's security, particularly from the fear of America's vulnerability in any future war. Many Jeffersonians, indeed, limited their commitment to a moderate protection only of manufactures that were of prime necessity and essential to defense.[23]

Significantly, however, such a commitment increasingly tended to include more advanced, large-scale manufactures. Madison referred explicitly in his 1815 annual message, for example, to "manufacturing establishments . . . of the more complicated kinds" that were in need of post-war support.[24] Certainly the Republican emphasis on household industry did not disappear, but the rigid association of useful manufactures, or "necessaries," with family and other small-scale manufactures had noticeably weakened. Perhaps a growing recognition of the need for a more developed domestic market on a national scale encouraged this new receptivity to large-scale manufactures. In any case, as they struggled to integrate more advanced, public manufactures into an acceptable republican mold, some Jeffersonians began to question the traditional association of large-scale industry with both poverty and luxury. If large-scale manufactures were not invariably luxuries, and if they did not necessarily entail the dehumanization of a poor, landless laboring force, then perhaps America might be able to absorb them safely after all.

In this regard, although some commentators continued to condemn all "very large and very expensive manufacturing establishments," other observers made a crucial distinction.[25] Large-scale manufactures that were part of a mercantilist system, in which a corrupt government promoted the production of luxuries (especially for export) by a degraded, viciously exploited working force, must always be condemned.[26] But large manufactories need not always take this treacherous form. Indeed,

23. See especially, Norris W. Preyer, "Southern Support of the Tariff of 1816—A Reappraisal," *Journal of Southern History*, XXV (1959), 306–322, and Murray N. Rothbard, *The Panic of 1819: Reactions and Policies* (New York, 1962), chap. 6.

24. Madison's seventh annual message, Richardson, ed., *Messages and Papers of the Presidents*, I, 552.

25. *Connecticut Courant* (Hartford), Feb. 25, 1817.

26. See, for example, Du Pont de Nemours to Jefferson, Mar. 31, 1816, Dumas Malone, ed., *Correspondence between Thomas Jefferson and Pierre Samuel Du Pont de Nemours*,

the American republic already had several large establishments that did not. The problem in Britain, where "disgusting exhibitions of human depravity and wretchedness" prevailed, was that "unequal laws and bad examples" perverted public industry. Under a mercantilist system ruthless employers pressed wages to a minimum, but in America, where emigration to free land was always an alternative and where government was not corrupt, "there are extensive manufactories, and yet no such consequences are observed."[27] Manufactures in themselves never caused poverty and misery. The culprit was usually a mercantilist system of political economy that promoted "a state of society" that Briggs and other pro-manufacturing Republicans continued to hope would remain "very distant from our happy land."[28]

One particularly vocal Republican proponent of manufactures, domestic commerce, and a home market in this period was Thomas Cooper. As editor of the *Emporium of Arts and Sciences* and in his private correspondence, Cooper articulated the full range of Republican reasons for an enhanced interest in manufactures and a more balanced national economy.[29] By 1814 Cooper was intensely worried about the oppressive lethargy and lack of energy that he detected in all spheres of American life. In this regard he even compared the young republic unfavorably to monarchical Britain. Pointing especially to the habitual idleness of the lower classes in America, Cooper ridiculed the fatuous delusion among Americans that their country was "the most enlightened nation on the face of the earth." On the contrary, the United States suffered from a dearth of manufactures, the advanced arts, and civilized refinement in general. Although Cooper conceded "to a great extent" the customary

---

1798–1817 (Boston, 1930), 180, and the *Emporium of Arts and Sciences*, N.S., II (December 1813), 161–167.

27. "Address of the American Society for the Encouragement of Domestic Manufactures," *Niles' weekly register*, Jan. 25, 1817, 368. See also the *American Mercury* (Hartford, Conn.), Jan. 21, 1817.

28. Briggs's address to Oneida Society, *Niles' weekly register*, Nov. 29, 1817, 213. Many supporters of manufactures also stressed that improvements in machinery made large-scale manufactures acceptable in a republican society, since these manufactures no longer required costly and burdensome human labor. See, for example, "On Manufactures," *Emporium of Arts and Sciences*, N.S., III (August 1814), 301–304.

29. Later in Cooper's life, when he had become a doctrinaire anti-tariff free trader in South Carolina, he would be somewhat embarrassed by the bold stand he had taken during and immediately after the war. See Malone, *Life of Cooper*, 293–294, and Joseph Dorfman, *The Economic Mind in American Civilization* (New York, 1946–1959), II, 527–539.

arguments against extensive manufactures, he insisted that in America the production of these manufactures need not entail the debilitating effects exhibited in Britain, where they were carried to far too great an extent under "a system congenial with the spirit that pervades the political government of the country." In a republican America free from such a corrupt mercantilist spirit, Cooper believed that the undeniable advantages of large-scale manufactures far outweighed their disadvantages.[30]

Nevertheless, Cooper always made it clear that he preferred to limit American production to articles "such as we feel the want of in time of war" and "such as may fairly be regarded as of prime necessity, or immediately connected with agricultural wants and pursuits." He wanted no frivolous superfluities produced in America, no luxuries like "the velvets of Lyons or the silks of Spitalfields—the laces of Brussels and the lawns of Cambray . . . the clinquaillerie and bijouterie of Paris and Birmingham."[31] America had no need to produce worthless gewgaws; its problem was that it remained dangerously dependent on Britain for more fundamental "necessaries," essential supplies that it must now manufacture for itself. Like most Republicans, Cooper also stressed the advantages of the home market this extensive manufacturing would create, but he surpassed many of them in his optimism that this market could grow large enough to absorb completely the republic's agricultural surplus for a century to come.[32]

Cooper's tentative hope that America might become a more advanced, dynamic, and self-sufficient society without succumbing to mercantilist corruption reflected a significant post-war trend in Jeffersonian political economy. Above all, many Republicans finally confronted the disturbing possibility they had evaded for so long: that an overwhelmingly agricultural economy was simply incapable of sustaining an industrious and fully employed citizenry. In one sense, their republican commitment to the fostering of such a citizenry had to take precedence over their pastoral sympathies, for it appeared that the Jeffersonians might continue to abjure manufacturing and social development through time only, paradoxically, at the expense of their character as a people. Haltingly and with much trepidation, but for good republican reasons, therefore, they

<hr />

30. Cooper to Thomas Jefferson, Aug. 17, 1814, Thomas Jefferson Papers, Library of Congress (microfilm).

31. *Emporium of Arts and Sciences*, N.S., I (June 1813), 9.

32. *Ibid.*, 7.

struggled to accommodate their traditional vision to a more modern economic order.

[II]

The Jeffersonians' accommodation to modernity was rarely carried far enough to overturn completely the traditional framework of assumptions that continued to guide their understanding of political economy. Most of the original fears and expectations associated with the idea of a republican revolution persisted well into the post-war period, especially in the minds of the elder statesmen, Jefferson and Madison. Jefferson's post-embargo acceptance of manufacturing, for example, is too often exaggerated. His commitment to a balanced economy prompted only a grudging approval of large-scale production, and even his limited concessions on this score were invariably hedged. As one of his biographers has persuasively concluded, he never wholeheartedly or enthusiastically embraced any manufacturing beyond "the household-handicraft-mill complex of an advanced agricultural society."[33]

Jefferson continued, above all, to put great faith in the potential of westward expansion to sustain a rough equality of wealth and power in a demographically explosive America.[34] In 1815 he celebrated the republic's rapid population growth for its role in "maturing and moulding our strength and resources," and he anticipated the day when a stable America would have no fear of "encountering the starved and rickety paupers and dwarfs of English workshops" in any test of commercial or military strength.[35] At the end of the second war for American independence, Jefferson remained confident that the expansion of America's growing population across the continent would nourish an even stronger republic, for he was still convinced that "a government by representation is capable of extension over a greater surface of country than one of any other form."[36] The illustrious Montesquieu had been wrong, as the American experience had already demonstrated and would continue

33. Merrill D. Peterson, *Thomas Jefferson and the New Nation: A Biography* (New York, 1970), 941.

34. Jefferson to Thomas Cooper, Sept. 10, 1814, Jefferson Papers.

35. Jefferson to Du Pont, Dec. 31, 1815, Malone, ed., *Correspondence between Jefferson and Du Pont*, 172–173.

36. Jefferson to Du Pont, Apr. 24, 1816, *ibid.*, 185.

to confirm. "My hope of its [i.e., the republic's] duration," Jefferson wrote in 1817, "is built much on the enlargement of the resources of life going hand in hand with the enlargement of territory, and the belief that men are disposed to live honestly, if the means of doing so are open to them."[37]

Yet Jefferson's post-war optimism was never completely unguarded. By the end of his life, in fact, it had rather suddenly and considerably evaporated. After the war he remained particularly suspicious of New England's susceptibility to the corrupt influence of English models in political economy, and this suspicion prompted him to look more and more to the South and the West as the true guarantors of American republicanism. During the war he had expressed to the South Carolinian Henry Middleton his growing belief that "in proportion as commercial avarice and corruption advance on us from the north and east, the principles of free government are to retire to the agricultural States of the south and west, as their last asylum and bulwark."[38] Jefferson was to become ever more wary of what he perceived to be the insidious schemes of northerners to impose on the republic their region's unsound principles and way of life; after 1819, this tendency to view the United States in terms of stark sectional divergences intensified. It was accompanied, moreover, by a strident assertion of the most rigid, uncompromising agrarian-mindedness that Jefferson had ever expressed in his long public career.[39]

Jefferson's frantic retreat to a sectional, narrowly agrarian outlook was fueled by a volatile mixture of fear, bitterness, and paranoia. The final years of his life were marked by an anxious revival of his long-standing fear of "corruption" emanating from a politically powerful clique. He came, once again, to see Federalists and conniving aristocrats lurking everywhere, now under the command of his own relative and fellow Virginian, Chief Justice John Marshall. In the 1790s Jefferson had fought Hamilton's conspiracy to subvert republicanism from within the Treasury department; now he was obsessed with the machinations of the

37. Jefferson to M. Barre de Marbois, June 14, 1817, Lipscomb and Bergh, eds., *Writings of Jefferson*, XV, 130–131.

38. Jefferson to Middleton, Jan. 8, 1813, *ibid.*, XIII, 203.

39. For an interesting analysis of Jefferson's republicanism, focusing on the post-1815 period, in relation to the antebellum southern mind, see Robert E. Shalhope, "Thomas Jefferson's Republicanism and Antebellum Southern Thought," *Jour. So. Hist.*, XLII (1976), 529–556.

Supreme Court. According to Jefferson, the Court under Marshall's leadership threatened in its revival of Hamiltonian principles to impose a system of "consolidation" on the young republic, a system that would unduly centralize political power while carrying out the selfish schemes of northern merchants and manufacturers.[40] In addition to castigating the activities of the judiciary, Jefferson unequivocally opposed Henry Clay's "American System," which called for the creation of an integrated economy based on a national bank, a protective tariff for manufactures, and a program of federally sponsored internal improvements. To Jefferson, this system was thinly disguised Hamiltonianism, part and parcel of the "consolidation" conspiracy. The fact that Clay and many other Republicans conceived of and defended the American System as the logical fulfillment of mature Jeffersonian principles, which sought the creation of a balanced, independent, and self-sufficient economy, did nothing to appease the Sage of Monticello himself.[41]

Jefferson's fixation on the threat of "consolidation" was perfectly consistent with his fundamental republican beliefs. Ironically, however, his fear of this tendency toward political centralization and the subsidization of manufacturing interests proved unfounded, at least in the short run. In the two decades after Jefferson's death, the Jacksonians would succeed remarkably well in preventing the implementation of any form of the American System. They systematically dismantled the remaining vestiges of Hamiltonianism (epitomized in their destruction of the Second Bank of the United States) and aggressively pursued, to the point of war in 1846, the Jeffersonian vision of a decentralized republic expanding rapidly across space. In fact, the triumph of "consolidation" in America would come only after a long and catastrophic civil war, and even then that triumph was probably not as complete or immediate as Jefferson feared it would be fifty years earlier.

But if consolidation did not actually pose a serious and immediate threat to the fulfillment of Jefferson's vision, there were other, comparatively unperceived dangers that did. Without a doubt, the institution of black slavery was the critical unspoken presence in American life that doomed Jefferson's republican vision. To the extent that American slav-

40. For further discussion of these matters, see Peterson, *Jefferson and the New Nation*, 992–1004.
41. *Ibid.*, 992–993.

ery had eliminated the need for a large, white, dependent, landless laboring class that would have made the espousal of republican beliefs much more dangerous (and perhaps impossible) for members of the Revolutionary elite like Jefferson, it played an important, though unacknowledged, role in the formation of the Jeffersonian perspective.[42] Moreover, slavery was the linchpin of the agricultural society Jefferson knew best, and during his lifetime the institution was becoming more solidly entrenched in the South instead of withering away in accordance with Revolutionary ideals. Nevertheless, on the conscious level of conceptualization, at least, slavery had never found a place in the Jeffersonian vision of a republican political economy. During the period between the Revolution and the War of 1812, slavery was generally disapproved of, generally regarded as inimical to republicanism, and generally expected somehow to die a natural death. There were scattered efforts to defend the institution in positive terms, but it was not yet a major subject of discourse in American reflections on political economy. Jefferson never seriously considered the role of slavery in his republican model of America, in large part because he continued to hope and expect that the institution would gradually die out.[43] He retained to the end of his life the naive but consistent faith that slavery, and not the republican vision that excluded it, was doomed to extinction.

In this regard, perhaps the saddest, most tragic irony of Jefferson's later years was his insistence on the right of republican farmers in the South to carry their slaves with them as they settled the western frontier. During the controversy in 1819 and 1820 over Missouri's admission to the republic, Jefferson adamantly asserted that the attempt of northerners to bar slavery there was nothing more than a partisan plot, part of a devious attempt by unreconstructed Federalists to rebuild a wholly northern party dedicated to the creation of a consolidated government that would subvert republicanism. Struggling to reconcile his defense of southern rights, his commitment to limited republican government, and his long-standing anti-slavery stance, Jefferson turned to a theory of

42. See Edmund S. Morgan, *American Slavery, American Freedom: The Ordeal of Colonial Virginia* (New York, 1975), esp. chap. 18.

43. See especially, John Chester Miller, *The Wolf by the Ears: Thomas Jefferson and Slavery* (New York, 1977). Miller's study is focused on Jefferson's encounter with slavery, but it effectively considers this specific problem in the broader context of Jefferson's political economy and moral philosophy.

"diffusion" as the best means of eradicating slavery. If slavery was permitted and even encouraged to expand geographically, his argument ran, its influence would be diffused, diluted, and irrevocably weakened. He hoped that this diffusion of slavery would result in the gradual breakdown of the large plantation system, which would not only improve the lot of the slaves, but also create the necessary environment for the slaveholder's innate moral sense finally to take control of his avaricious and tyrannical passions. The upshot of this diffusion, according to Jefferson, would be the voluntary emancipation that he had always regarded as inevitable.[44]

Jefferson's sincerity may be beyond question, but his naiveté and poor judgment were unequivocally confirmed by the subsequent course of events. With his outlook distorted by an inflexible preoccupation with the "consolidation" conspiracy, Jefferson unwittingly defended a form of expansion across space that betrayed the spirit and principle of his republican vision. Rather than weakening, the slave plantation system grew stronger than ever through diffusion; and by supporting a highly exploitative brand of agriculture, this system nourished the greed and avarice that Jefferson preferred to view as vices peculiar to the commercial and manufacturing regions of America. Jefferson's idealized farmer had never really been a simple subsistence farmer, but the Virginian had always clung to the hope that industrious, surplus-producing, republican farmers in America might somehow retain the spirit and character of the ideal yeoman in the traditional pastoral vision. One might conclude that, in the end, Jeffersonian political economy lost its battle both with human nature and with the exploitative character of a commercialized economy. In one sense, the Jeffersonians had hoped by the controlled and civilizing exploitation of land to avoid the exploitation of people. But the system of commercial agriculture that expanded westward across space entailed an exploitative cast of mind that could not be eradicated—a cast of mind well revealed in the rampant land speculation and profiteering of non-slaveholding Americans in the West, but undoubtedly best exemplified in the most vicious form imaginable of exploiting both land and people, the institution of slavery.

44. *Ibid.*, esp. chaps. 23–26. See also Peterson, *Jefferson and the New Nation*, 995–1001.

[III]

Jefferson's heightened attention to the artificial threat to his republican vision posed by political "consolidation" did not completely overshadow his continuing concern with the natural threat presented by the biological pressure of population growth. Although he continued to believe that westward expansion would forestall the development of dangerous social inequalities and dependencies in America, he also recognized that the supply of land would one day be exhausted. At the end of the War of 1812, Jefferson, along with most of his countrymen, still placed this dreaded moment in the distant future, but he could not afford to ignore completely the implications of population growth. In this regard, it is interesting that Jefferson greatly admired Destutt de Tracy's *Treatise on Political Economy*, translated it from the unpublished French, and prepared it for publication in America in 1817.[45] Tracy's manuscript included a penetrating analysis of the way in which population growth produced the ominous social decay that appeared to describe the fate of so much of the Old World. Jefferson's respect for Tracy's analysis is evidence not only of the Virginian's view of Europe's plight, but also of the traditional fears and concerns that continued to color his long-range view of his own country's social development.[46]

Tracy discussed at some length in his *Treatise* the process of "pression," a term he used to describe the results of an inexorable tendency for population to press against a finite supply of land. According to Tracy, pression occurred when "all the country is filled," and landless laborers, or "hirelings," were forced to work for the wages extended by property-owning employers. These hirelings no longer had an independent and secure source of subsistence in the form of their own land, but a lack of independence was only the beginning of their problem. As the number of hirelings multiplied in a populous society, the demand for their labor steadily diminished. The "perfection of the arts" (in the form of advanced

---

45. Count Destutt Tracy, *A Treatise on Political Economy* . . . (Georgetown, D.C., 1817). For brief but useful discussions of Jefferson and Tracy, see Yehoshua Arieli, *Individualism and Nationalism in American Ideology* (Cambridge, Mass., 1964), 142–155, and Gilbert Chinard, *Jefferson et les Ideologues* . . . (Baltimore, 1925), 45–55.

46. John Adams also found Tracy's volume convincing, but he characterized it as "a magazine of gunpowder" that would be badly received in America despite its "immutable truth." See J. J. Spengler, "Malthusianism in Late Eighteenth Century America," *American Economic Review*, XXV (1935), 705n.

manufacturing) might offer new sources of employment for these landless laborers and thus temporarily delay a serious crisis; but eventually "all lucrative employments being filled, without a possibility of creating new ones, there is every where more labour offered than demanded." As a result, many laborers "necessarily languish, and even perish, and a great number of wretched must constantly exist."[47] Simply stated, Tracy's crisis occurred when a society was no longer capable of providing sufficient incentives to industry and employment for its surplus population, and the tendency in such populous societies, Tracy stressed, was invariably toward greater and greater inequalities of wealth and power. Every civilized society, he concluded, would ultimately confront the onerous challenge of minimizing this social inequality to the greatest possible extent without endangering traditional property rights.[48]

Like the English population theorist Malthus, Tracy described an inevitable social crisis resulting from the natural "fecundity of the human species." Like Malthus, too, he warned that even the relatively youthful United States offered no exception to the general rule.[49] After noting that the expansion of manufacturing through the perfection of the arts could temporarily afford "if not riches, at least ease to the lower classes of people," Tracy went on to argue that "this happy and necessarily transient period" was also the best time for "the superior class of society" to be "sufficiently enlightened to give to the inferior ideas completely sound of the social order." Proceeding to apply this general insight to the American case, he suggested that if the United States failed to take advantage of the opportunity offered by this interim period, "their tranquillity and even safety will be much exposed, when interior and exterior obstacles, and inconveniences, shall have multiplied. This will be called their decline and corruption. It will be the slow but necessary effect of their anterior improvidence and carelessness."[50] Thus Tracy advised that everything possible be done at an early stage of American history to temper the potentially explosive effects of pression, thereby defusing the insidious threat of social chaos that inevitably awaited the young republic.

Even more than Jefferson, James Madison had worried since at least the 1780s about the potential for Tracy's "pression" to overturn Ameri-

47. Tracy, *Treatise*, xxiii, 114, 120.
48. *Ibid.*, 133–163.
49. *Ibid.*, 121.
50. *Ibid.*, 119–120.

ca's republican revolution.[51] After his retirement from public life in 1817, he gave this problem further attention. Indeed, Madison appeared to regard the natural threat of pression as far more serious to the republican character of America than the politically contrived threat of "consolidation" that so alarmed Jefferson. Madison was never entirely comfortable with the mature version of Jeffersonianism represented in Clay's American System, but his objections to this neo-Hamiltonian approach to political economy were much more restrained than Jefferson's.[52] Madison remained as committed as Jefferson to the original spirit of the republican revolution, but he proved more flexible in his ability to accommodate the social and political changes that rocked an aging Jefferson on his heels. Madison outlived his friend and neighbor by a decade and to that extent had a better glimpse into the future. Surprisingly, he retained, more than Jefferson did, the optimism that had characterized the early years of the Revolution, despite his unflinching recognition of the social and economic forces that would inexorably endanger its fulfillment.

As Madison pondered the development of American society in the 1820s, he looked ahead, as he had in the 1780s, to the day when the supply of arable land would be exhausted and the country would be as heavily populated as England and France. A majority of the community would then be "without landed or other equivalent property and without the means or hope of acquiring it." He predicted that a dangerous social inequality, including "a dependence of an increasing number on the wealth of a few," would take the form in the United States of "wealthy capitalists" and "indigent labourers," with the most severe dependencies stemming from "the connection between the great Capitalists in Manufactures and Commerce and the members employed by them."[53] Madison believed that this "crowded state of population" and its frightening consequences were not "too remote to claim attention." Within "a century or a little more," he predicted in 1829, the United States would have to face the challenge of maintaining republicanism in a society without a reservoir of land, a society that would be increasingly crippled by the

51. See above, chap. 5.

52. For a brief discussion of Madison's reaction to Clay's tariff proposals, for example, see Ralph Ketcham, *James Madison: A Biography* (New York, 1971), 635–636.

53. The quotations are taken from notes Madison made in 1821 on a speech he had given in the constitutional convention of 1787. These notes are conveniently reprinted in Marvin Meyers, ed., *The Mind of the Founder: Sources of the Political Thought of James Madison* (Indianapolis, Ind., 1973), 502–509. See pp. 504–505.

inequalities and dependencies resulting from this condition.[54] Once large numbers of Americans lacked the moral and political independence that freehold property conferred, the republic would enter a new, perhaps lethal, stage of its history.

Although the specter of a closed frontier persistently haunted Madison's view of the distant future, it is significant that he expressed other, related fears that could not be relegated to such a remote distance. These fears were tied to the nagging problem of an inadequate demand for America's surplus production, a problem that Madison had long regarded as particularly acute. Speaking in 1821 of Malthus, whom he generally admired, Madison noted that "he may have been unguarded in his expressions, and have pushed some of his notions too far." Specifically, the economist was vulnerable "in assigning for the increase of human food, an arithmetical ratio." In a country "as partially cultivated, and as fertile as the U.S.," Madison argued, "the increase may *exceed* the geometrical ratio." If anything, Americans were extracting too much subsistence from nature, so much, in fact, that it was impossible to dispose of it all. Referring to the devastating repercussions of the Panic of 1819, the Virginian observed that the surplus resulting from the fecundity of the American soil, "for which a foreign demand has failed," was indeed "a primary cause of the present embarrassments of this Country."[55]

To Madison, America's most pressing problem appeared to be this surplus production and the glutted markets that accompanied it, not an inadequate supply of land or natural resources. In this regard, he saw natural tendencies at work in the United States that were rather different from those Malthus had emphasized in the early editions of his *Essay on Population*. "It is a law of nature, now well understood," Madison wrote in 1829, "that the earth under a civilized cultivation is capable of yielding subsistence for a large surplus of consumers, beyond those having an immediate interest in the soil; a surplus which must increase with the increasing improvements in agriculture, and the labor-saving arts applied to it." It was the "lot of humanity," he continued, that of this human surplus, "a large proportion is necessarily reduced by a competition for

54. "Note During the Convention for Amending the Constitution of Virginia," *ibid.*, 518–519. This document is also printed in Gaillard Hunt, ed., *The Writings of James Madison* (New York, 1900–1910), IX, 358n–360n.

55. Madison to Richard Rush, Apr. 21, 1821, Hunt, ed., *Writings of Madison*, IX, 45–46.

employment to wages which afford them the bare necessaries of life."[56] Madison's "law of nature" was not the same natural law described by Malthus, because Madison referred here to the problem of population pressing on the available means of employment, not to the pressure of population on the earth's capacity to provide nourishment. The problem he envisioned was not a subsistence crisis occasioned by the exhaustion of natural resources; the problem was dwindling sources of employment for a surplus population whose labor could not be utilized in agriculture. He thus dealt with the prospective paradox of increasing poverty in the midst of a surplus of subsistence, a situation that Tracy had considered in his discussion of pression. In the end, Madison's problem, like Tracy's, was institutional, unlike Malthus's biological one: how might society be organized so as to overcome this paradox and bring about the comfort and happiness of a rapidly expanding population?[57]

Madison could only hope that a prodigious foreign demand for the republic's agricultural surplus might continue to postpone this crisis by permitting the vast majority of Americans to remain profitably employed on the land. But it also seemed clear to him that once America's agricultural surplus had finally glutted all available foreign and domestic markets, a crisis was unavoidable. Ironically, as Madison acknowledged, westward expansion might even hasten or exacerbate this dilemma, since bringing fresh land under cultivation only increased the size of the surplus, thus threatening to reduce further the value of American exports in glutted markets. He even conceded that such a possibility offered the best argument for restraining westward expansion and constructing a more balanced national economy.[58]

This potential for America's surplus production to exceed the combined demand of domestic and foreign markets persistently troubled Madison. He worried that if the republic's agricultural surplus could not be profitably disposed of for lack of a market, there would no longer be adequate incentives for its production. And this prospect suggested the alarming possibility that the United States might be forced into manufacturing as an alternative source of employment even in the presence of

---

56. "Note During Convention," Meyers, ed., *Mind of the Founder,* 516–517.

57. For an extended consideration of these matters, see Drew R. McCoy, "Jefferson and Madison on Malthus: Population Growth in Jeffersonian Political Economy," *Virginia Magazine of History and Biography*, forthcoming.

58. Madison to N. P. Trist, Jan. 26, 1828, Hunt, ed., *Writings of Madison,* IX, 304–305.

open land. "Manufactures grow out of the labour not needed for agriculture," Madison noted in 1833, "and labour will cease to be so needed or employed as its products satisfy and satiate the demands for domestic use and for foreign markets." "Whatever be the abundance or fertility of the soil," he added, "it will not be cultivated when its fruits must perish on hand for want of a market." Applying this general rule to his own state of Virginia, where "the earth produces at this time as much as is called for by the home and the foreign markets," Madison concluded that the Old Dominion "must be speedily a manufacturing as well as an agricultural State." The unfortunate consequence was that "the people will be formed into the same great classes here as elsewhere."[59] Thus glutted markets, as much as the absence of open land, could push an agricultural society like Virginia forward through time toward the social crisis Madison always dreaded, and it seems clear that by the end of his life he saw the former condition as much more imminent than the latter, both in Virginia and in the republic as a whole. As he had always feared, a deficiency of markets for this surplus could, just as readily as a deficiency of land, undermine the basis for a republican political economy.[60]

[IV]

Madison's final reflections on his country's future suggested a disturbing line of analysis for his fellow republicans to ponder. Perhaps America's agricultural productivity was so great, as Isaac Briggs had warned, that it would surpass the aggregate demand of foreign markets even in a utopian world of free trade and open markets. If so, any vision of America in which nearly all the citizens would remain industrious, surplus-producing farmers was unrealistic whether open land continued to be available or not. And if sufficient incentives to American industry in agriculture were impossible under any conditions, new sources of industry in alternative

59. "Majority Governments," Meyers, ed., *Mind of the Founder*, 527–528. This document is also printed in Hunt, ed., *Writings of Madison*, IX, 520–528; for the quotations cited, see pp. 525–526.

60. By the 1820s Madison also was reconciled to the apparent inevitability of an unfavorable balance of trade in America. He believed that this situation would persist until Americans changed their habits and renounced all luxuries, or decided to "manufacture the articles of luxury, as well as the useful articles" instead of importing them. See Madison to Henry Clay, Apr. 1, 1824, Hunt, ed., *Writings of Madison*, IX, 186–187.

occupations would have to be discovered to avoid the tragic irony of increasing inequality and poverty in a society that appeared to have the capacity to feed the entire world. America's dilemma seemed paradoxical indeed: new republican incentives to industry and employment, which would prevent idleness and indigence among surplus laborers, had to be generated in a society where Malthus's biological problem of subsistence had been decisively conquered.[61]

Despite the pessimistic implications of Madison's social analysis, his outlook in the 1820s and 1830s remained guardedly, even stoically, optimistic. His basic faith in republicanism did not die, and he continued to believe in the viability of a republican revolution in America. Yet he never doubted that serious and even radical adjustments to the relentless logic of social development would be necessary. If the republican revolution had initially been defined as an escape from time, Madison had always acknowledged that, in the long run, such a revolution was doomed. Eventually the New World would come to resemble the Old. America would become part of history and the human condition. And as Madison understood it, the challenge to future generations of Americans would be to redefine the republican revolution by adapting its basic spirit and principles to a form of society that was traditionally thought to deny them. Whether this challenge has been successfully met—and the spirit of Madison's republican revolution vindicated—are questions that must now bear on the conscience of the heirs to his republican tradition. Surely Madison would no longer permit them the luxury of regarding his crisis as prospective.

---

61. Madison's reaction to Robert Owen's New Harmony experiment is interesting in this regard. The Virginian was skeptical of this utopian community in part because its organization implied "that labour will be relished without the ordinary impulses to it." The problem of generating incentives to industry in a mature society could not be solved, in other words, by willing a revolution in human nature. See Madison to Nicholas P. Trist, Apr.—, 1827, Meyers, ed., *Mind of the Founder*, 453–454. Madison's response to Owen is interesting for another reason. Listing the "contingencies that must distress a portion" of the inhabitants of "every populous country," Madison first mentioned four problems and then asserted that "a freedom of commerce among all nations" was the best possible solution to them. Following this discussion, he finally raised the classic Malthusian problem of population outrunning the food supply. It can be inferred from this pattern, I think, that Madison relegated the classic Malthusian problem of a subsistence crisis to a position of secondary importance, in part because in America, at least, it seemed too remote a consideration to require immediate attention. *Ibid.*, 454–455. This letter is also printed in *Letters and Other Writings of James Madison* (Philadelphia, 1865), III, 575–578.

INDEX

View of the future

What could these men think if they came back today? commercial republican vision

what happened to the manufacturing vision — what was it

Tensions between past & future? True n venture
Caught   what was   what was

Tensions within
    colonial economy?
    slavery?

Manufacturing (home market / domestic commerce)

→ The vision of republican virtue temporal /
    hierleval — wealth needed to be
    channeled